CROSSING THE THRESHOLD

CROSSING THE

The Story of the Marriage Equality Movement

Edited by Gráinne Healy
Photographic editor Orla Howard

THRESHOLD

First published in 2017 by
Merrion Press
10 George's Street
Newbridge
Co. Kildare
Ireland
www.merrionpress.ie

© Gráinne Healy and individual
contributors, 2017

9781785371165 (Paperback)

9781785371172 (PDF)

British Library Cataloguing
in Publication Data
An entry can be found on request

Library of Congress Cataloging
in Publication Data
An entry can be found on request

Design by iota (www.iota-books.ie)
Typeset in 10.5 pt on 15.5 pt Calluna with Whitney display
Cover front: Courtesy of Anthony Kinehan.
Cover back: Activists and politicians unite to celebrate the passing of the Civil Marriage Bill outside Dáil Éireann, October 2015. Courtesy of The Irish Times.
Back flap: Dr Gráinne Healy.
p. i: Ireland counts down 12 days to marriage equality vote. © Robin English, Demotix/Corbis.
This page: Joe Caslin's iconic artwork pictured on George's Street, Dublin, courtesy of Paul Sharp at Sharppix.ie.
Printed and bound by Gráficas Castuera, Spain

Contents

Acknowledgments   ix

Foreword   xi

Editor's Introduction   xvii

1   The Journey Towards Winning: Our Story
Katherine Zappone and Ann Louise Gilligan   2

2   Socio-Political Developments Creating the Context for
Marriage Equality for Same-Sex Couples in Ireland
Gráinne Healy   20

3   From Little Acorns: Mobilising the Million in the Middle
Moninne Griffith   44

4   The Equality Authority and Same-Sex Marriage
Niall Crowley   68

5   The Making of a Movement: Communications and its Role
in Marriage Equality, 2008–2010
Andrew Hyland   82

6   Across the Pond: Connections to Marriage Equality Ireland
Íde B. O'Carroll   102

7   Legal Mobilisation and the Movement for Marriage Equality
in Ireland: From Missing Pieces to a Yes Vote
Justine Schönfeld-Quinn   114

8   Making Noise
Anna MacCarthy   130

9   The National LGBT Federation and Marriage Equality
Olivia McEvoy   140

10   The Labour Party and Marriage Equality
Ronan Farren   154

11   The Story of an LGBT Marriage Equality Activist:
From Canvassing for Equality to Canvassing for a Yes
Ross Golden-Bannon   172

12   Lesbians in Cork (LINC) and Marriage Equality
Kate Moynihan   190

13   Marriage Equality Champion Volunteers
Anthony Kinahan   198

14   Leading the Marriage Equality Volunteer Team
Carol Armstrong   210

15   Raising Funds for Marriage Equality
Darina Brennan   218

16   Our Families and Our Children for Marriage Equality
Denise Charlton and Paula Fagan   228

17   Faith in Marriage Equality and the Pilgrimage for Yes
Richard O'Leary   240

18   Challenges of the Personal and the Political
Orla Howard   250

19   Making Short Films for Marriage Equality
Linda Cullen   264

20   GLEN and the Remarkable Journey to Marriage
Brian Sheehan and Kieran Rose   276

21   BeLonG To and Marriage Equality
Michael Barron   292

22   Working Together: The Student Movement and Marriage Equality
Laura Harmon   306

23   Hands Across the Water: Freedom to Marry and Marriage Equality
Thalia Zepatos   316

Notes   333
Contributors   345
Index   351

We would like to dedicate this book to the Marriage Equality 'Widows'. These are the group of underappreciated partners, spouses and friends of the Marriage Equality Board and staff, who generously and graciously supported the years of work and activism in the journey to achieve equal marriage.

Acknowledgments

The editor wishes to acknowledge Conor Graham, Fiona Dunne and the team at Merrion Press; Orla Howard for the hours of work editing photographs; a special word of thanks to Karl Hayden for the beautiful shots of contributors and finally to each of the contributors, the Marriage Equality and Yes Equality activists and the people of Ireland who made marriage equality a reality.

Photographs and images have been kindly supplied by: Karl Hayden, Paul Sharp at Sharppix.ie, Conchubhair Mac Lochlainn, LGBT Noise, *The Irish Times*, Gráinne Healy, Justine Schönfeld-Quinn, Kieran Rose, GLEN, NXF, Gearóidín Charlton, Peter Clifford, John O'Shaughnessy, Kelley Mackey, Olivia McEvoy, Anna McCarthy, Trevor Hart at trevorhart.com, Brian Finnegan, GCN, Margaret Lonergan, Joan O'Brien, Orla Howard, Clare O'Connell, Yes Equality Dundalk, Anthony Kinahan, Linda Cullen, COCO TV, Ronan Healy, Adam May, Ivana Bacik, Paul Rankin.

A heartfelt thanks also to Gail Birbeck and Colin McCray of The Atlantic Philanthropies for financial support towards this publication.

Foreword

Marriage is so personal. Whether you get married, who you marry, how you stay married, whether you like being married, whether you don't – marriage is such an intimate thing. At the same time, it is highly political – who can get married and under what conditions – and it's hugely symbolic, too, in terms of how we see ourselves.

Despite the hard-won decriminalisation of male homosexuality in 1993, the absence of the right to marry was a denial of equal citizenship, a denial which was profoundly insulting to all LGBTI people, whether we wanted to marry or not. Quite simply, it designated us as different and lesser. Homophobia was still on the statute books.

I became involved in the campaign for the right to marry in the mid-2000s, when I was Chair of the National Lesbian & Gay Federation (NLGF). I vividly remember the afternoon I got a call from Katherine Zappone and Ann Louise Gilligan, telling me they had decided to take a case to have their Canadian marriage recognised in Ireland and were building support for this audacious move. I was intrigued by the challenge, attended meetings and briefings, and raised it with the NLGF board where we all agreed it should be a major issue on our agenda.

At that stage there was a diversity of views on marriage, so it was very much about having conversations and working through why this was an important issue for the LGBT community. I say LGB and T, because although it was about the right to marry of lesbians and gay men, it was clear that this was a fight for equality, and therefore mattered to everyone whose sexuality was marginalised and who was made to feel less of a citizen, and unequal because of that.

I became part of KAL, the loose organisation set up to support Katherine and Ann Louise in taking their case, and when that morphed into Marriage Equality (ME), I stayed on the Board, along with other NLGF representatives including Patrick Lynch and Orla Howard. I am very proud that the NLGF (now NXF) was part of the fight from the get-go. We held a seminar entitled 'Marriage Matters', which made an impact, and of course *GCN* (*Gay Community News*, which is published by the NLGF), was raising the issue and beginning to publish more and more about it. Marriage – often to our own surprise – was becoming part of the everyday conversation within our LGBT communities, with wide agreement that it did indeed matter on so many levels: our personal and family lives, our human and civil rights, our status and equality, our hopes and dreams for the future.

The six or seven years before equal marriage became centre-stage on the political agenda were fascinating. When you're opening up a topic, as we were, you are always listening to what other people are saying, always trying to understand and interpret their views and feelings. It is slow, backroom work, looking for opportunities to raise the issue, to frame it so that people have an understanding of the issue and why it matters so much. That was our job in ME at the time: explaining within our own community, and more broadly to our elected representatives and to the people of Ireland and to our politicians, why this was such an important goal.

The symbolic dimension of the campaign for equal marriage was quickly recognised, which meant that people and organisations across a very broad spectrum could get involved. It was difficult for some at first. Feminism, for instance, has always had an acute and profound analysis of marriage as a patriarchal institution, so discussions in the early days were lively and often robust, as I well know. Like many of my friends, I had to argue with myself through my own long–standing feminist positions, misgivings and personal experience, to arrive at an understanding that the right to marry is about having the freedom to choose to marry – or not. I understood that I couldn't argue for choice in one area of my life, and not fully support and fight for it in another. I also believed, along with friends and co-campaigners, that marriage as an institution was not static or fixed, and that lesbians and gays would do it differently, which I believed – and still do – to be a very healthy proposition.

From the beginning, marriage (hardly a surprise) was the focus of ME as an organisation. Civil partnership, therefore, was problematic for us, even as a 'step-along-the-way'. While according some basic rights, it signalled second-class citizenship: 'You were second-class citizens before, and now you are second-class citizens – grade one'. That was absolutely unacceptable. We were not interested in anything less than the full shilling of equality. We were either equal, or we were not, no fudging.

Ailbhe Smyth

We were also concerned about the splitting of precious energies and resources which we reckoned would be best placed in a focused campaign for a common goal, and this inevitably led to differences of opinion between ME and GLEN (Gay & Lesbian Equality Network). To the abiding credit of everyone involved in what was to become the Yes Equality campaign, that clear common focus ultimately happened. The disagreements and tensions were not just put to one side, we moved beyond them to create a remarkable unity. It was quite an extraordinary achievement. I know from my own political experience that it rarely happens, and so thoroughly. I believe it says a lot for community spirit.

At the same time, it is important to acknowledge that an advantage of the halfway house of civil partnership was that almost all of the legal issues relevant to equal marriage began to be sorted out through the work on drafting and lobbying for the Children and Family Relationships Bill (it was eventually enacted in 2015). That work made a real difference, not only in terms of campaign unity but because it meant that when it came to the referendum campaign, there was a piece of legislation which answered questions and countered the doubts and fears people had (perhaps sometimes for vexatious and strategic reasons, mind you) about 'what would happen to the children' if equal marriage were to become legal.

I have to say that those questions have always both irritated and amused me, in more or less the same measure. Did the questioners genuinely think that LGBTI people are less kind, less caring, less intelligent, and basically less able to raise children than straight people? Did they not look at the children we already have for an answer? Did they not think about how we've all been children ourselves and have the same immensely diverse 'parenting models' as they do? Those questions made me realise both how silly people can be, and at the same time how difficult it is to root out deeply embedded homophobia.

The Constitutional Convention in 2013 provided the occasion for ME, GLEN and the Irish Council for Civil Liberties (ICCL) to build unity by working together on our submissions and preparing a joint presentation to the Convention members. We understood exactly how important it was for us all to articulate essentially the same messages. The powerful presentation to the Convention, in which our children played such a key role, was an eye-opener for many members, with several – including politicians – changing their minds. It resulted in an overwhelming vote by the Convention in favour of marriage equality. It marked the real beginning of a referendum campaign and set up a sound and durable working model for the way in which we could all pull together to win that referendum.

The detail of that campaign and the emotions that were part of it – politics is always fundamentally about emotion, whatever people may say – is brilliantly captured by the many contributions in this collection, and I won't go over it here. It's all before you in the reading. Our individual analyses, personally grounded experiences and feelings are here in all their uniqueness and diversity. The story of ME that emerges is like a kaleidoscope: many-coloured and wonderful to behold.

It's very hard, for me and for anyone who was involved in the campaign at any point, not to feel and sound intensely proud and pleased about it all. That is not to say, for one moment, that it was easy. The campaign was hard-fought all the way, and it was often very tough indeed out there. But it was also uplifting. I think of the young people out on the canvass encountering levels of homophobia they had never experienced before, but dealing with it staunchly, and coming back to base telling stories of kindness, humour and warmth, often in unexpected places, which outweighed the nastiness and restored their faith – all our faith – in humanity and decency.

I never thought we would lose, which is not quite the same as being convinced we would win. But it seemed to me that the Irish electorate would find it very difficult, en masse, to say 'No to Equality'. We had shifted perceptions and understanding and challenged people to think about what equality truly means, and why it is so important to us individually and as a country. As long as any one of us is not free and not equal, we do not have equality and freedom in Ireland. This was a chance for people to stand up for something we say we believe in.

And they did, in huge numbers. Almost two-thirds of the country voted in favour of marriage equality. It was a tremendous victory, and a rare one in my experience. No wonder we were ecstatic, with joy unbound on the day of the count and the historic announcement. To be very personal for a moment, I can tell you that I've never been kissed and hugged by so many people who are not my natural political allies, and I'm sure I wasn't alone in that. We had somehow managed to bring the country over deeply embedded dividing lines, not only of sexuality, but of class, gender, ethnicity, generations, political ideologies and a whole lot more besides. It was glorious.

I remember thinking on that wonderful day that something I had only dreamed of had come to pass in my lifetime: the hierarchical divide between straight and LGBTI people had been breached in a profound way. Yes, I'm lesbian and will go on being lesbian; yes, that person is gay, or trans or intersex or bi or straight, but those are not differences that should ever separate us in the social order, or on the scale of humanity and rights. I think that breach we made is something that we can hold on to in this country, now and for our future.

No more than marriage means 'living happily ever after', none of us is so naïve as to think that marriage equality solves all the problems of the LGBTI community (I have in mind particularly the needs of trans people, of older LGBTs, of young people and mental health among other issues) or that it magically resolves a whole raft of long-standing inequalities. Of course it does not.

But I think we surprised and delighted ourselves quite a bit in Ireland on that wonderful sunny May day. We surprised ourselves by showing how much more open and generous and understanding we have become as a country. It's a victory which taught us something important and which has undoubtedly stiffened our backbone for the struggles that most surely lie ahead, both here at home and in the wider rapidly darkening world.

All the years we spent preparing for this referendum were desolate years of hardship for so many, years of mind-numbing, hope-destroying austerity. The marriage referendum gave people a chance to be our best selves, and to express our hopes and our dreams. Those hopes are for an Ireland which can reach beyond the taboos of history, tradition and prejudice, wholly capable of generosity, willing and able to cherish equally all who live here. We did it spectacularly in 2015, and we can do it again and again, for as long as it takes. Equality matters. Let's hold on tight to that.

Ailbhe Smyth with her daughter Lydia as she collects the 2015 Lifetime Achievement GALA award.

Each and every single person who fought this campaign made a crucial contribution, but I want to finish by expressing my special thanks to Gráinne Healy, ME Chair, Yes Equality Co-Director, and strategist *extraordinaire*, who led us so steadfastly towards victory. Thank you for assembling this important record of our long campaign, for your vision and determination, and above all for keeping us going through thick and thin, hell and high water. It was entirely worth it.

Ailbhe Smyth, January 2017

Editor's Introduction

The idea of gathering a collection of writings from key figures in the marriage equality movement in Ireland arose from conversations at Marriage Equality (ME) Board meetings as we reflected on the success of our goal: marriage equality for same-sex couples in Ireland.

The story of the Yes Equality campaign, particularly of the 107 days of Yes Equality from its launch in March 2015 to the referendum result of 23 May 2015, had begun to be told in *Ireland Says Yes: The Inside Story of How the Vote for Marriage Equality Was Won* (Healy, Sheehan and Whelan, 2016, Merrion Press). What that book did not do, nor was it intended to, was tell the story of the decade-long struggle to reach that day in May 2015. This collection is a first attempt at capturing key elements of that story, told by some of those who were involved over the previous decade.

Hans-Georg Gadamer, the German philosopher, speaks about interpreting events through 'a fusion of horizons'. The contributions in this collection are just that: a fusion of unique viewpoints; some are specific and some are personal, while others are more historical, sociological or biographical.

This book is the opening of a conversation inviting others to document their involvement in this successful movement. The essays are sometimes conflicting and critical, overlooking some contributions, while other recollections strive to be more inclusive. Some

The Board of Marriage Equality, 25 June 2015. *From left to right:* Clare O'Connell, Denise Charlton, Darina Brennan, Ronan Farren, Carol Armstrong, Andrew Hyland, Gráinne Healy, Moninne Griffith, Ross Golden-Bannon, Olivia McEvoy, Katherine Zappone, Ann Louise Gilligan, Orla Howard and Ailbhe Smyth. Linda Cullen not pictured.

partners in the movement were invited but were unable to contribute. As former Director of Marriage Equality (ME) Moninne Griffith expresses it, the Yes Equality campaign put the roof on the ME house that had been carefully constructed over a decade, with the foundations, walls and windows designed and built by ME and its allies and supporters.

This fusion of writings from ME staff, Board members and volunteers was developed in consultation with Orla Howard and Denise Charlton of the ME Board. We agreed that the spectrum should widen to include significant allies, long-time friends of ME, and others thrown together by political realities into the Yes Equality campaign.

The journey to marriage equality has been life-altering and, as co-founder and Chairwoman of ME, for a decade, it has been a pleasure to work with the talented, passionate Board, staff and consultants over so many years: Carol Armstrong, Ross Golden-Bannon, Olive Braiden, Darina Brennan, Linda Cullen, Denise Charlton, Paula Fagan, Ronan Farren, Ann Louise Gilligan, Deirdre Hannigan, Orla Howard, Patrick Lynch, Anna MacCarthy, Oliva McEvoy, Feargha Ní Bhroin, Kieran O'Brien, Clare O'Connell, Justine Quinn, Christopher Robson, Ailbhe Smyth, Judy Walsh and Katherine Zappone (on the Board); Moninne Griffith,

Andrew Hyland, Dawn Quinn, Kirsten Foster and Joan O'Connell (on the staff); and Ronan Farren, Andew Hyland and Michelle Thomas (consultants).

I also want to thank Brian Kearney-Grieves and Atlantic Philanthropies for their generous support of ME until 2012 when their funding ended, leaving us with a hard road ahead and the added job of having to divert attention to fundraising. Thanks to the vision and the skills of our Board, staff and volunteers, however, we kept our doors open.

The animosity that existed between GLEN (the Gay & Lesbian Equality Network) and ME seeps through into some of the chapters – it was no secret that ME and GLEN had adopted differing strategies on the road to same-sex relationship recognition. My friend and former GLEN and ME Board member, Christopher Robson, stayed on the Board until we both agreed that, as GLEN was taking the civil partnership-first route to marriage equality, he would step down, but we looked forward to working together again for marriage equality after civil partnership. It was a great loss when Christopher died suddenly in 2013. I believe he would have been particularly pleased to see ME and GLEN work so closely together in Yes Equality.

Creating a unified campaign with the Irish Council for Civil Liberties (ICCL) and GLEN was imperative when fighting a referendum became the only route open to us after the 2013 Constitutional Convention recommendation for a referendum. It was not an easy transition to form Yes Equality; old histories had to be put aside and long-standing frictions parked. After the Constitutional Convention, I emailed Mark Kelly of ICCL and Brian Sheehan suggesting a meeting to discuss forming a unified coalition. The success of our work at the Convention gave each of us hope that ME and GLEN might put aside their differences, now that the road to marriage equality was clear. I want to thank Mark and Brian for agreeing to move ahead together. There were suspicions to overcome, past comments critical of either organisation to forget, and a lack of mutual respect due to differing strategies to be addressed, but the staff and boards of GLEN and ME moved forward together, certain that only unified leadership focusing on the values of equality, inclusion, fairness and love would win the day – that day in May when Irish LGBT people and our families finally felt we belonged.

I had come across 'Belonging' as a concept central to same-sex relationship recognition while pursuing my doctorate in Dublin City University, also completed in 2015. The couples I interviewed for my research all either had a civil partnership or a foreign marriage that was recognised only as civil partnership in Ireland. Each of them spoke, without prompting, of how their relationships being recognised was a way of showing they belonged: to family, to friends, to community and to the Irish State as equal citizens.

Marriage Equality team members. *From left to right:* Kirsten Killoran and Dawn Quinn with John Lyons TD, and Director of Marriage Equality Moninne Griffith.

Ailbhe Smyth, long-time feminist activist and campaigner, provides the foreword and, as a founding Board member of ME, shares insights into the efforts and sacrifices made by staff, Board members, volunteers and allies to bring about this historical civil and human rights victory in Ireland.

The two women who lit the spark under the marriage equality movement in Ireland when they took a court case to have their Canadian marriage recognised in 2003, Katherine Zappone and Ann Louise Gilligan, open with their ten-year battle from High Court to Supreme Court and finally to a local constituency campaign to win Yes votes in their local area in Tallaght in Dublin.

Detailed descriptions by Co-Directors of ME, Moninne Griffith and Andrew Hyland, outline how they mobilised support and volunteers, building a marriage equality support base so that when a referendum was called, a clear approach and strong base were in place to win the hearts of the 'million in the middle' so needed by the Yes Equality campaign.

Campaign elements of fundraising and political strategic support are provided by ME Board members Darina Allen, Ronan Farren and Orla Howard. The legal context for marriage equality and the KAL case is outlined by ME Board member Justine Schönfeld-Quinn. Carol Armstrong describes how the army of volunteers were managed and Ross Golden-Bannon, a long-time LGBT rights activist, recalls the support and abuse he and his canvassing team experienced on the campaign trail. Denise Charlton, co-founder of ME, narrates how she, her partner Paula Fagan, and others put their families central to the campaign for marriage equality and LGBT family equality, while ME champion Anthony Kinahan recounts the story from County Louth. Key allies of ME describe how their organisations came to support the issue and their campaigns to bring together the widest gathering of civil society activists ever assembled on an equality social-change issue.

Kate Moynihan tells the story of how LINC in Cork flew the marriage equality banner proudly for the Yes Equality campaign. Michael Barron of BeLonG To details how his organisation built a campaign for young people who supported marriage equality to encourage their families to vote Yes. Niall Crowley, former CEO of the Equality Authority, describes

Marriage Equality Co-Directors Andrew Hyland (*left*) and Moninne Griffith.

his role in forming groups to support the fledgling marriage equality movement while Anna MacCarthy, former ME Board member, chronicles the radical work of LGBT Noise, and its successful marches for marriage and actions to 'make noise' for equality that drew many younger and more radical supporters into the movement. Laura Harmon sets out the nationwide campaign for marriage equality organised by the Union of Students in Ireland when she was USI president, and ME Board member Olivia McEvoy describes the long-time support of NLGF (National Lesbian and Gay Federation, now NXF) for marriage equality.

Richard O'Leary narrates how his organisation, Faith in Marriage Equality, made an extraordinary pilgrimage across Ireland to inspire people of faith to vote Yes. Brian Sheehan and Kieran Rose give their account of how GLEN moved from achieving civil partnership in 2010 to being one of the three partner organisations that came together to form Yes Equality with the Irish Council for Civil Liberties and ME.

The success achieved through the development of video resources is detailed by award-winning film-maker and ME Board member Linda Cullen of COCO Television. These short films ensured that social media would play a huge role in mobilising support for the marriage equality campaign.

Two contributions with a US twist are by Thalia Zepatos from Freedom to Marry USA, who shares her insights and contribution to the achievement of marriage equality in Ireland, and former evaluator of ME, Ide O'Carroll, academic and activist, now living between the US and Waterford, who gives her insights into the marriage equality campaign and the final win.

Thank you to each contributor for your story of the decade-long campaign for marriage equality in Ireland, and thank you to all those who voted Yes in May 2015.

Gráinne Healy
Chairwoman of Marriage Equality Ireland

Opposite: Activists and politicians unite to celebrate the passing of the Civil Marriage Bill outside Dáil Éireann, October 2015.

CROSSING THE THRESHOLD

Katherine Zappone *(left)* and Ann Louise Gilligan

The Journey Towards Winning
Our Story[1]

Ann Louise Gilligan begins

Fellow campaigners,

On behalf of Katherine and myself I want to thank you for the invitation to share our journey to marriage equality. We are doing so in the hope it will inspire you to continue to fight for what is fair, right and just – no matter what obstacles, challenges and setbacks you encounter.

It is right that we gather to celebrate the momentous referendum result and recall the joyous scenes not only at Dublin Castle but, perhaps more importantly, in family homes right across the country just one year ago. But it is equally important that we should accurately recall the long journey to that historic point.

In fact, it would be a disservice to those who are now campaigning and indeed will be fighting the campaigns of the future not to give an accurate account of the sleepless nights, the discrimination and the threat to our very livelihoods that had to be overcome along the way.

I am conscious that many of you are not familiar with our story, but that story is important because it was our driving force, inspiration and source of strength. The long road we travelled from 1981 to 2015 had many twists and turns, hills and vales but we never gave up. A campaign for equality cannot be time-bound. Practising resilience is therefore an integral feature of the journey. Resilience, as we discovered, is the capacity to hold hope in the face of strong resistance to a campaign for social change. What made it possible for us was that we had each other; we had love in our sails and a passionate longing for justice.

THE BEGINNING

Ours is a love story. Furthermore, our story illustrates the significance of the feminist insight 'the personal is political'.

It seems hard to believe now – but it started way back in September 1981, it was the autumn (or the Fall depending on which one of us tells the story!). We were each beginning studies in Boston College, we were strangers in town, Katherine from Seattle via New York and, of course, I was from Ireland. I recall the exact moment – an orientation day for graduate students.

Irish Times report of the KAL case proceedings, Monday, 8 November 2004.

4 THE IRISH TIMES Tuesday, November 9, 2004

HomeNews

Court to rule today on lesbian couple's recognition challenge

MARY CAROLAN

The High Court will give its decision today on whether an Irish lesbian couple who married in Vancouver, Canada, a year ago may take legal proceedings to have their marriage recognised here and to have the Revenue Commissioners treat them under the Tax Acts the same as a husband and wife.

Ms Katherine Zappone and Ms Ann Louise Gilligan claim there is no legal impediment to recognition of a same-sex marriage.

They say the refusal of the Revenue to grant them the same tax reliefs as available to an opposite-sex married couple discriminates against them on grounds of gender and/or sexual orientation and breaches their rights under the Constitution, European Convention for the Protection of Human Rights and Fundamental Freedoms, and the charter of Fundamental Rights of the EU.

They claim their rights to marry and to respect for their private and family life have been breached as have their rights to benefits under tax law. The conduct of the Revenue and State has, they claim, caused them distress, inconvenience, loss and damage.

Yesterday, Mr Gerard Hogan SC, and Ms Ivana Bacik, for the couple, applied for leave to take judicial review proceedings in which they will seek, among various reliefs, orders compelling the State and Revenue to recognise their marriage in Canada and to treat them as a married couple under the Tax Acts.

Mr Justice McKechnie said he wished to consider the matter overnight and would give his decision this morning. The respondents in the proposed proceedings are the Revenue, Ireland and the Attorney General. If leave is granted, the outcome of the case will have significant implications for the tax rights of same-sex and cohabiting couples.

According to the 2002 census, some 1,300 couples described themselves as same-sex couples while there were 77,600 family units based on cohabiting couples. The judge heard yesterday that Ms Zappone, a public policy consultant and member of the Human Rights Commission, and Ms Ann Gilligan, an academic, have been living together for 23 years and are joint owners of a home at Glenaraneen, Brittas, Co Dublin, and a holiday home at Kinego West, Caherciveen, Co Kerry.

They married in a ceremony in Vancouver, British Columbia, Canada, on September 13th, 2003, before family and friends and describe themselves as a lawfully married couple living together.

However, when they applied to the General Register Office here for confirmation that their marriage was legally binding in Ireland, they were told that was not a matter which came within the remit of that office. While there is no mechanism in law for having a foreign marriage registered here, the couple say a foreign marriage certificate, accompanied by a reputable translation from a reputable translation agency if necessary, is acceptable by the State for most legal and administrative purposes.

The couple wrote to the Revenue on April 26th last informing them of their marriage and enclosing a copy of their marriage certificate, plus an affidavit from a Canadian lawyer confirming their marriage was legally recognised under Canadian law. They claimed to have the same allowances as a married couple under the Taxes Consolidation Acts.

The Revenue informed them on July 1st, 2004, that it would not allow their claim for allowances as a married couple. The couple say that while the Tax Acts do not define the terms "husband and wife", the Revenue had told them that the Oxford English dictionary defined "husband" as a married man and "wife" as a married woman and justified its refusal on that basis.

The couple claim that, if they were an opposite-sex couple resident in Ireland who married in Canada, then their marriage would be recognised here and they would receive the various reliefs available to a married couple under the Tax Acts. Under those Acts, persons legally married and living together as husband and wife are entitled to certain income tax and capital gains benefits not available to cohabiting couples.

Outlining the basis of the case, Mr Hogan said he would be contending that the Constitution, the ECHR and the Tax Acts contain no definition of what constitutes marriage.

While the Constitution did not stipulate that marriage involves a husband and wife, Mr Hogan said he accepted that was the understanding in 1937 when the Constitution was drafted. However, the Constitution "did not freeze constitutional standards in the permafrost of 1937".

Matters had moved on and the Constitution must be interpreted as a living document.

Ms Ann Louise Gilligan (left) and Ms Katherine Zappone leaving the High Court in Dublin yesterday. They have been living together for 23 years, married last year in Canada and are seeking to be recognised as "husband and wife" by the Revenue Commissioners

Beocheist
Alex Hijmans

Críost ar fud na háite

Tá muid ag tiomáint tríd dheisceart Ohio, gar don teorainn le Kentucky, agus ar raidió an chairr tá amhráin ceol tíre ag dánamh ingairr d'Íosa Críost i ngach dara líne. Athraíonn mo chara an stáisiún – agus aimsíonn sé seanmóir ar stáisiún reiligiúnda éigin.

Ligeann sé osna mhór. "Thabharfainn an Bíobla air," a deir sé ag leathmhagadh "ach níl raibh Íosa Críost thart an oiread sin nuair a bhí mise ag fás aníos. Anois tá sé ar fud na háite."

Tá an ceart aige, agus is í uileilíthreacht Íosa Críost ta tsochaí Mheiriceánach an phríomhchúis gur éirigh le George W. Bush an dara treimhse a fháil sa Teach Bán i dtoghchán na seachtaine seo caite, an uair seo le móramh na phobail taobh thiar de. De réir anailís sa Washington Post, is Críostaithe den chine geal a "rugadh arís" iad 42 faoin gcéad de na daoine a vótáil do George W. Bush i dtoghcháin na seachtaine seo caite.

Is agallamh ar stáisiún raidió NPR chuir Rosa Gonzalez, ón eagraíocht dheonach The League of Pissed-Off Voters (ceann de na heagraíochtaí deonacha a choinnigh súil ghéar ar chórsaí vótála ar eagla go "ngoidfí" toghchán eile) ar muir seo é: "Cuireann sé iontas ar dhaoine nuair a deir duine atá 19 bliain d'aois, agus a chaitheann éadaí ó lipéad faiseanta, go vótáileadh sí do George W. Bush, toisc go bhfuil sé i gcoinne ginmhillte.

"Duine a admhaíonn nach bhfuil sé cinnte faoin chogadh san Iaráic ach go vótáiladh sé"

Irish Times report on the expected High Court ruling of the KAL case, 9 November 2004.

I was reserved by temperament, and Katherine appeared confident, with an air of authority and stunning black curly hair. It was later I found out about her passion and love of life, and the orange Volkswagen Beetle she drove. We were the only two students that year accepted into a PhD programme in Theology, Philosophy and Education. So it is correct to say that our studies brought us together but what was not expected was the magic of love that took us both by surprise. It was just a short six weeks later – on 10 November 1981 – that Katherine asked me to spend the rest of my life with her – it was what I can only describe as an eternal euphoric moment ... and so begins our lives together.

Those early days of the 1980s saw enormous social change. As feminists, it was an extraordinarily exciting time to take courses in a consortium of universities, including Harvard and Boston University. In October 1982, we gathered twelve close friends in Rockport to share a Eucharist together, to witness our life-partnership vows and to pronounce our union. We exchanged rings – ruby for Katherine, as it is my birthstone; topaz for me, Katherine's birthstone – both engraved 'God is Love – KAL'. It was a perfect occasion – the only cloud that dampened the day was the absence of family. While we had spent time in each other's homes during our first year together, we lacked the courage in those early years to live as an openly lesbian couple.

A year later we were in Ireland.

LIFE IN IRELAND

Crossing the Atlantic brought us face to face with recession, the fallout of a mismanaged economy and emigration stripping a country of its young people. But perhaps more strikingly, Ireland had not kept pace with social change. Claims that personal privacy was respected rung hollow when the reality was that people were expected to comply with the social norms.

The Catholic Church influenced every aspect of Irish life: women were largely excluded from political, business and public life – and while the courts condemned male homosexuality, the rights of lesbians were not even being discussed.

Upon returning to Ireland I resumed my position in St Patrick's College, but all had changed, changed radically. Studies in feminist theology and philosophy over previous years, insights into liberation movements in Latin America, and work on philosophies of imagination and creative education, meant disregarding all previous lecture notes. Katherine was appointed to a half-time position in Trinity College. On the home front we both moved into our small house in Dublin.

Ann Louise Gilligan (*left*) and Katherine Zappone speak to reporters outside the Four Courts,
15 December 2006.

Although neither of us experienced direct discrimination in our places of employment, we both experienced the insidious consequences of indirect discrimination. In my own case, I was appointed by an academic board from UCD to chair the Department of Religious Studies of which I was a member. Within a month, the Archbishop of Dublin intervened and withdrew his ratification of the appointment. As manager of a State-funded college, it is within his remit to approve all appointments to the College! Only the threat of legal action on my part, partially resolved this injustice. I eventually moved to the Department of Education in St Patrick's College, Drumcondra, and stayed there for the rest of my career. There are many other examples of how we both faced obstacles and were challenged by figures in authority. But we stood firm to our equality agenda, deeply rooted in feminism.

That agenda was to bring us to The Shanty – many of you will be familiar with our beautiful home in the Dublin hills – but it was also where we laid the foundations for our community activism. Deeply influenced, not only by the ideas from various liberation movements, but also shaped and influenced by the organisations for social change in the Boston area, we returned to Ireland determined to purchase a home together that we could share as an education and training centre with women who did not get the opportunity to reach their potential in their early experience of school. For fifteen years we worked with women from the Tallaght community (and beyond) to provide second-chance education in a purpose-built centre nine feet from our back door.

As the demand for our courses increased, with the local community we decided to build a large and beautiful Education, Early Years and Enterprise Centre in the heart of Jobstown, West Tallaght. It happened above all because of a ground-up campaign led and owned by hundreds of people, alongside the mutually owned determination of a fundraising/development committee of eighteen women from outside the West Tallaght community. This campaign was marked by fun, meals together and lots of laughter. Our shared mantra was 'Image the possible'. As we all campaigned to raise the million pounds required to build An Cosán in Jobstown, we knew that 'What you image is what you get.' We wanted the building to be beautiful and spacious. When some people tried to dampen our enthusiasm, we'd hold on to what for them was an impossible dream and, thankfully, together we built what the locals now call a 'beacon of light' for the people.

Over the past thirty years it has been exciting and rewarding to see our work flourish into An Cosán: A Centre of Learning, Enterprise and Early Childhood Education in the community of Jobstown, West Tallaght. Together with the local community we have served over 15,000 adults and 5,000 children. One hundred jobs have been created through the establishment of a social franchise of Fledglings Early Childhood Centres throughout the wider Tallaght region. I mention this work because it is important in another way. It showed us the huge thirst from people across West Tallaght and surrounding communities for knowledge on how to work together, to organise and to bring about real change which impacts on not only their own lives but the lives of their neighbours every day. Through training, courses and readings, women were empowered – and were making a difference.

You may ask what has all this to do with marriage equality – but what I have recalled are the foundations. It is where both of us have come from, how our experiences on both sides of the Atlantic gave us vision, courage and strength. It illustrates how our relationship has been generative. Now we have set the scene.

Our Lives Out Loud by Ann Louise Gilligan and
Katherine Zappone, October 2008.

First (joint) recipients of the Person of the Year GALAS award, 2009.

MARRIAGE EQUALITY

Preparations for the trip of a lifetime to Chile in 2001 highlighted that, despite our lives being full, we were not treated as equals. Before setting off we decided to catch up on outstanding paperwork. During a stocktake of our wills, we discovered that, in the event of a bereavement, a co-owned property in Kerry would be taxed differently than if we were a married couple. The realisation that the Revenue Commissioners could in an hour of grief suddenly target one of us was a shock. This was never about money or possessions. The question was: could we as feminists, campaigners and believers in equality tolerate or accept this? After working with a community to act – could we just sit back and allow ourselves, as a loving couple, to be treated differently?

Two years of research, advice and many coffees with close friends and legal experts followed to weigh up the pros and cons of taking on politics and the Church – which were at best benign and often hostile on lesbian and gay rights. Part of our consideration had to be the fact that the Archbishop of Dublin was the official manager of St Pat's College, my place of employment for twenty-seven years. Dismissal was a real possibility if he determined that the sexual identity of an employee undermines the College's religious ethos.

Our final decision came in a transatlantic phone call when I was in Vancouver to deliver a paper at an academic conference in July 2003. Katherine's brother Mark was also there in

Ann Louise Gilligan and Katherine Zappone *(right)* at the 2011 March for Marriage.

the same city at the same time, to act as best man at a wedding. I met Mark for lunch and he revealed that the celebration was for two gay friends, David and Chris, who lived in Seattle. It transpired that they were one of the first couples to come over the border from the United States to avail of the new law in British Columbia that opened the institution of marriage to gays and lesbians. There was no requirement to be a citizen or a resident. With great excitement I rang Katherine (who was back in Ireland) with the glorious news. We ran up an enormous phone bill but the decision was 'Yes, Yes, let's do it.' We were 6,000 miles apart but united in our passionate desire to push for justice ahead of naked fear. Everything happens for a reason – or to use an old-fashioned sounding phrase, 'providence'. The meeting with Mark made us realise our dream could also become a reality.

A short time later, a surprise birthday dinner for myself during a summer break ended with a moonlight stroll on the strand and our agreement to marry. Loved ones received the news with excitement and joy. Sharing with one's family that one is choosing to get married is coming out *par excellence*. On 13 September, in the home of the commissioner who had officiated for Mark's friends, we were married in Canada. It was an extraordinary moment for us both, and equally it was profoundly moving to watch the gaze of affirmation that

Senator Katherine Zappone's first day at Seanad Éireann, with Ann Louise Gilligan *(right)*, May 2011.

extended to us from faces aged from twelve to eighty-two. Our return to Ireland brought us back to the reality.

With no national organisation willing to campaign on the issue of marriage and others in our situation still closeted, it was clear we would have to go it alone. In early 2004 our legal team devised a strategy: first, we were to apply to the Revenue Commissioners to recognise our marriage and request a change of tax status. If they accepted, we had won, if they did not, we were heading to the High Court. Upon receiving a negative response, our lawyers set to work immediately. Nothing prepared us for waking up on the morning of 8 November 2004 to hear our application to the High Court all over RTÉ's *Morning Ireland*, after featuring on the front page of *The Irish Times*. Headline writers sent the message worldwide – the battle for marriage equality in Ireland was on.

The court decided yes, there was a case to answer, but this was just a prelude. Weeks and months of huge public support came to a crashing halt with another *Irish Times* front page, and the news was not good. The government at cabinet level had discussed our case and decided to challenge us. The full gravity of what we were about to take on suddenly hit us. It took time to regain our energy and drive. A fundraiser at a packed Mansion House reminded us of the enormous gift of solidarity. Four and a half years after we discovered Ireland's discriminatory tax system, our legal challenge began.

Judgment Day was 15 December 2006. We arrived early at the Four Courts to be greeted by family and friends. The judgment is 138 pages, but in reality it was over in ten minutes. We lost. Despite the disappointment and hurt, we lodged our case with the Supreme Court as we reached for hope. Our case remained active and we were ready to take that option until the prospect of the Marriage Equality Referendum came into view. As we now delve into politics, I will hand over to the politician of the KAL team to continue.

Katherine Zappone continues

Ann Louise has really shared our roots, our foundations and our vision as a feminist couple that believes in equality for all – it is our core, it is at the very heart of our personal journey, and I suggest Ireland's journey, to marriage equality.

Campaigners in the United States say the first step to success is to be able to tell the 'Story of Self'. It is normally the very reason for a campaign's existence, or personal involvement in a campaign. By being comfortable in telling your own story, you convince family, friends, neighbours, and many others. Ann Louise has given you our story of self. There are others who also have a story to tell – Gráinne Healy, Denise Charlton, Paula Fagan, Moninne Griffith and so many of our friends and fellow campaigners. Through each other the 'Story of Self' became the 'Story of Us' – of course, we didn't know it at the time but that is what happened, albeit organically in our context. That 'Story of Us' led to the establishment of Marriage Equality. We were feminists looking for equality because it is our right – we were not going to accept watered-down marriage, we were seeking what is right, fair and just. Like so many successful organisations, it is actually quite hard to pin down a moment when it started – but suffice to say the legal case was the genesis.

There were so many legal arguments to the case, but the one that I would single out today is this: 'Everyone should have the right to marry *the person they choose to love* (italics mine).' This legal argument – in a public interest law case – eventually became a prime public communications message in the Yes campaign during the marriage referendum.

However, I am getting ahead of the story now. Forgive me. For the past to become the present, out of which we image new horizons, is part and parcel of the journey of social change. It is an integral characteristic of 'social intelligence' and it can be learned. Always stay in the present, knowing that a rich past has shaped it, and then we will have the confidence to do new work. So, let us reach back to one dimension of the past.

Senator Katherine Zappone *(left)*, Tánaiste Joan Burton and Minister for Communications, Energy and Natural Resources Alex White at the launch of the Yes Equality campaign, March 2015.

In February 2008, what had been a close support base of friends, feminists and supporters gathered around our kitchen table had transformed into the organisation, Marriage Equality (ME). We were a not-for-profit, national, single-issue, grassroots-advocacy organisation. Our goal was to achieve equality for lesbian, gay, bisexual and transgender people in Ireland through the extension of civil marriage rights to same-sex couples. Now it was about the 'Story of Us'! Our mission was supported primarily by the work and experience of the KAL case – our legal battle before the courts – and those extraordinary and generous people who made up the KAL Advocacy Initiative.

There were also public pieces of work dating back to the time of our case; a report by the Law Reform Commission on Co-habitants (2007); and findings of the Oireachtas Committee on the Constitution (2006). Those findings were in favour of legal recognition of same-sex relationships for 'marriage-like' privileges. It was a mixed bag – accepting marriage equality as the only true equality measure but favouring civil partnership as possibly the only option in legislation. Ann Louise is very clear on this – we did not want some second-class marriage, we would not ask others for permission to marry, and full equality is the only acceptable outcome. Gráinne Healy, Denise Charlton and many others shared our views.

It would be dishonest not to tell you that these were difficult times in our community, while others favoured civil partnership and a piecemeal approach there were those of us who would only accept one end goal.

You will be aware that civil partnership did become a reality and, in fairness for many couples, it did overcome obstacles: I am thinking of immigration issues, inheritance and other areas of law. But for us it was not enough. Political changes, a new government with Labour in power and the appointment of Alan Shatter (TD) and then Frances Fitzgerald (TD) as Ministers for Justice brought new hope. It seems like so long ago now, but in June 2011 the establishment of a Constitutional Convention reignited our campaign. Through this mechanism we were able to reassure nervous politicians that the support was there for a referendum – and a referendum that would pass. We shared our stories – stories that struck a chord with fellow citizens. It was the foundation on which the referendum was built, and a model, which I am sure, that will deliver more much-needed social change in our country, not least Repealing the Eighth amendment. There is no doubt in my mind that the Constitutional Convention probably more than anything else set us on the road to achieving marriage equality. You will have heard about the grand coalition building it sparked, reinvigorating our community. There was the emergence of new allies, and not just in politics. The need to work together, one voice, agreed messaging – culminating in that glorious day in Dublin Castle.

SIGNIFICANCE OF MARRIAGE EQUALITY

What is the significance of that result? The significance is first and foremost in family homes across Ireland. Our marriages are equal, and are celebrated and rejoiced by our family, friends and neighbours. It is significant for wider changes, too. Recently, I was in County Mayo and together with Taoiseach Enda Kenny met local members of BeLonG To.[2] There the Taoiseach sat on a couch with three young lesbians, easily discussing how their lives had changed since the referendum. Would any political leader have hosted such a visit two or three years ago? The image of that morning is etched forever in my memory. That is why Ann Louise and I took our case oh so long ago now. We took it for ourselves, yes, but we also took it for young LGBT people. We wanted them to grow up free to be themselves, free to be L, G, B or T.

Those of you on Twitter would have seen news of the result of the referendum last year explode, not just here at home, but across the globe. It was hugely significant that Catholic Ireland was the first country to introduce marriage equality by popular vote. It has been a

Katherine Zappone (*left*) and Ann Louise Gilligan at the launch of the 'I'm Voting Yes. Ask Me Why' campaign, 9 April 2015.

Ann Louise Gilligan speaking with Moninne Griffith at one of the final YES Equality photocalls, 21 May 2015.

huge journey – for us personally, for LGBT people and their families and friends across the country and for Ireland. For Ann Louise and myself, it was a privilege to be there at the start and to celebrate its finish.

There are three roots in this movement – the courts, the lawmakers and the people. The recent referendum result was a seismic shift of the cultural foundations of Ireland. The impact of such change only 'drops slowly' and the ripple effect moves into streams and rivers and oceans that we can't even see right now. Whether inside or outside the courtroom, the changes involved the enormous, effective, intelligent and emotional mobilisation of the people.

Earlier this year in City Hall, President of Ireland Michael D. Higgins and his wife, Sabina, Members of Government and other friends, joined us for a moving ceremony, facilitated by our friend Miriam O'Callaghan.[3] We not only renewed our vows – we brought our marriage home! And that is the significance of what has unfolded in this country for the past two decades.

Ann Louise and Katherine conclude together

There are so many things that we have learned on the journey towards winning, and we want to share a few of them now.

ON LEADERSHIP

Formed in early 2008, the Board of ME was composed of strong feminist women and generous men, in solidarity. The feminist leadership in the presence of the Co-Chairs, members of the Board and members of staff utilised a dialogical, relational approach to our work together, and this was owned and promoted by all men who joined the Board and staff. In short, the leadership of any campaign is vital. Katherine and I recall one campaign in the 1980s where we lived in tents outside the fence of Greenham Common. Our objective in the women's peace camp was to protest the nuclear missiles sited at the Greenham Common Air Force Base. The 'leader' of the campaign insisted that true to her version of feminism there could be no leader, which resulted in no clear structure for the campaign. The fact that we didn't all die of hypothermia, given the freezing nights and frozen ground water pipes in the campsite, was miraculous. The lesson of the powerlessness of leaderlessness was learned forever! Leaderless campaigns are structureless and are usually ineffective.

The Marriage Bill passes through the Oireachtas, 30 September 2015. *From left:* Ann Louise Gilligan, Senator Katherine Zappone, Minister for Justice Frances Fitzgerald and Gráinne Healy.

ON TIME

Shifting indelibly engrained prejudice takes time. We always believed that shifting conscious-ness beyond the orthodoxy of Church teachings and dominant political and legal practice is a lengthy educational task that cannot be underestimated. Over the years, we never refused a chance to speak on media through television, radio, newspapers and Twitter whenever the opportunity presented itself. It is true that an invitation in 2004 to go on Ireland's *Late Late Show* – the most popular talk show in the country – was a watershed moment. Still, shifting the cultural norms of resistance takes time, and so we need to cultivate the virtues of patience and perseverance.

ON RELATIONSHIP

The journey towards winning the referendum happened predominantly through a ground campaign. The campaign conducted in the constituency of Dublin South West,[4] led by Darragh Genockey and Katherine, was marked by an ethos of relationality and empathy.

Each night campaign volunteers were welcomed by name and given time to catch up and chat before the work of the evening in small teams began. Bonds were built between people and this significantly impacted the empathic listening and dialogue that was exchanged at each house. At the end of each evening, there was genuine jubilation when a campaigner narrated with deep respect how someone changed her or his mind from an adamant 'No!' to marriage equality to a faltering 'maybe' and sometimes a 'YES'!

Campaigning is hard; it is tiring but it is energising as it calls on all of our creative resources to find the *mot juste* (the exact word) or the empathetic silence and stillness that respects the diversity of perspectives. The experience of campaigning reflects the relational continuum of all human life, from the very positive to the opposite. One evening, alone, Ann Louise called on a house that was dark and dilapidated. As the door was opened by a timorous Spanish *au pair*, a voice boomed up the corridor from the back kitchen. The interrogation that ensued was peppered with shouts of condemnation and threats of hell for all who were campaigning for marriage equality. To say Ann Louise was afraid of what would happen next is no exaggeration. When she escaped, she swore that she would never concede to an 'invitation' of this hue again!

ON GLOBAL CONNECTIONS

In 2004, we made a visit to the Boston GLAD (Gay and Lesbian Advocates and Defenders) offices. We had travelled to meet with GLAD after receiving Court permission to take our own case in Ireland. We received assistance from Mary Bonauto, who was involved in the *Goodridge* case in Massachusetts, which was the first US state to legalise same-sex marriage. Bonauto had also worked with GLAD in Boston following the *Marshall* judgement and was one of the lawyers in the *Obergefell v Hodges* Supreme Court case, the case famously depicted by President Obama with the #LOVEWINS.

Our visit to GLAD shaped our campaign and a decade later we achieved marriage equality, followed swiftly by the USA itself. In a conference call with Mary, we shared key legal arguments and strategies with other lawyers around the table, creative strategies and tactics of advocacy and public communications that went along with the legal strategy. The global impact of public interest law in the twenty-first century is huge. Yes Equality had substantive links in the USA, including Evan Wolfson and others of Freedom to Marry. That's the way it gets done today – those who fight us organise internationally, and so we do, too.

Katherine Zappone *(left)* and Ann Louise Gilligan attend the Road to Equality Summer School, July 2016, with Denise Charlton *(behind)*.

ON IMAGINATION

Arrogance and orthodoxy are anathema to the flexibility required for a creative and imaginative campaign for social change. The Yes campaign in the final months leading up to the referendum held strong to the belief that 'What you imagine is what you get.' The intuitive insights of 'what to do next' often bubbled to the surface as we listened carefully to stories from the doorways; for example, the heartfelt plea from a family member that his gay brother's recent suicide would not be in vain. Intuitive insight and soul-filled longing for a different Ireland energised this campaign and fuelled hope for a more equal country for all.

Gráinne Healy

Socio-Political Developments Creating the Context for Marriage Equality for Same-Sex Couples in Ireland[1]

CATALYSTS FOR CHANGE

The socio-political changes in Ireland in the late twentieth and early twenty-first centuries created the conditions allowing for the emergence of civil partnership in 2010, and then five years later marriage equality in 2015. The change in family size and structure, the emergence of same-sex-headed households led to key societal changes. These changes include the changing roles of men and especially, women in Ireland. These three key catalysts for change in Ireland from the 1960s onwards challenged the prevailing Catholic habitus and led to a liberalisation of attitudes towards lesbian and gay rights. The legislative progress towards equality and civil partnership was a significant milestone for equality for gay and lesbian people, but an incomplete and unequal one.

IRELAND: CARNALLY COMING OF AGE

Twenty-first-century Ireland is in the 'throes of a delayed sexual revolution, as a country long accustomed to a strict policing of sexual morality, has carnally come of age' (Ferriter, 2009, p. 1). The history of sexuality in modern Irish society is complex and perhaps some aspects of it are unique to the Irish. 'The sexual is always about the individual as well as the social constructions, discourses and struggles for power that are part of society's quest for control over the individual life' (Ferriter, 2009, p. 2). It is a story of great change, a power struggle, set in the wider story of the Irish sexual revolution, a complex process criss-crossing a multitude of discourses: 'A constellation of interests and an alliance of power, especially between Church and State, and between mothers and priests, drove sexuality into the dark recesses of Irish society' (Inglis, 1997, p. 5).

Exploring how Foucault's 1978 examination of the deployment of sexuality is relevant to Ireland, Inglis (1997) suggests Foucault's interest in examining sex in a genealogical way will help us to discover who does the speaking, their positions and viewpoints.

Inglis describes three major discourse formations on sexuality in Ireland: firstly, that which forms discourses on policing of bodies in marriage, family and property relations, initially the sphere of experts, theologians and scientists in the late eighteenth and early nineteenth century. That discourse then becomes embodied in everyday life in homes, schools, churches and hospitals, under the watch and control of priests, doctors, nuns and mothers; finally, sexuality becomes central in the late twentieth century to 'an intensive system of care, knowledge and appreciation of the self' (Inglis, 1997, p. 9). This last discourse is concerned with 'rooting out the forces of sexual repression and the search for the truth and emancipation of the sexual being' (Foucault, 1986, p. 77). The move towards same-sex-relationship recognition is part of this search.

For Inglis (1998) growing up, Ireland of the 1950s was an Ireland with an absence of physical affection, an obsession with sex and an emphasis on self-denial. This he claims is what makes Irish sexuality different. It was an Ireland where the greatest sin was sex and where this belief was inculcated deeper and lasted longer in the bodies and souls of the Irish than among the rest of those living in the West. Ferriter (2009, p. 3) maintains 'there was dissent, different opinions, double standards and a more complex sexual identity and practice' than Inglis allows. The experiences of lesbians and gay men show the lived reality as somewhere in between.

In relation to the suggestion that the Church was consulted on impending legislation by the founding legislators and policy makers, Ferriter says that it was more a case of politicians looking to the Church for guidance on how to, 'protect Irish citizens from sexual immorality,' (Ferriter, 2009, p. 6). This is ironic given the litany of clerical sexual abuse committed by Catholic clergy and subsequently hidden and denied by the Catholic hierarchy (O'Gorman, 2002 & 2006; Raftery, 1999, 2002 & 2013). It was the media 'that did most to shatter the Church's dominance of sexual discourse' (Inglis, 1997 p. 6). The separation of Church and State was 'gradual and initially amicable' (Breen, Hannan et al., 1990) and became most obvious when the Catholic Church's special place in the Constitution was removed in 1972 (Canavan, 2012).

Listening attentively at the official launch of Marriage Equality, Mansion House, Dublin, February 2008.

Gráinne Healy wins Volunteer of the Year GALA award, March 2015.

Patricia O'Connor *(left)*, Conor Irwin and Gráinne Healy with their dog Keeper as part of the 2010 'We are Family' campaign.

CHANGING FAMILIES

Central to an examination of same-sex relationships and their recognition in Ireland is the emergence of same-sex-relational households as new and emerging family forms in an Irish context. 'What family is, what family does, and how it does it are ongoing questions for Irish society and its government' (Canavan, 2012). Same-sex families and LGBT-parented families (Pillinger and Fagan, 2013; CSO, 2012) are a feature of twenty-first-century Irish family life. Irish family life and patterns have greatly changed since the distinctive patterns of the twentieth century where family forms were, in the vast majority of cases, based on marriage and the characteristics of the Irish family then included late age at marriage, a high rate of single women who never married, and very low levels of births outside marriage, while, due to the lack of birth control, Irish families were large and few women participated in the Irish labour force (Kennedy, 2001).

Launching the 'Just Love campaign'. *From left:* ME Board members Judy Walsh and Paula Fagan, Director of ME Moninne Griffith, Board member Justine Schönfeld-Quinn and Deputy Chairwoman of ME Orla Howard, October 2011.

Ireland has moved from a predominantly socially conservative agricultural economy in the 1950s to a more open service-based economy in the twenty-first century with a more educated people and fewer children in most families; contraception is widely available and used, and divorce taken up when needed, despite the Catholic Church's opposition to both. Kennedy (2001, p. 2) maintains that compared to our European neighbours, while 'the pace and timing of modernisation in Ireland differed ... the pathway travelled was similar'. Fighting Catholic Church authoritarian positions on matters of public and private morality was not just a feature of Irish society (Dillon, 1999), but with a Catholic majority, those within the Catholic community and those just living in a Catholic-dominated society worked to effect change, 'redrawing the borders of Catholic identity' to achieve a transformative change (Dillon, 1999, p. 11).

Gráinne Healy speaking at the Amnesty International launch of their campaign for the marriage referendum, 'Let's Make History', March 2015.

SAME-SEX-HEADED HOUSEHOLDS

The 2011 Census was the first time a question was asked which allowed same-sex-headed households to declare themselves and become visible and counted. The emergence of same-sex-headed households in the 2011 Census is an indicator of yet another change of family patterns in Ireland. There were then 4,042 same-sex-headed households (2,321 males and 1,721 females). Of these, 230 of them had children and 166 stated that they were 'married', which means that they were married outside of Ireland as same-sex marriage was not then available (CSO, 2012). As civil partnership was only enacted in 2011 and marriage equality later in 2015, it is thought that the full extent of same-sex-headed households may be more visible in the next census. It is estimated that 5–7 per cent of the population may be lesbian, gay or bisexual (GLEN, 2007). To June 2013, 1,088 same-sex couples have had their relationships registered and recognised by the Irish State in civil partnerships (GLEN, 2013). An unknown additional number of same-sex couples have had foreign civil partnerships or foreign civil marriages recognised as civil partnerships by the Irish State. Such new family forms are increasingly prevalent (Fine-Davis, 2011; Canavan, 2012; Pillinger and Fagan, 2013) and their views, attitudes and behaviour form an important area of new research in Ireland.[2]

Looking to possible future same-sex family patterns in Ireland, Pillinger & Fagan's (2013) Irish study of LGBT people who are parents, and those who are planning parenthood, would indicate that this new family form is present, and their study provides the lived experiences of LGBT people 'as a backdrop to the legal, policy and other changes' that the study participants themselves see as urgent for family and relevant policy changes in Ireland (Pillinger & Fagan, 2013, p. 5).

So, what have been the key socio-political changes that have happened, which account for this changing face of families in modern Ireland, in particular the emergence of same-sex-headed households and families?

Constitutional Convention campaigners. *From left:* Stephen O Hare, Olivia McEvoy, Gráinne Healy, Moninne Griffith, Ross Golden-Bannon, Tiernan Brady, Conor Pendergrast, Brian Sheehan, Walter Jayawardene, Orla Howard, Dawn Quinn and Mark Kelly, April 2013.

Jean-Philippe Imbert of DCU *(left)* marches with Gráinne Healy, March for Marriage, August 2014.

KEY SOCIAL CHANGES IN IRELAND

An examination of sexuality-related issues in Ireland, including the emergence of same-sex-relationship recognition, will have as part of its basis an understanding that Irish sexual morality was traditionally based on Catholicism (Smyth, 1995). Central to this understanding is the non-separation of Church and State that existed since the foundation of the State (Breen, Hannan et al., 1990), indeed so-called 'sexual immorality became one of the new adversaries' of the newly formed Irish State (Duffy, 2011, p. 17).

A number of cultural factors have contributed to a changing Ireland that has seen the introduction of same-sex-relationship recognition in 2010 and led to the heightened demand for access to civil marriage for same-sex couples and LGBT-headed families in the subsequent years (Pillinger & Fagan, 2013).

CHANGING ROLES OF MEN AND WOMEN

While the 1937 Constitution defined the role of woman in Ireland as primarily within the home, it is evident today, with more than 50 per cent of Irish women in the labour force (CSO, 2012), that women's role has changed in Irish public and family life. The work life balance required of women is evident in the fact that 57 per cent of mothers in a recent study are engaged 'predominantly in employment outside the home' (Williams et al., 2010, p. 9). The move from women's role as homemaker and mother to one of active participant in the labour force has meant greater economic independence for women. The decoupling of the exclusive link between marriage and motherhood has also coincided with a change in attitude towards marriage in Ireland (Kennedy, 2001). Marriage has come to be seen as an option for women and men, not a destiny. Increased emphasis on parenting and partnership roles of men, coupled with a widening of women's career opportunities, has supported a shift away from the exclusive male breadwinner pattern of the Irish family towards a broader sharing of both paid work and work in the home by couples.

Studies of 1970s Ireland show that by the end of the twentieth century, 'the patriarchal, authoritarian model of the family was largely replaced by a more egalitarian model' (Hannan and Katsiaouni, 1977, p. 100). The earlier male-dominated, Church-ruled private space of marriage and family was being replaced with notions such as the growing importance of love and intimacy within Irish marriage (Ryan, 2012). It is within this context that we begin to see how a more general openness to gender diversity, sexuality and diversity of family forms is the seedbed within which the seeds of same-sex-relationship recognition could be sown.

As more and more women entered the workforce, their male parenting partners, the new generation, got more involved in home duties and child rearing (Kennedy, 2001). The traditional family unit of male and female married couples raising children remains high, at 71 per cent, with cohabiting male/female couples at 15 per cent and lone parents at 14 per cent (Williams et al., 2010, p. 9). Through an absence of childcare and paid parental leave,[3] only 1.2 per cent of Irish fathers are primarily engaged in home duties (Williams et al., 2010). Women's lives have changed far more than men's, at least with regard to family and parenting responsibilities. A further factor which pushed women into the labour market and broke down the traditional gendered roles of men and women was the desire to own family homes and the need for two salaries to allow that purchase to take place. Irish men's, and especially Irish women's, roles have altered in response to economic and social demands of modern life. But there were some notable catalysts to this process.

THE WOMEN'S MOVEMENT

Increased job opportunities for women, in both the private and public sector, drew women, post-1960s, towards greater economic independence. Overcoming the marriage bar (where married women had to resign their jobs in the public service – completely removed in 1973 – on foot of a European directive to do so) women could now both work and be married or work and have children. The vast majority of women's groups and organisations pre-1960s focused on children and homemaking and were replaced (Kennedy, 2001; Connolly, 2005) in the 1970s with the emergence of the Women's Liberation Movement (WLM) and subsequent women's rights organisations and bodies, seeking rights for women, not just in relation to their role as wife and mother, but rights for women as independent agents requiring control over their own economic, reproductive and relational lives. These events were highlighted and gained access to living rooms across Ireland by the advent of Raidió Teilifís Éireann (now RTÉ) and the famous *Late Late Show* programme in 1971. Inglis (1997), Ferriter (2009) and Ryan (2012) hold that the advent of mass media, especially television, and the women's movement, which challenged attitudes towards gender and sexual inequality, were major catalysts for change in Ireland at that time. While former editor of *The Irish Times* Conor Brady (2012) tells us that 'the struggle between those who wanted to silence dissent and criticism and those who believed ideas should be free and should be debated took place on a much wider stage than television alone' (*The Irish Times*, 27 July 2012, 'RTÉ history of television screened out bigger picture'). Not embraced by all women, organisations such as Women in the Home tried to hold onto the constitutional view of Irish women and the traditionally defined roles of men and women established in 1937, greatly infused with Catholic Church teaching and traditional values on such matters (Ferriter, 2009; Connolly, 2005).

Rose (1994) and Hug (1999) place the early lesbian and gay activists at the heart of many feminist campaigns in the 1970s, which were training grounds for strategies and tactics used to begin the work of the initial gay rights movement in Ireland, which sought to challenge discrimination and invisibility and attain fundamental rights for lesbian and gay citizens of Ireland.

IRELAND JOINS EEC: A CATALYST FOR CHANGE

A second event that pushed change forward in Ireland was when Ireland entered the European Economic Community (EEC, later to become the European Union) in 1973. As mentioned earlier, by 2012, 50 per cent of Irish women were in the labour force. In 1973,

The Yes Equality bus launched to take the Yes message nationwide, 22 April 2013. *From left:* Tony Glavin, Colm O'Gorman, Gráinne Healy, Eithna and Andy Hyland (parents of Andrew Hyland).

only 7 per cent of married women worked outside the home, the male breadwinner model was still firmly in place, but membership of the EEC, which promoted equality legislation to underpin gender equality, pushed the Irish government to make changes to employment law (*Equal Pay Act*, 1974, *Employment Equality Act*, 1977), social welfare law (introduction of individualised payments to women and men), and reform of taxation codes. All of which strengthened women's economic independence and loosened the gendered roles which kept both women and men so bound to traditional notions of what men and women could and should be in Ireland (Hug, 1999). In 1960, women earned only 53 per cent of what men did; this rose to 59 per cent in 1971; it was the EEC's equality policies which sought to outlaw this discrimination and in doing so promoted the economic independence of women in the EU – including from 1973 on, Ireland (Ryan, 2012).

John Lyons TD with Gráinne Healy at the RTÉ studios following an appearance on *Morning Ireland*, as the votes were counted, Saturday, 23 May 2015.

THE MEDIA: A CATALYST FOR CHANGE

The media played a key role in pushing social change – the new RTÉ television station, the rise in women's magazines, radio and TV shows which discussed matters like marital breakdown or domestic violence and phone-in radio shows, where the voices of men and women began to be aired over the airwaves, increasing the dissemination of voices depicting the lived realities for men and women in Ireland, and elsewhere. It was on these chat shows and in these magazine and newspaper columns that issues such as homosexuality or contraception or abortion were often aired and views different to those held in an earlier, more closed society, were shared and understood (Ryan, 2012). Brady (2012) says television was part of a process, combined with print media, which worked to 'create change in a society where values had scarcely altered since the famine' (*The Irish Times*, 27 July 2012, 'RTÉ history of television screened out bigger picture'). The earlier, less questioning, acceptance of how life was to be lived by men and women, until the 1960s, coupled with second-level education extended to all children following primary school, contributed to the production of 'a counter culture' to traditional Catholicism, especially in the area of the Church's teaching on sex and morality

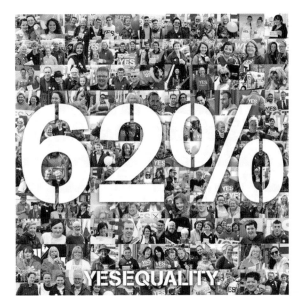

Result!

2015 Dublin Pride Marshalls. *From left:* Gráinne Healy, Brian Sheehan and Mark Kelly.

(Kennedy, 2001, p. 118). It was the media which played the most effective role as a catalyst for social change in Ireland and shattered the Catholic Church's dominance of sexual discourse (Inglis, 1997; Layte et al., 2006). The mass media as Nic Ghiolla Phádraig (1995, p. 617) pointed out were 'the church's main competitors in the interpretation of Irish society.'

CHANGING RELIGIOUS AND SEXUAL IDENTITY IN IRELAND

'Religious identity in modern Ireland has been as socially significant as gender, class, ethnicity or sexual orientation' (Inglis, 2005, p. 59).

To understand how religion is tied in with everyday life and the struggles to control and police moral areas, Inglis (2005) insists that one must understand why religion was such a strong force in Irish society. There is no doubt that in the colonisation of Ireland, the Catholic Church was close to the oppressed Catholic people and, as the State moved towards post-independence, it was to the Church the largely uneducated masses turned for guidance. Likewise, as the State was founded, its foundational document, the Irish Constitution, placed the Catholic Church in a privileged space, which it would retain for decades. However, as 'feminism and secularism have gained ground, the Catholic Church has lost ground in politics and in daily life' (Canavan, 2012, p. 4).

Working with the media on polling day, 22 May 2015: Patricia O'Connor (*left*) and Gráinne Healy.

Likewise the emerging bourgeois, who were to be the ruling and governing class of the new State, often sought guidance from the Church on matters of legislation and policy (Ferriter, 2009). While some may have sought guidance, the reality was that Irish education, at all levels, including teacher training colleges and Irish health services, were (and continue to be) mostly provided by and predominantly under the management of Catholic religious bodies and Catholic religious institutions. Such bodies did not have to be approached for guidance in many instances, the Catholic Church provided effective guidance and regulation of the population through these institutions. The Catholic Church controlled Ireland both through its dissemination of ideology and also control of resources (Nic Ghiolla Phádraig, 1995). Kilfeather (2005) tells us that, in trying to compensate for the loss of its historical role as the public voice of a wronged nation, 'The church, fearing revolutionary discourse, set out to demonise the attractions of liberalism or socialism as "foreign" and that usually meant English. It was the battle against secularism which the church targeted and in particular the regulating of sexuality' (Kilfeather, 2005, p. 106). This 'war' built to a height in the 1960s, led by Dublin Archbishop McQuaid. He built thirty-four new churches in that decade while the censorship board drew up banned lists of publications which saw international writers like Sartre and Hemingway banned. Irish writers like Frank O'Connor, John McGahern and Edna O'Brien also were banned for dealing with matters sexual and forbidden for Catholic consumption (Ryan, 2012).

CATHOLIC HABITUS

Bourdieu's (1984) concept of *habitus* applies to Catholic influence on sexuality in Ireland. *Habitus* or 'know how' is created through a social, rather than individual process, leading to patterns that are enduring and transferrable from one context to another and can shift in relation to specific contexts over time. *Habitus* is not fixed or permanent, and can be changed under unexpected situations or over a long historical period (Navarro, 2006, p. 16). The Catholic Church's influence on Irish society, as a result of Catholic *habitus*, pervaded all aspects of society, but it particularly dominated sexual discourse (Inglis, 2005). Much of the maintenance and development of economic capital in Ireland in the twentieth century was dependent on controlling marriage, 'the deployment of alliance' as Foucault (1978, p. 106) termed it, which in turn meant the need to control sexual relations. In particular, keeping all sexual activity solely within marriage and for reproductive purposes, was its aim.

Irish society in the late twentieth century saw a decline in agriculture, an increase in urbanisation, and the introduction of television and mass media, the latter being the most influential of all in shifting the traditional *habitus* of Irish sexuality (Inglis, 1997). All of these changes caused the decline of Catholic *habitus* of Irish sexuality; 'the unreflective, immediate, ongoing disposition which people had when encountering sexuality, began to change from fear, doubt, suspicion, guilt and shame more towards positive pleasure and enjoyment' (Inglis, 1997, p. 6). This led to a reduction of the power and control of the Church. In this more secularised society, religion becomes more private in expression and thus restricted in its influence. We now realise, with the clerical sex scandals and child abuse terrors uncovered in the nineties and noughties, that alongside 'the religious discourse emphasising celibacy, purity, innocence, virginity, humility and piety, there existed practices of child abuse, incest, paedophilia, rape, abortion and infanticide' (Inglis, 1997, p. 60).

Ferriter (2009), like Kennedy (2001), rejects the notion of a strict clerical/laity divide in Ireland; neither does she accept the idea of a docile laity, taking all direction from a dominant conservative clergy. Citing the case of how Catholics took up the widespread use of contraceptives, contravening the ban on them, Kennedy supports the view that religious doctrines 'will be disobeyed' when they run strongly against the interests of Church members (Kennedy, 2001, p. 151). Many Irish Catholics lived lives outside of or in contravention to the strict sexual prescriptions of the Catholic Church. Ryan (2012, p. 201) describes this phenomenon of the 1960s/1970s as the emergence of the 'new Catholic'. We can see more recent evidence of this new Catholic in *Census 2011*, where over 84 per cent of Irish people declare themselves Catholic (CSO, 2011), yet the numbers of those divorced, remarrying, managing the birth of their children, cohabiting or living in same-sex partnerships, indicates that these people are living their lives according to their own conscience and needs and no longer slavishly following all Catholic guidance and dictats regarding private and public morality.[4]

LIBERALISATION OF ATTITUDES TO SOCIO-SEXUAL ISSUES

Hug (1999) suggests there were four socio-sexual issues prevalent in Ireland in the 1980s and 1990s – contraception, abortion, divorce and homosexuality. The first approval by Irish parliamentarians of a measure in favour of homosexual rights was a vote in 1989 on a law prohibiting incitement to hatred (Incitement to Hatred Act, 1989), which included homosexuals and Travellers in its remit (Hug, 1999, p. 220). Resistance to decriminalise homosexuality during this time was based on beliefs that 'by extension, these practices corrupt society at large because they undermine the family, the institution on which moral order is built, the basic unit of society whose main function is to maintain order, economic as well as ideological' (Hug, 1999, p. 3).

Happy activists. *From left:* Brian Sheehan, Gráinne Healy, Orla Howard, Moninne Griffith and Andrew Hyland as the Marriage Bill passes through Dáil Éireann, 7 October 2015.

Many lesbian and gay rights activists were involved across these socio-sexual campaigns, leading to what Hug calls the emerging 'new moral order' (Hug, 1999, p. 7). It was in January 1990, when the then Archbishop of Dublin, Desmond Connell (later criticised for covering up the truth about child abusing priests) (Raftery, 1999), reflected Church teaching when he spoke of homosexuality as 'an objective disorder' (Hug, 1999, p. 201). However, within three years, legislation to decriminalise homosexuality was passed by both houses of the Oireachtas (Irish parliament) without a vote. Some signs of 'tolerance' for lesbian and gay people and their rights were emerging.

Key to the development of acceptance on social-sexual matters was a series of public debates over issues on privacy and reproductive rights and child abuse which took place in the 1980s and early 1990s. Kilfeather (2005) recalls the death of Ann Lovett and her baby in a graveyard in Longford, where the teenager died in secretive childbirth (1984); the trial of Joanne Hayes for her alleged role in the murder of two Kerry babies (1984); Lavinia Kerwick's decision to waive anonymity and speak about her rape (1990); the rape of a 14-year-old girl known as 'X', prevented by the State from travelling to England for an abortion (1992); the exposure of Bishop of Galway Eamonn Casey as having fathered a child seventeen years previously (1992); and the conviction of a Catholic priest, Fr Brendan Smyth, a serial child abuser protected by the Catholic Church and shielded from extradition by the Irish government in 1994[5] (Kilfeather, 2005, p. 111). All of these scandals and their exposure by the media moved public opinion and served to further dent Catholic *habitus* on sexuality in Ireland. Perhaps the election of Mary Robinson as President of Ireland in 1990 was an indication of how far public opinion had moved. Robinson had been the senior counsel in the David Norris case on homosexuality[6] and an advocate of choice in abortion matters. Her election by popular acclaim is another indicator of how attitudes and values were changing in Ireland (Kilfeather, 2005).

It can be argued that recently reported clerical sexual abuse scandals in Ireland, 'The Ferns Report' (2005); 'The Ryan Report' (2009); 'The Murphy Report' (2009); and 'The Cloyne Report' (2011) have harmed the Catholic *habitus* regarding sexuality and Catholic authority on moral issues generally. McGarry (2012) commented that the fall by 22 per cent in religious sentiment by Irish people (WIN-Gallup International, 2012) since 2005 (69 per cent in 2005 considered themselves to be religious – 47 per cent considered themselves religious in 2011) – may reflect the effect of the publication of the above reports. 'Ireland has experienced the second-greatest drop in recent years in the percentage of the population that claims to be religious' (McGarry, 2012; *Irish Times*, 8 August 2012).

In Kennedy's view, changes in family patterns and attitude to social issues have also been driven by economic factors. The increase in diversity of households, relationship types and family forms in the twenty-first century reflects the demands and needs of the individuals and couples residing in the State at this time. Change in family life has been 'people'-driven she maintains (Kennedy, 2001, p. 258). These changes have led to a plurality of values, to 'an Irish society that is more open and tolerant than in the past' (Norman et al., 2006, p. 6). The pace of change has been, particularly in the last thirty years, immense (Layte et al., 2006).

The push for access to marriage by same-sex couples was a movement toward foundational change to the traditional meanings of marriage and family in Ireland; it would also prove to be just one more change in the two institutions of family and marriage which have changed so much over time.

GAY AND LESBIAN LEGISLATIVE PROGRESS IN IRELAND

On 23 June 1993, the Minister for Justice proposed 'The Criminal Law (Sexual Offences Bill 1993)' to the Dáil (the lower house of the Irish parliament), which provided for equality between heterosexuals and homosexuals and effectively decriminalised homosexuality in

'Bráinne' at the victory party, Ballsbridge Hotel, Dublin, 23 May 2015.

Ireland. The bill passed all its stages without a vote: 'while the equality-based law reform is fundamentally important in removing the taint of criminality, it must be remembered that it only provides the basis for achieving equality in everyday lives' (Rose, 1994, p. 60).

Subsequent to decriminalisation in 1993, significant rights legislation, including that protecting lesbians and gay men, was introduced. The 1998 Employment Equality Acts included bans on discrimination based on sexual orientation from employment, recruitment, training and pay; and the 2000 Equal Status Act included bans on discrimination in relation to supply or sale of goods and services (but allowed different treatment in relation to pensions and insurance policies). These significant equality acts offered protection on nine grounds – including sexual orientation. These acts were helpful in moving gay men and lesbian women, away not just from the criminal taint but also towards a sense of the possibility of real equality in their everyday lives. The journey was moving inexorably towards examining relationship recognition rights.

Gráinne Healy speaking at the post-referendum press conference at the Radisson Hotel, Dublin, on Sunday, 24 May 2015.

The Equality Authority's call in 2002 for equal access to civil marriage for gay and lesbian couples was a significant policy milestone for relationship recognition (Equality Authority, 2002). Various political party positions on gay and lesbian partnerships (Fine Gael, 2004; Green Party, 2006) were pushed along by the publication of significant policy reports such as the *Colley Report*, 2006. A Private Members Bill on Partnership Rights (Norris, 2005), and the Labour Party Civil Unions Bill in 2007, were unsuccessful but the Zappone/Gilligan High Court case pushed for marriage recognition for same-sex couples as the parliament struggled to put forward civil partnership between 2009 and 2010.

In June 2010, following debates in both upper and lower houses of the Oireachtas, the Civil Partnership and Certain Rights and Obligations of Cohabitants Act, 2010 was passed without a vote in the Dáil and only four Senators voted against it in the upper house (Seanad). The Act was enacted in January 2011 and the first same-sex couples applied to have their relationships registered and recognised by the Irish State. Pivotal in pushing the issue centre-stage in Ireland were Dr Katherine Zappone and Dr Ann Louise Gilligan, two lesbian women who had married in Canada and took a case seeking the legal recognition of their 25-year relationship and their legal Canadian marriage conducted in Vancouver in 2004. 'The deepening of our desire to do something that could bring about change, had more to do with the fact that our lifelong partnership was being denied proper legal recognition' (Gilligan & Zappone, 2008, p. 223).

Although their case failed (the couple subsequently withdrew their appeal of the decision in favour of taking new proceedings in 2012 to challenge directly two acts which prevent recognition of their marriage and they halted their proceedings on announcement of the proposed referendum on the issue), it left a legacy of a strengthened lesbian and gay rights movement – an advocacy group going from strength to strength (Marriage Equality/ ME) – and achieved an ambition to stir up a grassroots revolt against the inequality of a lack of same-sex-relationship rights. While GLEN[7] had committed itself to seek civil partnership rights as a stepping stone to equality, ME,[8] NLGF,[9] LGBT Noise[10] and others had taken up the baton to push for full equality for same-sex relationship recognition by continuing to advocate for civil marriage rights in Ireland.

Key differences between civil partnership legislation provision and marriage rights were identified (Ryan, 2010; Fagan, 2011; Pillinger & Fagan, 2013; Marriage Equality, 2012) and include those relating to a civil partner and his/her partner's children. The adult/child relationship is not acknowledged in the Act (Ryan, 2010, p. 5). The recognition of children in the Civil Partnership Act (2010), which extends to non-biological parents who are a co-parent, extends only to their rights to seek access in respect of a child if the child is in the custody of the other civil partner. In relation to maintenance, courts must only take into account a civil partner's obligations towards his/her own biological children, similarly after the dissolution. Thus, no specific financial support is required for the child by the non-biological parent who is a civil partner to the child's biological mother or father. Ryan (2010) and Fagan (2011) conclude that full equality undoubtedly demands equal access to civil marriage, however for Ryan, civil partnership 'both practically and symbolically ... represents real and substantial progress in the recognition and protection of non-traditional families' (2010, p. 18). These major gaps in provision for LGBT families motivated many in the ME group to continue the fight for full relationship recognition by winning marriage equality for same-sex couples.

Some 169 differences in treatment 'covering rights and protections across a range of legislation including, areas of family law, immigration, housing, inheritance, taxation, freedom of information, and other miscellaneous provisions, which apply to married heterosexual couples, but not to same-sex couples who are registered civil partners' are identified in Fagan's report (2011, p. 10).

In April 2013, the Constitutional Convention (a citizens' forum with 100 members including sixty-six citizens and thirty-three parliamentarians or Senators) was convened by government to discuss marriage equality. Seventy-nine per cent of the body called for government to make provision for same-sex marriage by holding a referendum on the matter. The Irish government had to respond to the call by November 2013 and this took place when Taoiseach Enda Kenny agreed to hold a referendum on the issue some time in 2015. Meanwhile, 1,088 civil partnerships were registered since 2011 – 2,176 lesbians and gay men – 423 lesbian couples and 655 male couples (GLEN, 2013). The battle for full and equal relationship rights in Ireland continued.

Gráinne Healy speaking at the 'Road to Marriage Equality' Summer School, Dublin, July 2016.

TOWARDS THE CAMPAIGN WIN

The socio-political background which created the fertile seedbed for the KAL case, ME, the Constitutional Convention and ultimately the successful Yes Equality campaign – the hundred days that got the issue across the line in a historical referendum – sits firmly on the shoulders of the decade-long campaign for equality that preceded it. The story of those hundred days is told in *Ireland Says Yes* (2016) and also contributes to the kaleidoscope of viewpoints and perspectives of this multi-perspectival story of the road to marriage equality.

Moninne Griffith

From Little Acorns
Mobilising the Million in the Middle

In November 2007, a group of enthusiastic equality activists met up in The Shanty[1] in West Dublin to plan how to achieve marriage equality for same-sex couples in Ireland. Katherine Zappone and Ann Louise Gilligan had lost their High Court case to have their Canadian marriage recognised in Ireland, but their courageous strategic litigation put the issue of marriage equality for lesbian, gay, bisexual and transgender people in Ireland on the political agenda and in the media spotlight.

I was employed by the KAL Advocacy Initiative, the advocacy group set up to support Katherine and Ann Louise's case, to run a new campaign which was as yet unnamed. For a newcomer to LGBT life like me, it was the most exciting, inspiring and exhilarating meeting I'd ever attended. We spoke about an equal Ireland for all families and discussed strategies and tactics to reach that goal. That weekend, the advocacy group Marriage Equality (ME) was born and we agreed a strategy that led to the historic win on 22 May 2015. The 100 days of Yes Equality is often referred to by those of us who have dedicated years to this win as the 'roof on the marriage equality house'. The foundations, structure and walls were already built by the time the referendum was even called.

It is hard to capture everything that we did over the eight-year lifespan of ME that led to such a monumental win. Leading the organisation for that time, save for a brief few months after the birth of my daughter Edie, I have many wonderful memories. What follows are a sample of those arranged around the five strategies we decided on right from the beginning, over that weekend in November 2007.

1. Legal strategy – to support the Zappone and Gilligan case for recognition of their marriage with legal analysis and rationale;
2. Communications strategy – to increase visibility of the LGBT community and the rationale for equality through access to civil marriage;
3. Mobilisation strategy – to engage supporters from all sectors of people across Ireland and to ensure that there was demonstrated support for change from the public;
4. Political strategy – to work with public representatives to ensure that marriage equality legislative change was implemented;
5. Funding strategy – to sustain the organisation.

LEGAL STRATEGY AND COMMUNICATIONS STRATEGY

Having worked as a solicitor for almost a decade prior to ME, I knew how controversial it is to try and influence the judiciary in any way. To do so openly could have jeopardised the Zappone and Gilligan case as judges can be very sensitive about campaigns. I gathered some legal friends and supporters around the campaign including Judy Walsh, Michael Farrell, Fiona De Londras, Tanya Ward, Noeline Blackwell and Brian Barrington to make sure that our language and messaging would align with current legal trends, support the case and also to identify opportunities for awareness-raising in the human rights, equality and legal sector.

Back in 2008, proposed civil partnership was on people's minds, so my job was to help people understand that it wasn't enough, it wasn't equality. Brian Barrington worked with me to distinguish the very real practical legal ways the difference would impact on same-sex couples' lives. Versions of Brian's legal opinion were disseminated to politicians, the media and other stakeholders, published on our website (www.marriageequality.ie) and used for speaking engagements, especially aimed at academic and legal audiences. I felt strongly that if we wanted to get the general public's attention on the matter, however, we needed a number, a media hook, to define the gap between civil partnership and civil marriage.

Marriage inequality itself wasn't news. Back then, LGBT people were not really considered as ordinary citizens who might want to get married by the vast majority of people. Marriage was seen as something you did when you were in love, wanted to have children and you got married in a church. 'So why would gay and lesbian people want to get married?'

Moninne Griffith addressing the audience at the formal launch of Marriage Equality, Mansion House, Dublin, February 2008.

Marriage Equality at the Dublin City Council Civic Space during Dublin Pride, 2009.

was a question we were often asked. I needed a big number and personal stories to illustrate those differences to get media coverage and the general public's attention.

The United States General Accounting Authority, an independent, nonpartisan agency that works for the US Congress, carried out an audit in 2004 of federal rights and obligations afforded to married couples in the US. These were rights that same-sex couples could not avail of even if they had a civil partnership or had a marriage recognised at State level.[2] There were 1,138 benefits, rights and protections provided on the basis of marital status in US federal law that weren't available to same-sex couples. Carrying out the same kind of research in an Irish setting was vastly more challenging, not least because we didn't have funding to employ a specialist research team. Irish legislation relating to marriage (or any other subject) is not entirely accessible in one database. You can't just use a computer to find and list all the relevant Acts and Statutory Instruments. We also have a common law system, which means that some rights and responsibilities are 'judge-made' and not listed in any one place and only familiar to family law practitioners.

My plan to carry out an Irish 'Marriage Audit' meant I had to be creative and ask for support from many legal volunteers. Ruth Kelly led the volunteer team of eighteen legal volunteers who scoured volumes of Irish legislation to list some of the relevant laws. It was a painstaking exercise but without it we would not have been able to produce 'Missing Pieces' in 2011,[3] our report which showed that, in stark contrast to claims that civil partnership provided most or all the rights of marriage, same-sex couples who registered a civil partnership were denied a range of rights which they would be entitled to if they could legally marry.

Armed with the raw data I secured some funding and, with the help of some of the most generous legal experts in the country, we were able to translate the hundreds of pages of excel spreadsheets into what this meant in LGBT people's everyday lives. Paula Fagan worked tirelessly with me as a consultant on the project from early 2011, pulling together the research, liaising with legal experts and writing it up. It was a mammoth project but without this report and the follow-up advocacy work, we might never have galvanised the support and momentum to lead towards marriage equality so soon after the Civil Partnership Act at the end of 2010.

Some of the learnings and wins in our communications strategy are well captured by Andrew Hyland, who worked as our communications manager, in his chapter in this book. However there are other stories from along the way that I want to share. These stories illustrate how our strategies overlapped and how, with a small team, we made sure they had multiple layers of impact.

One of Marriage Equality's 'Just Love' series of posters, 2011.

The success of the ground-breaking Children and Family Relationship Act 2015, which at the time of writing has still not been fully commenced (but when it is will give equal protection to children in same-sex families), has its roots in a working group that I was involved in putting together following our historic 'Voices of Children' report and conference in 2009. This report was inspired by a young man, Evan Barry, who has two mothers and who was fed up listening to anti-marriage equality campaigners 'worrying' about the potential impacts for children. As he said himself, 'If they are so worried about us, why don't they ever ask us for our opinions?' It became a goal of Board member Denise Charlton's and mine to do exactly that.

We put out a call for adult children with LGBT parents to come to Dublin to share their experiences of what it was like growing up in Ireland and what they thought about marriage equality. With the generous support of children and youth advocates and experts, including author Iris Elliott, workshop designer/facilitator Dr Celia Keenaghan, fieldwork support by Emily Bent, Kieran O'Brien in UNICEF Ireland, who provided us with space for the workshop (and who later joined our Board), and many more who gave their time to this exciting project, we published exactly what young people with LGBT parents thought about the issue.

The report outlined some of the legal and everyday challenges faced by children growing up in Ireland with lesbian and gay parents, such as lack of recognition and therefore protection of many parent–child relationships, and documented their experiences of public (churches,

Marching for Marriage Equality, August 2014.

media, schools, health services) and private (family, social circle) homophobia. This was the first report of its kind in Ireland. Some of the participants had never met another person with an LGBT parent and indeed back then the vast majority of Irish people were not aware that they existed. The report led to a conference in Dublin City Council's Wood Quay venue in September later that year. Conor Pendergrast and Christine Irwin-Murphy, who had taken part in the original workshop and who had set up 'Believe in Equality' for adult children with LGBT parents who supported marriage equality, shared their stories on the day. Both became important advocates for the campaign and the legislation in the ensuing years.

As well as Irish and international child law and psychology experts on the issue, however, we had some uninvited guests at the conference. We hadn't anticipated that a group of protestors would arrive to hurl abuse and try to storm the venue. Paula Fagan and Dawn Quinn, our volunteer manager, and my partner, Clodagh Robinson, literally had to physically keep the door shut to stop the angry group from disrupting the event. They were great 'bouncers' for the morning and no one noticed the 'inconvenience'. Karl Hayden, who had been filming the event, very cleverly popped outside with camera in tow during one of the breaks and filmed them. Once the mob believed they had been included in footage for the news later that day, they packed up and headed off.

2009 Fundraising initiative for Marriage Equality.

After the conference I worked with colleagues from One Family,[4] Women's Aid[5] and Barnardos,[6] lobbying for legislation to provide legal protections for children in many diverse families, including LGBT families. We also supported LGBT Diversity's[7] excellent research project 'LGBT Parents in Ireland', conducted by Dr Jane Pillinger and Paula Fagan, which once again pointed at the lack of marriage equality as a major issue for children and parents. While I was off after the birth of my daughter Edie, then-Minister for Justice Alan Shatter published the headings of a far-reaching innovative and child-centred bill. That bill sought to drag Irish family law into line with the lived realities of thousands of children in diverse families. Andrew Hyland, who returned to work with ME after a couple of years' break, was acting Director at this time. Andrew organised a follow-up conference to Voices of Children to shine a light on the urgent need for the proposed legislation. I brought Edie to the conference and we thanked the Minister and his officials who were working on the bill in person. The following day a photo of Edie and the Minister appeared in many of the newspapers. It was the first but not the last time that I had taken the step of sharing our story and it was a daunting experience.

Above: At Marriage Equality's second birthday February 2010. *From left:* Brian Kennedy, Moninne Griffith and Ross Golden-Bannon.

Right: 'Missing Pieces' launch invite, October 2011.

On my return to work I was more determined than ever to secure legislation that would ensure Edie and many children with families like ours would have the same rights and protections as any other child. We worked with Tanya Ward in the Children's Rights Alliance[8] to form a broad coalition of children and family rights advocates and allies. Tanya is an advocacy pioneer in this area and co-wrote *Equality For All Families*[9] with the exceptionally talented lawyer, Judy Walsh, while in the ICCL.[10] This was the first report in Ireland to point out many of the legal gaps faced by non-marital families, including co-habiting same-sex couples. The working group spent hours reading over complicated draft legislation. I was grateful to have a few years' family law practice under my belt which helped me think through the various family structures that exist in Ireland and the challenges some children face to have their family relationships recognised and their rights vindicated.

One thing after another delayed the Bill's progress. Alan Shatter stepped down as Minister for Justice and there were constant rumours of a general election being called. Minister Frances Fitzgerald replaced him and, thankfully, with her experience as a former Minister for Children shared his vision and determination for achieving equality for children in Ireland. When Taoiseach Enda Kenny announced a referendum on marriage equality would be held in mid-2015, he made it clear that the Children and Family Relationship Bill would have to be passed first.

There was pushback from the Attorney General's office on parts of the draft legislation and some of that was around children with lesbian and gay parents. We knew the legislation had to be completed as soon as possible but not at any cost. With the help of Justine Quinn, who had joined the ME Board a few years previously, and Jeanne McDonagh in the Bar Council, we enlisted the help of two of the most respected lawyers in the country – Mary O'Toole, who had been senior counsel in most of the highest profile family law cases of recent years, including cases around surrogacy, and John Rogers, former Attorney General. Armed with their joint opinion, I went back once again to the Department of Justice to make our case for ensuring that LGBT families would have equality before the law.

After many lengthy conversations, meetings, briefings and conferences, our working group, made up of Children's Rights Alliance members, finally helped shape an historic piece of family law legislation with just the right balance of persuasion and support for a determined Minister for Justice; and a small team of brilliant civil servants who were tasked with creating this mammoth Bill. We didn't get everything we wanted included, but it was a proud moment for me personally as so many of my friends and their children would have a legal pathway to recognition and protection once the legislation was enacted and commenced.

Current media coverage in relation to political debate relating to referenda issues is skewed by an interpretation of what 'balance' means for media organisations. As a result, those of us who took part in debates around marriage equality often took personal insults on air where journalists focused on equal time but let the opposition away unscrutinised or without the usual interrogation. This silencing effect was so bad that many people working in the media were afraid to voice any opinion at all. It was extremely frustrating to take part in or to watch or listen and no doubt left many viewers and listeners confused. It is not easy debating with people about your capacity to love or parent, especially when they weave unchallenged myths and untruths.

The last story I want to share relates to a TV debate in 2012 I took part in against David Quinn, Director of the conservative religious group, the Iona Institute.[11] RTÉ's *Prime Time* had called to see whether I would take part, and without hesitation I said yes. I had plenty of radio and print media interviews under my belt at that stage, even a few pre-recorded soundbites for the news; however, this was my first live TV debate. I was nervous. Michelle Thomas, our media trainer, put me through the hoops in preparation. I felt like pulling out, but my partner Clodagh wouldn't hear of it. This was a prime-time chance for people to hear why marriage equality mattered to someone personally as opposed to hearing from someone whose life wouldn't change one little bit whether it was introduced or not. The make-up, waiting room, and bright lights of the studio added to the adrenalin rush.

Ben and Jerry get on board, 2013.

I took my seat opposite Mr Quinn. Donogh Diamond, the presenter of the programme, was sitting between us asking the questions. I could feel my heart beat in my ears as he introduced the piece. It was a heated debate with all the usual scare tactics about the effect on children and society. I don't remember much of what I said but I know the last line before Donogh closed the programme went to me. I said that Ireland was ready for marriage equality and that soon Mr Quinn would be on the wrong side of history. I am so proud of and grateful to the generous, fair-minded Irish electorate who made this a reality.

MOBILISATION STRATEGY AND POLITICAL STRATEGY

Mobilisation work was always focused on growing our base of supporters and empowering them to demonstrate their support for marriage equality. It was about empowering ordinary LGBT people and allies to become agents for positive social change themselves.

I spent much of the first few years in ME travelling around Ireland speaking at meetings and conferences, anywhere I could get a platform to raise awareness about why marriage equality mattered with audiences that I thought would be natural allies: trades unions, women's groups, children and youth advocacy organisations, human rights and equality organisations, lawyers and faith-based groups working for LGBT inclusion. Sometimes it was simply a casual meeting with a staff team over lunch, but nurturing those relationships and working together built trust and respect over years. Other times I addressed large groups of people such as the Family Resource Forum in Killarney in October 2008, where I met some fantastic allies. Later, so many colleagues who worked in civil society organisations became champions for marriage equality in their own sectors.

Back then most of the general public didn't understand why same-sex couples would want to get married, so engaging with people who already were passionate about equality, rights and social justice was where we decided to focus our energy. This meant collaborating and planning with colleagues on how best to secure support and a mandate from member organisations. It involved bringing motions to AGMs, joining boards and supporting the work of other human rights and equality organisations such as the National Women's Council, Amnesty International, the Equality Rights Alliance, the Irish Congress of Trade Unions and many more. Building trust and respect amongst colleagues meant they were ready to roll up their sleeves and answer our call when we needed them.

Sharing our stories of why marriage equality mattered was also intrinsic to the success of our political strategy. We could lobby 24/7 but having a constituent contact their elected representative to make the issue local and personal was always much more powerful. However, I knew it wasn't enough to just ask people to visit their TDs. We needed to build people's confidence and capacity if we wanted a grass-roots approach. Ronan Farren worked with me to produce our first 'Out To Your TD' pack and Tom Duke in Digital Revolutionaries built the web-based technology for us to make it simple for supporters to contact their TDs and send feedback to us. What made 'Out To Your TD' a standout success, albeit a slow-burning one, was our amazing volunteers. Laura Sheahan, one of our first volunteers, who had worked as a young volunteer in the Democratic Party in the US, helped me design our telephone outreach model, and Sarah Benson in Women's Aid helped us to put our volunteer training and policies together.

Every Tuesday and Wednesday evening, our dedicated teams of trained volunteers called supporters who had signed up for the campaign to encourage and support them to contact their TDs and Senators. Armed with a script and the latest information we had on file in relation to the politicians in their constituency, gleaned from Dáil reports or from previous meetings, our team of brave volunteers called supporters week after week, month after month. We celebrated every time we achieved a visit or any contact at all. It was hard work but thanks to a remarkable team and Dawn Quinn, our volunteer manager on the staff who kept up morale, it worked. Once emails, letters, phone calls and visits started to happen, we could track the change in opinion. Often it only took one or two visits to humanise the issue, make it local and relatable and win the TD's support. There were some notable exceptions. One TD told a lesbian couple from Galway that some inequality was necessary to maintain social order. He is right – if you believe in maintaining patriarchy!

As well as running the 'Out To Your TD' campaign, we designed and ran lobbying workshops to build supporters' confidence and capacity. Long-time ME friend and advocate Kieran Clifford in Amnesty International co-designed our workshop with me and delivered some of them, too. One of my favourite memories of one such workshop was with TOST!, an LGBT group in Mayo. We spent an inspiring day with the group but afterwards some of the women admitted to us that, although they found it very useful, and that they would use what they had learnt to effect social change, they couldn't put it to use in relation to marriage equality. They weren't out. It's a stark reminder of where we were at eight years ago.

I am happy to say however that this very group of amazing women, and a few amazing men, led Yes Equality Mayo and the county to a resounding Yes. They came out to everyone in Mayo, shared their stories and changed hearts and minds all over the West. In fact, many of the leaders in the seventy-plus Yes Equality groups in May 2015 were led by people who had volunteered with or supported marriage equality in one way or another over the eight preceding years. Some visited TDs, some shared their stories in local and national media, some fundraised for the organisation and many more marched with us in their hundreds in Pride marches all over the country each summer.

Other stand-out memories from our mobilisation work involved joining the celebrations with One Family's annual Family Day in May. Each year we took a stand and painted faces, gave away balloons, cupcakes and leaflets, and chatted with parents, grandparents and guardians about why our families needed legal recognition and protections. The solidarity we experienced from one-parent and other diverse families reached a crescendo during the referendum campaign when the No side put up posters denigrating families that didn't fit the mum, dad and baby picture. In fact, it solidified soft Yes supporters to hardened Yes voters and helped with our fundraising efforts for our own posters.

Pride was a huge mobilisation opportunity for us. Year on year, the numbers of supporters who marched with us grew at Pride in Dublin, Cork, Galway, Limerick and Sligo. Whether our theme was 'Missing Pieces' to highlight the differences between civil partnership and civil marriage, or 'Marriage is …' left blank on T-shirts so people could fill in what it meant to them personally, volunteers and supporters joined staff and Board members to show their support. Some parades were sun-soaked fun events, whereas at some we were just soaked. The smaller parades meant so much as people bravely outed themselves as we marched along with them, clinging to our banners and chanting 'What do we want? Equality. When do we want it? Now!'

Marching for marriage, 2014.

A personal favourite project for me was working with Richard O'Leary of Changing Attitudes Ireland (see Richard's chapter elsewhere in this collection), a network of LGBT and heterosexual Anglican Christians working for a more inclusive Church. Richard is a passionate advocate whose beloved partner had sadly died after they were civil-partnered in their home city of Belfast. I learnt so much from Richard and he introduced me to many friends in Anglican churches and of the Roman Catholic faith who were supporters of LGBT equality. With my support, Richard set up and led 'Faith in Marriage Equality' during the referendum. This brave outspoken group of people of faith – Anglican, Roman Catholic and Jewish – persuaded many voters in Ireland that you could be a person of faith and also support marriage equality.

Michelle Thomas worked her magic again, volunteering her time with media training, planning their launch and some media relations advice, and then they were ready. Faith in Marriage Equality members attended conferences, took part in debates and placed opinion pieces in print media. They were the voices other people of faith needed to hear, assuring them that being a good person of faith meant loving your neighbour. Richard himself decided to take to the Wild Atlantic Way on a 'Yesvena' – distributing Faith in Marriage Equality leaflets outside churches and asking people to vote Yes. He met some colourful people along the way and many many supporters who thanked him for his bravery. Richard is one of the many heroes I met over my eight years working for ME.

Other people and organisations took on their own projects to mobilise, whether it was LGBT Noise's annual Marches for Marriage in Dublin (see Anna MacCarthy's piece elsewhere in this collection), which grew year on year from a respectable fifty to a glorious 5,000 people in August 2014 or GAZE, the LGBT Film Festival that took the film *The Case Against 8* on tour to eleven venues around Ireland in February to May 2015. The film told the story of the landmark US Supreme Court case that overturned the notorious Proposition 8 and its ban on marriage for same-sex couples in California.

The Yes Bus opposite the Yes Equality HQ, prior to the countrywide tour, April 2015.

POLITICAL WORK

ME's political work consisted of meetings, briefings, submissions, and appearances in front of Oireachtas committees. It was tough going to begin with. Even some of our friends in the Labour Party said to us that they didn't think it would happen in their lifetime, but we weren't put off. With help from some seasoned political advisors such as Ronan Farren, Paul Daly and Andrea Pappin, we engaged with politicians in their constituency offices, Leinster House and through each party's structures. We shared our personal stories and brought in young adult children with lesbian parents to tell theirs. We supported party members to bring motions of support to party conferences and local councillors to bring them to council meetings. Belfast City council started this trend and Cork city followed, leading the way for a wave of discussions at local level and a large pool of supportive candidates in the 2011 General Election. The issue grew from being described by one TD as not one he could recall being raised by any constituent[12] to one where almost every TD knew the personal story of someone locally whose life was affected because of the lack of marriage equality.

As part of the programme for government, the Labour Party secured a promise to have marriage equality discussed and considered at a citizens' assembly along with other issues that might require constitutional change. This Constitutional Convention was seen by many as a controversial compromise for the Fine Gael–Labour coalition government. However, the Convention gave rise to a significant sea change among politicians, once they witnessed what unfolded over that weekend in April 2013. The Constitutional Convention was also the first time that the three founding organisations of Yes Equality (ICCL, GLEN and ME) came together to work as a united team for the common goal of securing a majority of supporters for the referendum on marriage equality.

Our work was to ensure the Convention delegates overwhelmingly recommended to government to call a referendum on the issue of marriage equality. The three organisations played to our strengths with the choreography from Michelle Thomas once again. ME made the case for equality and addressed some of the most common concerns people had with same-sex couples marrying (presentations were made by myself and our Chairwoman, Gráinne Healy). We also brought the personal stories with our beautifully made *Yes to Love*[13] video showing ordinary couples telling their stories with the end line saying 'Ireland is ready – Say Yes to Love'. The Gay and Lesbian Equality Network (GLEN) set the historical scene, setting out a timeline for LGBT rights since decriminalisation in 1993, and the ICCL (Irish Council for Civil Liberties) set out the legal precedence for marriage equality from a human rights framework.

However, it was Conor Pendergrast and Clare O'Connell, who had both grown up in 'gay' families and shared their stories, who stole the show. Conor and Clare had worked with us on the 'Voices of Children' seminar and research and were seasoned spokespeople for ME. When they spoke, you could hear a pin drop. The children of Ireland were heard and delegates didn't have to fear what would happen in the future any more. When the result of 79 per cent in favour of marriage equality and 81 per cent in favour of equality for children with LGBT parents came through, we couldn't contain our delight and neither could the delegates. We hugged and cried and thanked them and they were so proud of their decision and what they had achieved. It was like a premonition or glimpse into the future and what was to come nearly two years later in May 2015 – a picture of our best selves – generous, fair, and caring.

Moninne Griffith *(left)* with Mary McDermott, Yes Bus organisers, April 2015.

YES EQUALITY - THE RAINBOW ROOF

By the time the referendum was called, ME had our 'Roadmap to Victory' (see p. 66) ready. We knew from our mobilisation work and polling that Irish people wanted to support family members and friends, and the people in their clubs and communities. ME had been supporting people to share their stories in local, regional and national media, at local events and in the local elected representatives' constituency offices for eight years, and we knew this worked. The key to the win was personal relationships. We wanted people to have conversations – friend to friend, co-worker to co-worker, club member to club member. We knew that our personal stories and our relationships were the strongest tools we had for both persuading people to support marriage equality and to mobilise a majority Yes vote on polling day. Yes Equality's success was due to the incredible face to face work undertaken by supporters, coalition partners and allies from all sectors of Irish society.

ME's 'Roadmap to Victory' had three phases:

1. Base-building.
2. Education & Persuasion.
3. Motivation & Getting Out the Vote.

The Roadmap (see p. 66) depicts more or less the timeline of our work, although we didn't launch the campaign until later than originally planned, for a number of strategic reasons. It does capture what we envisaged would need to happen to get a win and in hindsight is a pretty close representation of what actually happened during the Yes Equality campaign.

Phase one was all about building capacity amongst our supporters and launching our 'Register to Vote' campaign. Working with our base (LGBT activists and long-term active supporters of ME), we began to build and train teams of volunteers to work with us nationally for the duration of the campaign. Armed with our research, our tested messages and our strategy, these volunteers persuaded voters in the moveable middle and recruited hard Yes supporters. This work focused on three groups:

1. The Platform (LGBT groups) – we kept them engaged and ensured that their groups/ members were informed, active and engaged with all campaign activities.
2. Regional/Constituency – this work established and supported local Yes Equality groups. This was to ensure the campaign was successful nationwide and was not just Dublin-centred.
3. 'Sector' or strategic partnership development – this ensured we reached voters in every sector of Irish society, persuading them to be supportive and to come out and vote Yes.

Some of the work we did during this period included:

- A National Volunteer Day, which brought together and trained supporters from all over Ireland in preparation for going back to their local areas/organisations and mobilising.
- Appearances at public events such as AGMs, Trades Union regional meetings, members' meetings.
- Constituency work with local Yes Equality groups – building capacity locally.
- A national 'Register to Vote' campaign – which with partners like USI and BeLonG To delivered the biggest voter registration drive ever seen in Ireland.
- Continued communication and engagement with platform members and sector partners.

Phase two was about education and persuasion. Based on polling we had commissioned, we knew that 76 per cent of the electorate supported marriage equality. However, 34 per cent of this group was made up of a 'moveable middle', those who could as easily vote No as they might vote Yes. Their Yes was easily disrupted to a No if certain messages or fears were invoked. A No vote on their part would jeopardise the referendum. This cohort wanted to support us, but could have easily been persuaded by the opposition for many reasons to vote No, e.g. fear of what introducing marriage equality would mean for Irish society or fear of LGBT people parenting. We had to persuade this group of people and inoculate them against the opposition's arguments to win middle Ireland's vote and the referendum.

Some of this work would be done in phase three, through our media work, but from our research and experience we knew that grassroots mobilisation would play a major role in persuading voters and in getting out the vote (GOTV) in the final week. Face-to-face conversations with friends, neighbours, work colleagues and family members was crucial to our success.

Some of the work we did in phase two included:

- Launch of Yes Equality: Yes Equality was a massive public awareness campaign that integrated multi-media, fieldwork, online and offline communications, mobilisation and fundraising methods to talk with Irish voters.
- Sector outreach work to secure support from all sections of Irish society: youth sector/young people, students, women's groups/women, sports fans, civil society, trade unions, employers, religious people, older people, parents, Irish speakers and people living in rural Ireland. This work involved weekly meetings with representative bodies to devise targeted plans, visible endorsements, tailored messaging and identifying key influencers in each sector. One of those allies was BeLonG To, the national LGBT youth organisation (detailed elsewhere by Micheal Barron).
- Identifying and briefing key influencers, champions and unexpected allies from constituencies and sectors.
- Launch of Faith in Marriage Equality (detailed elsewhere by Richard O'Leary).
- A joint Dublin City University and ME conference in March 2015 on the international experience of marriage equality, with guest speaker Professor Lee Badgett (US-based international academic expert on the global movement for marriage equality), whose book *When Gay People Get Married* (2010) quelled fears about what happens in countries after marriage equality is introduced and dispelled arguments around levels of 'gay' divorce.

Moninne Griffith *(right)* with Minister for Justice Frances Fitzgerald, Yes Bus, May 2015.

Phase three focused on GOTV. We knew that voter apathy, even amongst our supporters, was a risk to success. Many supportive people believed that a win was a 'shoe-in'. Positive figures in polls had added to this belief. We had to convince supporters that every vote counted and make sure that they got to the polling stations on the day.

In order to motivate supporters and get them to the polling stations, we used the following:

- A high impact/high visibility GOTV Campaign (heavily branded, pulling all mobilisation groundwork together, large multi-dimensional multi-media campaign with attractive merchandise and materials e.g. T-shirts, badges, bumper stickers, posters, posters for supportive businesses).
- Field work and canvassing project: door to door, shopping centres, public events, local hubs/centres events, telephone banking, email reminders, daily motivational messaging updates to local leaders. Not all the political parties helped out with this work, but there were notable individuals from across the political spectrum like Averil Power (then Fianna Fáil), Aodhán Ó Ríordáin and John Lyons (Labour), Thomas Pringle (Sinn Féin) and Jerry Buttimer (Fine Gael) who came out night after night with the Yes Equality canvassers.

- We had a Countdown Calendar in Yes Equality head office so that in the month leading up to the referendum we had one planned tactic for each day without clashes, e.g. launch of the National Women's Council's 'Women for Yes', BeLonG To's #BeLonGToYes, Amnesty's 'Let's Make History' and Mayors for Marriage Equality were some of those key events keeping up momentum.

What took up most of my time during those last few weeks, and where some of my fondest memories of the referendum campaign were made, was the Yes Bus tour. This was our full-scale national tour of every county in Ireland during the last four weeks. I persuaded a good friend of mine, Mary McDermott, to plan and run the project with me. We learned all about bus sizes suitable for getting down narrow roads in towns around Ireland and how to wrap a bus with colourful messaging from Kathleen Hunt[14] who was working with us in head office and who had organised many bus tours for elections. Route plans mapped out, Stephen O'Hare from the ICCL and Ross Flanagan, one of our amazing volunteers, worked out parking permits and licences for us to pull up in towns and shopping centres all over Ireland. We travelled 11,000 kilometres and visited twenty-six counties in twenty-nine days with our team of energetic volunteers and our skilled driver, Andy Wilkinson. KerryAnn Conway of Conway Communications announced our arrival each day with local colourful press coverage.

Moninne Griffith at the 'I'm voting Yes. Ask Me Why' launch, March 2015.

Moninne Griffith speaking from the Yes Bus, May 2015.

With the help of local champions, local couples or celebrities, each stop was a mini event in itself, organised in collaboration with the local Yes Equality groups, with speeches, music, conversations and lots of colour. Ben & Jerry's joined us in some locations to scoop ice-cream for passers-by. Some stops were like mini festivals. In Galway, hundreds of people, including Maire Geoghegan-Quinn,[15] gathered to welcome the arrival of the bus and canvass the city centre with us. Friends in Trade Unions organised lunches for us at stops all over the country and supporters brought Yes Equality cupcakes to the bus stops for us to eat on the sometimes long journeys on the road between towns.

Other stops were hugely challenging, where people told us that we were disgusting, going to hell and should be locked up; but we kept going and focused on gaining middle Ireland's support. We spent nights away from our families and loved ones and got to know our teams of inspiring volunteers, swapping stories of why we were on the bus. One young man, Karl Ryan, took all his annual leave together to volunteer with us for the whole month! Some volunteered in memory of loved ones they had lost to suicide or HIV-related illnesses. Others did it to show siblings and friends their support. Many did it because this was an opportunity for them to take part in something that would change Ireland and their own futures for the better, forever.

Moninne Griffith with her partner Clodagh Robinson at the Dublin count centre, RDS, 23 May 2015.

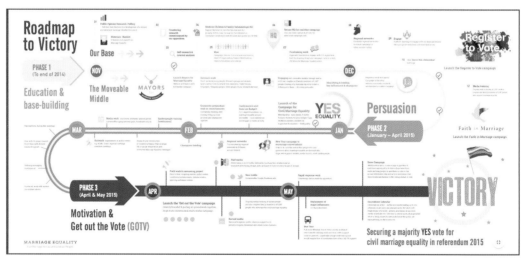

Devised by Marriage Equality Co-Directors Moninne Griffith and Andrew Hyland, Marriage Equality's 'Roadmap to Victory' plots the final six months to the referendum, October 2014.

I heard so many stories on that bus tour from young people, parents and grandparents about why they were voting Yes. On one of my last days on the road, a woman a bit older than me expressed how humiliated she was standing on the road asking people to vote so she could marry her partner of over twenty years. She told me how it took all her willpower to suspend that humiliation so she could keep on doing it until polling day. I went back to the bus and cried. She was right. It *was* humiliating, when people rushed by or said no, or hurled abuse in your direction. The Yes Bus tour was physically and emotionally exhausting, an experience I will never forget but by the end of it, we were confident that Ireland was ready to say Yes.

And on 22 May 2015 that is exactly what happened. That day the citizens of Ireland voted Yes to marriage equality, Yes to a fairer, more inclusive Ireland, and put the roof on our rainbow-coloured marriage equality house. All our work over many years culminated in achieving our goal and putting ourselves out of business – every advocate's dream.

When Ireland voted Yes to marriage equality we sent a message to LGBT people in Ireland that they belong and are loved, that they are equal citizens and part of our culture, our identity, our families and our communities. We sent a message to the world that Ireland is a modern secular nation where difference is okay and discrimination because of sexual orientation is not. Our resounding Yes told young lesbian, gay, bisexual and transgender people and parents that it was safe to come out, that we had changed what it meant to grow up LGBT in Ireland. Of course, we did not wipe out homophobia and transphobia overnight. That will take lots more work. We secured a bright and equal future for young LGBT people, but the present can still be a scary place of isolation, fear of rejection and bullying because of who you are. We must keep saying Yes so we can achieve the kind of Ireland we voted for.

Niall Crowley

The Equality Authority and Same-Sex Marriage

A STATE AGENCY STEPS UP

This is the story of a State agency contributing at an early stage on the long road to the achievement of marriage equality. The Equality Authority was established in 1999 with a mandate to promote equality of opportunity and combat discrimination on nine grounds including the ground of sexual orientation. It was responsible for implementing the Employment Equality Acts, which prohibit discrimination in employment, and the Equal Status Acts, which prohibits discrimination in the provision of goods and services, education and accommodation.

It is the story of people like Mervyn and Richard, Myra McGurk and Eileen Twomey, and others who did not wish to be named. They stood up against discrimination and, with no little courage, took cases under the equality legislation, cases that ultimately rendered discrimination against lesbian and gay couples unacceptable. It is the story of people like Eilis Barry, legal advisor to the Equality Authority, and other staff in the Equality Authority who contributed with determination and creativity to achieving progress on the ground of sexual orientation.

POINT OF DEPARTURE

'Implementing Equality for Lesbians, Gays and Bisexuals' was launched in May 2002 by Kate Hayes, Chairperson of the Equality Authority, Maureen Gaffney, Chairperson of the National Economic and Social Forum, and Ailbhe Smyth of the Women's Education, Research and Resource Centre in UCD. Each played key roles in championing this report and its recommendations. The report was agreed by the Equality Authority and had been developed by an advisory committee we had convened.

Under Section 48 of the Employment Equality Acts, the Equality Authority had the power to appoint 'advisory committees' which would advise it on matters relating to its functions. In 2000, we set up an advisory committee to establish the equality agenda for lesbian, gay and bisexual people. It was drawn from the full spectrum of lesbian, gay and bisexual organisations and included representatives of relevant State agencies and government departments. It was chaired by Barbara Cashin and supported by Marie Mulholland, both from the Equality Authority.

The issue of partnership rights was neither obvious nor easy to address for the advisory committee. It emerged slowly onto its agenda and raised disquiet. In the final report there was a chapter on 'Partnership Rights'. The recommendations were directed at individual government departments and sought action to address the disadvantages for same-sex partners in the absence of legal partnership rights.

We recommended that the Department of Justice Equality and Law Reform extend the right to nominate a partner with legal rights to same-sex couples, comparable with those recognised for a spouse in a heterosexual couple. This addressed issues of succession, next of kin, pensions and guardianship. The Department of Enterprise, Trade and Employment, and the Department of Justice Equality and Law Reform, we argued, should address statutory leave entitlements for partners caring for children and ensure residency and work entitlements for foreign partners of same-sex couples.

We recommended that the Department of Finance should amend the taxation system to address disadvantage for same-sex couples and the Department of Social, Community and Family Affairs, should do likewise in relation to welfare benefits. We sought that the Department of Environment and Local Government would ensure provision of and support for housing of same-sex couples on a par with heterosexual couples. We recommended that the Department of Health should ensure that rights in relation to parenting, fostering and adoption should operate on an equal basis with heterosexual couples.

These recommendations were important in being made by a State agency. However, the groundbreaking recommendation was tucked away in the section prior to these recommendations. 'Key principles for legal reform' was almost hidden under the subheading 'Diversity'. It stated that 'a legal framework should encompass a range of different kinds of partnership arrangements for which couples or households could opt. These should cover a range of different situations including legal marriage, registered partnerships and recognised households'. In seeking to implement equality for lesbian, gay and bisexual people, the report was recommending civil marriage for same-sex couples.

Ailbhe Smyth played a key role in championing the Equality Authority's report 'Implementing Equality for Lesbians, Gays and Bisexuals', which was launched in May 2002.

The report stressed that 'any system of social and legal provision for LGB people (including those in same-sex partnerships) in Ireland must recognise and reflect the diversity of that community. The different rights and choices of individuals, couples and households need to be respected in a broadly based legal framework'. This captured and sought to address the concerns on the advisory committee about this issue.

These concerns were held by lesbian, gay and bisexual organisations but these organisations had not yet fully grappled with the issue and did not have an agreed or final position. This was not surprising given the pace of change for lesbian, gay and bisexual people. Decriminalisation had only been achieved seven years earlier in 1993.

There were strands on the advisory committee that argued that any recommendation on partnership rights ran counter to gay culture in seeking to organise sexual relations in a monogamous heterosexual form. There was a reluctance among other strands to recommend civil marriage and thus further an institution, marriage, that is patriarchal in nature and not conducive to gender equality.

The Equality Authority pushed the equality agenda in accordance with our mandate. The advisory committee was originally planned to remain in place for a year; however, it was extended to work over a two-year period. We sought to use the additional time to stimulate and support discussion on the issue of partnership rights, and hosted a number of regional seminars on the report and its possible recommendations with the lesbian, gay and bisexual organisations on the advisory committee.

We commissioned research by John Mee and Kaye Ronayne on partnership rights to establish the disadvantages accruing to lesbian, gay and bisexual people in the absence of a legal basis for their relationships, and identifying disadvantages including pension rights, succession rights, and adoption rights. These disadvantages accrue because diversity was not acknowledged and taken into account when legislation in areas concerned with relationships was being drafted and enacted. We were, however, keen to move beyond an acknowledgement of difference to a valuing of difference, which would point towards equality objectives.

The issue of partnership rights did not raise a stir when the report was launched. The media gave it an uncritical focus and there was no negative public reaction. This was an indicator of the shifts in Irish society that would ultimately and overwhelmingly vote Yes in the Marriage Equality Referendum. The media questioned the issue of adoption by same-sex couples but, in most instances, this involved mild and polite interrogation. There was some negative reaction, from predictable quarters. David Quinn[1] in the *Sunday Times* was neither mild nor polite in writing 'by recommending that homosexual couples be allowed to adopt, it showed how a blind attachment to the notion of rights and equality could run a horse and four through common sense and reason'. Kevin Myers, never in the mood to be polite where the Equality Authority was concerned, stated in *The Irish Times* that 'adopted children should not be the tools for yet another social experiment by the latest generation of barking ideologists or playthings of the barren'.

CONCEPTS

Equality was not defined in the equality legislation that gave the Equality Authority a mandate to promote equality of opportunity and combat discrimination. We set a high bar for our understanding of equality in each of our strategic plans. It is most succinctly put in the Strategic Plan 2006–2008.

We seek progress in achieving equality outcomes that have economic, political, cultural and caring dimensions. These dimensions encompass:

- Redistribution and greater access to jobs, income, education, accommodation and health for those who currently experience inequality.
- Representation and increased access to participation in decision making that impacts on groups experiencing inequality and to the skills and resources necessary for an organisational capacity within these groups.
- Recognition and enhanced access to status and a valuing and accommodation of different identities, experiences and situations.
- Relationships and access to relationships of trust, care, respect and solidarity.

An ambition was evident in the focus on 'equality outcomes'. We sought substantive equality rather than a limited formal equality. Substantive equality is concerned with outcomes and change in the situation of groups experiencing inequality. Formal equality is merely concerned with a limited equality of opportunity and the elimination of discrimination.

The focus on recognition of diverse identities in part responded to the issue of invisibility that is often the fate of communities experiencing public hostility and for whom coming out becomes a burden. An early meeting with lesbian and gay organisations had impressed on us the importance of visibility. They were clear in stating that in the nine grounds covered by the Equality Authority they did not want to be 'the etceteras', as in 'we cover the nine grounds of gender, race, disability etc.'! This was a neat way of marking our cards.

Our focus on recognition went beyond acknowledging difference, to seeking a valuing of difference. When difference is acknowledged it becomes visible, and a concern to address discrimination and disadvantage can be asserted. When difference is valued it is recognised as a source of benefit and a concern to make changes to take account of the practical implications of difference and to achieve equality can be asserted.

BUILDING ON THE REPORT: NATIONAL ECONOMIC AND SOCIAL FORUM

One issue with reports like 'Implementing Equality for Lesbians, Gays and Bisexuals' is the challenge to sustain a focus on the recommendations and engage the relevant authorities to implement the recommendations. The Equality Authority developed a unique and strategic approach to this challenge with the National Economic and Social Forum (NESF). This is where Maureen Gaffney, Chairperson of the NESF, and Seán Ó hÉigeartaigh, Director of the NESF, made such an important contribution. The NESF agreed to process the recommendations in the report through the various government departments. They set up a project team to examine the recommendations, engage the relevant government departments and agencies on their implementation, and report to government on how best to move forward on the recommendations. The project team was drawn from the four strands of the NESF, involving all the social partners. It reported in 2003.

The NESF kept the recommendations to the forefront for government departments and allowed the lesbian, gay, and bisexual organisations on the project team to build the relationships with key officials that would drive change into the future. The NESF report recommended that partnership rights 'should include rights to: nominate a beneficiary of pensions and inheritance; designate a next-of-kin for medical reasons; nominate a partner as co-parent or guardian of a child; the right of a non-EU partner of an Irish person to live and work in Ireland; and the civil recognition of the partnership'. While this was not civil marriage, it brought the social partners into play as supporters of partnership rights.

BUILDING ON THE REPORT: EQUALITY AUTHORITY CASEWORK

Casework under the equality legislation supported by the Equality Authority helped to keep the issue of partnership rights to the forefront of public debate over the following years. A number of groundbreaking cases were widely covered and provoked national debate. Behind each of these cases was a couple with the nerve to take on the exposure involved in legal action and the determination to see a process through that often took an inordinate length of time. One measure of the courage required can be seen from the high level of under-reporting of discrimination on the ground of sexual orientation. We received few cases on this ground despite evidence of widespread discrimination. There were, for example, research findings of high levels of homophobic bullying in schools. Yet we received no cases of harassment on the ground of sexual orientation in educational establishments. In 2004, the Equality Authority had only one case on the sexual orientation ground and we reported that, since our establishment, the annual case files opened on this ground ranged from 1.5 per cent to 4 per cent of the total number of our case files.

Free travel passes on buses and trains are given to people once they reach the age of sixty-five and to their married or cohabiting partners, even if they are under sixty-five. The Department of Social and Family Affairs had given a 65-year-old gay man his free travel pass while refusing to provide his cohabiting partner with one. The Equality Authority intervened with the Department on behalf of the couple. In 2003, the Department accepted that the scheme was at odds with the Equal Status Acts, granted the free travel pass to the younger partner and paid compensation of €1,500.

Many media commentators opposed the granting of marriage rights.

Marriage Equality's 2011 message.

The government took action to undermine this result by enacting the Social Welfare (Miscellaneous Provisions) Act 2004. Section 19 of this Act established that applicants for schemes had to be a married couple or a man and woman cohabiting as husband and wife. The government sought to block further casework by taking advantage of section 14 of the Equal Status Acts. This exempts any action required under other legislation from prosecution under equality legislation. The Equality Authority had repeatedly identified this exemption as a licence for government to discriminate. The Residential Tenancies Act 2004 introduced the same formula to the definition of a couple. This was particularly problematic as the legislation included provisions for a tenancy to pass to a partner in a relationship, now exclusively heterosexual, when the other partner dies. The Equality Authority stated that the government could be in breach of the European Convention of Human Rights as a result.

A lesbian woman went for an interview and was told at interview that her curriculum vitae was the best. She had a discussion about working conditions and an offer of a job. On leaving the interview, she was chatting with one of the interviewers who asked if she was married. She said she had a partner who was a woman. A week later she was told she had not got the job. The Equality Authority took up the case, under the Employment Equality Acts, and, in 2004, it was settled with a payment of €8,000.

Myra McGurk and Eileen Twomey kissed in Malone's Pub: a 'peck on the lips' as one of them moved away to play pool. This simple signal of affection brought the house down around them. The pub is in Blarney, which one reporter noted is the 'traditional home of the kiss'. Nonetheless, the publican asked them to stop kissing. The pool table was closed down. The situation became so intimidating they felt they had to leave. They noted a group of people engaged in 'antics' with a blow-up doll as they left, with no action taken against them by the publican. They took a case with the support of the Equality Authority. In 2006, a judge of the District Court found in their favour. With apparent reluctance, he found that there was a 'technical breach' of the Equal Status Acts but awarded no compensation. Nonetheless the two women were satisfied and vindicated.

Mervyn and Richard's relationship had been recognised under the Civil Partnership Act 2004 in Northern Ireland. Mervyn had a terminal illness and could not work. He was on invalidity pension and his partner Richard took unpaid leave from his full-time job to care for him. He applied for an adult dependent allowance under Mervyn's pension. This allowance is provided under the invalidity pension for unmarried co-habiting heterosexual couples, but Richard was refused. Richard had to return to work, which was upsetting, and also detrimental to the care available for Mervyn. The couple lodged a case under the Equal Status Acts with the support of the Equality Authority. It took a government decision in October 2006 to settle this case. The Department of Social and Family Affairs agreed to make a payment to the couple, including arrears due because of the initial refusal, and to process their application for the adult dependent allowance to his partner. The outcome reflected an important recognition, in the most difficult circumstances, for same-sex couples and their relationships no matter how often the Minister, Seamus Brennan, insisted that this was not precedent-setting.

Niall Crowley *(left)* with Anne Motherway and Professor Gerard Quinn NUIG at the launch of Katherine Zappone and Ann Louise Gilligans's book *Our Lives Out Loud,* October 2008.

Niall Crowley with members of his godchild's family in a photo-still from one of a series of five Yes Equality videos produced by COCO TV. *From left:* Gráinne Courtney, Niall Crowley, Eileen Courtney, Clare O'Connell, Colm Kelly, Orla Howard, Michael Clancy, Daire Courtney and Shane Howard, May 2015.

BUILDING ON THE REPORT: NATIONAL DEBATE

The Equality Authority sought ongoing media debate on these issues to stimulate public support. This media presence was built around the recommendations of our original report and was enabled by extensive reporting on the cases supported. We also played a reactive role in the media to keep the debate alive.

The Vatican provided one such opportunity to react that was particularly heated. A Vatican Directive was published in 2005 that stated that homosexual practices were intrinsically immoral and contrary to natural law and banned homosexuals and their supporters from the priesthood. It added that 'these people' must be received with respect and delicacy. In an opinion piece in *The Irish Times* (December 2005) we suggested that the Vatican's position was 'clearly damaging to any ambition for equality in relation to gay or lesbian people. It ends up diminishing, degrading and lowering the status of lesbian and gay people in society and when that status and standing gets diminished it creates a context where abuse and discrimination can happen'. We stated that there is a need for the State to respond to the context created by the Vatican Instruction. This response could usefully include steps to put in place a legal recognition for (lesbian and gay) relationships on a par with heterosexual relationships.

In the *Irish Independent* David Quinn defended the supposedly embattled Vatican. 'The equality agenda is the new orthodoxy,' he wrote. 'It is the modern version of 1950s Catholicism and its officers are the new Bishops. Like the Church of old, the new and decidedly secular "church of equality" is trying to use a combination of the law plus moral intimidation to impose its values on us all and bully us into submission. Don't let it.'

Gerard Casey, a philosophy lecturer in UCD, told the *Irish Catholic* that 'the Equality Authority is like the new Curia with leader Niall Crowley as its high priest turning its fire on anything or anybody which contradicts its new heterodoxy. It is opposed to any real differences and proper diversity in that it only allows differences it accepts.' Christopher McCamley wrote to *The Irish Times*: 'Mr Crowley talks about celebrating diversity and accepting difference: is he prepared to accept and tolerate a religion which teaches that homosexual acts are sinful and that the condition is disordered?'

It was strange that, in many of the negative media responses in this and other instances, commentators sought to portray the Equality Authority as a church, while ultimately defending positions that drew from the Catholic Church. In 2004, Kevin Myers wrote in *The Irish Times* that 'perhaps we could have a new civil egalitarian ceremony for such unions solemnised by Archbishop Crowley'. In 2006, Mary Kenny, in the *Irish Independent*, went down the church road too with 'Mr Niall Crowley of the Equality Authority is the true heir of Archbishop John Charles McQuaid, the Dublin Primate who virtually controlled civil society over the span of his reign.'

BUILDING ON THE REPORT: INSTITUTIONAL CHANGE

Another strand of the Equality Authority's work was supporting change in the policies, procedures and practices of organisations to better promote equality, accommodate diversity and eliminate discrimination. Partnership rights emerged in this work, in both public- and private-sector organisations.

The Equality Authority assisted the Irish Congress of Trade Unions in the publication of its 2003 guidelines to prevent discrimination against lesbian, gay and bisexual employees, including guidance in responding to workers in same-sex relationships in terms of spousal benefits. This was not a new issue for Congress but needed to be refreshed.

We published research on 'Recognising Sexual Identities in Health Services' in 2008. This addressed a number of concerns about the recognition of same-sex partners in health-care settings, including being denied visiting rights and information on their partner's health in the absence of legal recognition for same-sex relationships.

NEGOTIATING CHANGE

Michael McDowell, Minister for Justice, Equality and Law Reform, established a Working Group to report to him on options for domestic partnerships in March 2006. The Working Group considered three groups of relationships outside of marriage: opposite-sex couples; same-sex couples; and non-conjugal relationships. The options to be identified related to giving legal recognition to these relationships. The Working Group included representatives from the Gay and Lesbian Equality Network (GLEN), the Family Lawyers Association, the Equality Authority, officials from various government departments, and the Office of the Attorney General, and was chaired by Anne Colley. This offered a key opportunity to make progress. Eilis Barry represented the Equality Authority, to great effect, as the final set of options reflected. She also found a great partner in equality in Eoin Collins of GLEN.

In May 2006, the Working Group, the Equality Authority and GLEN organised a seminar on the 'Legal Status of Co-habitants and Same-Sex Couples'. At an early point, we had to call the Gardaí. Members of the Ancient Order of Hibernians[2] had infiltrated the audience. They stood up shouting 'Shame' and throwing anything that came to hand at Michael McDowell when he got up to speak. I stood bravely by as a copy of the Constitution whizzed close to his head. His speech was, after all that, disappointing. He acknowledged that some people wanted full marriage but, in his view, 'the vast majority of gay men did not'. We had also hosted a fraught dinner the night before for the speakers. One speaker from abroad espoused a theory of gradual change. All countries had followed the route of civil partnership and then civil marriage and Ireland, to his mind, must follow suit. We saw no reason we should have to take the scenic route just because everyone else had. We did not want Michael McDowell to be let off the hook. The speaker was not for turning, however.

This ultimately emerged as a divisive issue in the search for change in Irish policy for marriage equality. Significant tensions emerged between those groups and individuals committed to seeking the immediate introduction of civil marriage, the equality now option, and those groups and individuals seeking the introduction of partnership rights and some model of civil partnership, the building change over time option. At one point I was invited to chair a platform that met to seek to address these tensions. This appeared to work at the time and there was some useful airing of the tensions and commitment to addressing activities that were leading to these tensions. However, the divisions continued and were only really put aside when the demands of winning the referendum for marriage equality imposed themselves.

In a significant achievement for those involved in the Working Group, however, the first option for same-sex couples presented in the Working Group report later in 2006 was, against all the odds, civil marriage:

Niall Crowley launches Marriage Equality's 'Out To Your TD' campaign, 2011.

The introduction of civil marriage for same-sex couples would achieve equality of status with opposite-sex couples and such recognition that would underpin a wider equality for gay and lesbian people. Civil marriage offers legal certainty and predictability in terms of the consequences for each partner. It would be administratively straightforward as the registration arrangements already in place for marriage would apply and would also be straightforward in terms of recognition.

The report went on to point out that 'introducing civil marriage for same-sex couples is likely to be vulnerable to constitutional challenge', while acknowledging that the case of Katherine Zappone and Ann Louise Gilligan had been heard recently by the High Court and judgement was awaited.

The second option identified was civil partnership. It noted 'full civil partnership falls short of full equality for same-sex couples' but concluded that 'in the absence of civil marriage the full civil partnership option is seen by the Group as one which would address the majority of the issues encountered by same-sex couples'. This was the option pursued by the government.

A STATE AGENCY GETS TAKEN OUT

The Equality Authority was effectively taken out of the debate in late 2008 on foot of a 43 per cent cut in its budget. A plethora of resignations followed but the government was not for turning. The Equality Authority was effectively put in abeyance until its eventual merger with the Irish Human Rights Commission in 2014 and the formation of the Irish Human Rights and Equality Commission.

Andrew Hyland

The Making of a Movement
Communications and its Role in Marriage Equality, 2008–2010

In 2008, Ireland was a more tense and hostile home for its lesbian, gay, bisexual and transgender (LGBT) citizens. Homosexuality was only decriminalised in 1993; the Roman Catholic Pope of the period, Benedict XVI, writing as Cardinal Joseph Ratzinger, in his 1986 document 'On the Pastoral Care of Homosexual Persons' labelled homosexuality a 'condition' and an 'intrinsic moral evil'. Homophobic bullying in schools was at record levels, and society, including LGBT people, didn't give much thought to the issue of LGBT people marrying.

Put simply, equal marriage rights were not high on the social justice agenda prior to and including 2008. From 2004, Ann Louise Gilligan and her wife Katherine Zappone brought a court action against the Revenue Commissioners to have their Canadian marriage recognised in Ireland. Their legal challenge, while a critical milestone in Ireland's history, and the *raison d'être* for the existence of Marriage Equality (ME), didn't embed the issue in the national psyche. Instead, their love inspired a group of committed friends to start the ME campaign, which eventually reversed multi-generational discrimination against LGBT relationships in Ireland.

Marriage Equality, the campaign and the movement, didn't just happen overnight, or in the short few months from when the referendum was called, leading to 22 May 2015. Yes Equality, a partnership formed by ME, with the Irish Council for Civil Liberties (ICCL), and the Gay & Lesbian Equality Network (GLEN), to lead the referendum campaign in 2015, was the culmination of years of strategic thinking, campaigning, communicating, and organising by ME and other groups. The strong foundations laid by ME across multiple areas from 2008, with communications as one of the central pillars, successfully penetrated the public and political psyche more than any other social justice campaign in the history of the Republic of Ireland.

In 2008, ME was a fledgling NGO. There was little awareness or understanding of the issue, low support for the campaign, and few allies. Communications, and a strong media presence, was vital to transforming it from a little-known group to an NGO with substance, political punch, and a trusted and credible voice.

To make strides and assert marriage equality as a political issue, the campaign had a number of audiences to reach with a variety of messages. Stakeholders included the LGBT community, the general public, politicians, the legal community and, of course, the media. The storyteller, the narrative, and their tone, was of huge importance and included staff, and members of the Board for serious news and current affairs issues, and lesbian and gay couples for more personal 'human touch' stories.

ME staff in 2008 comprised Moninne Griffith as Director, Dawn Quinn as Administrator and general all-round superwoman, and myself as Director of Communications. In 2010, Kirsten Fjoser would join to primarily concentrate on social media. It was a small team. It never got bigger; in fact, it got smaller. However, with zeal, determination and incredibly dedicated staff, Board and volunteers, it realised its dream. This is the story of how ME, with its well-thought-out communications strategy, achieved that dream.

FOUNDATIONS: STRATEGY AND RESEARCH

Underpinning every campaign and every company is a strategy. Lawrence Freedman in *Strategy: A History* tells us that having a successful strategy suggests an ability to look up from the short term and the trivial to view the long term and the essential, to address causes rather than symptoms, to see woods rather than trees.[1] ME crafted a strategy for each of its central pillars of operation, namely communications, mobilisation, fundraising, and political lobbying. Communications was one of these pillars, with the long term in mind. Civil marriage rights for LGBT people would be hard won and take years to achieve, and so ME's strategic success relied on future thinking. Storytelling, the sharing of personal stories specifically, was part of the communications strategy from which we never strayed. The organisation instinctively knew that Irish people would support equal marriage rights when they heard stories which demonstrated that the love between LGBT couples was no different to their own, and clearly placed LGBT people as family, friends and community members.

Iconic Yes. *From left:* Jerry Buttimer TD, Kieran Rose, Brian Sheehan, Gráinne Healy, Ailbhe Smyth, Andrew Hyland, Senator Averil Power, and Councillor Chris Curran at Dublin Castle, 23 May 2015.

Once this strategy was in place, ME swiftly moved to understanding current attitudes among the LGBT community and the general public's attitude towards the issue. This was done by conducting research, which was pivotal for ME in developing both the narrative and messaging of the campaign. Lansdowne Market Research was commissioned in 2008 to conduct focus group research with the core objective of understanding gay and lesbian attitudes to marriage, civil partnership, and to uncover 'hot button' topics. Led by Richard Warring, the research team returned with an incredibly insightful presentation that greatly assisted ME in crafting its messaging. Gay men and lesbian women were recruited from Dublin, Cork and Limerick, with the criteria that they were (i) apathetic or against extending civil marriage to same-sex couples and/or (ii) content with the civil partnership scheme being proposed. In addition, they had to be comfortable with being out gay and lesbian citizens.

The research revealed many things, but a core insight was that when the focus group participants reflected on the meaning of marriage in Irish society, and the meaning of their exclusion from it, there was an 'aha' moment that converted them to supporters of marriage equality. This was a wow moment for those of us developing the communications strategy – a gold nugget of information. Campaign communications had to educate around the importance placed on marriage in Irish society, and how LGBT exclusion from marriage was a form of oppression. If ME could do this, it would ignite a fire that would eventually lead to equal marriage rights in Ireland.

Brilliant in its foresight, considering Yes Equality didn't form for another seven years, the research conclusions included the following: 'Equality is and will possibly always be the key word' [for garnering support]. In other words, Irish people understood the word equality deeply and keenly. Its use in campaign literature and messaging was critical to success. These research results gave ME superb insight into its community and supporter base. It could motivate and engage people by conveying the importance of marriage in Irish society, mobilise with the knowledge that same-sex couples could not avail of marriage rights and, critically, frame the issue through the lens of equality. The research also showed that Irish people believed in equality and fairness. They did in 2008, and they remain committed to these principles now. This is something that consistently came through. ME needed to talk without the jargon of loaded and often inaccessible human rights speak, and opt instead for more personal and emotive conversational language.

Andrew Hyland *(left)* with Aengus Ó Snodaigh TD at the TÁ launch at the Clarence Hotel, Dublin, April 2015.

When focus-group participants explored the differences between the proposed civil partnership scheme and marriage rights, the campaign gained insight into what irked or angered participants. The knowledge that civil partnership would hold far fewer rights to civil marriage disappointed people. Participants became angered when they reflected on this as a further act of discrimination against LGBT people. The inequality of civil partnership when compared to marriage was an issue of great concern to focus groups. There was resentment that the same-sex family unit would not be recognised in civil partnerships, only through civil marriage. In a civil partnership, a couple's home would become 'a shared home', while in marriage it was 'a family home' with Constitutional protection for that family. Lesbian- and gay-headed families, through their exclusion from marriage, were being denied equal family status.

Significant differences between civil marriage and civil partnership needed to be communicated if we were to win the battle for hearts and minds at this stage of engagement. Some research participants viewed civil partnership as a step backwards, as a two-tiered scheme for recognising relationships, with lesbian and gay couples as second-class citizens at the bottom of the pile. The research said, 'There is an opportunity to generate more support by highlighting that the differences between civil partnership and civil marriage lie not just in a word disparity, and communicating the extent of those inequalities, especially those that seem trivial. This may help to affect and turn attitudes and gain support.'

A second piece of quantitative and nationally representative research, undertaken in 2008 by Landsdowne Market Research and Richard Warring, examined public attitudes to same-sex civil marriage. Critically and worryingly, it revealed that 51 per cent of people surveyed supported the statement that same-sex couples should be allowed to marry in a registry office. That 51 per cent statistic was of huge importance to the campaign. ME was not supportive of a referendum in 2008; instead it believed it could work to get parliamentarians to introduce same-sex marriage rights via legislation. For this to happen it needed far more numbers supporting the proposition and publicly calling for marriage equality than this statistic showed. There was an uphill struggle ahead to bring far greater numbers of supporters over to become active marriage equality supporters.

Incredibly, 62 per cent of those polled in the 2008 research said they would vote Yes in a referendum to extend equal marriage rights to same-sex couples. In 2015, 62.1 per cent, or 1,201,607 people, did vote Yes.

From 2008, when a referendum was not on the cards, to 2015, when the referendum took place, were crucial years in building and hardening support for marriage equality through strategic communications tactics by ME. Strategy and research was always critical to the foundations of ME. With an agreed long-term path, and the armoury of informed research findings to hand, ME moved into a space of developing messages for the LGBT community and the general public, which would harden support and bring greater public visibility and political support for marriage equality in Ireland.

DEVELOP YOUR MESSAGE AND STICK TO IT

Knowing what people needed, or wanted to hear, pushed the campaign to develop a set of concrete messages that we would repeat over and over again whenever we were given the opportunity. The messages were split into categories and included narratives on marriage (supportive of the institution); the exclusion of same-sex couples from marriage (real stories of the costs to these couples); and same-sex couples as second-class citizens (real examples of how that felt). Building on what it had learned from the research, the staff and Board of ME knew that messages must be carefully constructed with research informing and guiding the choice of each word. ME also knew that people, LGBT people specifically, would be vexed by the discriminatory differences between rights gained through marriage, and those gained through civil partnership. Civil partnership gave ME multiple opportunities to engage in effective communications and drive home the message that equal marriage rights for same-sex couples should be made law, and that anything else was discriminatory and further enshrined LGBT inequality.

Through research, knowing the appropriate triggers, the campaign produced a subset of messages when communicating on civil partnership. These messages became central to communications as the Civil Partnership Scheme was brought through the Oireachtas and then became law on 1 January 2011. Significantly, ME carefully constructed messages on children within LGBT families to explain how children suffered when their parents were excluded from marriage. These messages acknowledged the reality of the lives of children with LGBT parents, and also examined the fact that civil partnership virtually ignored these same children, giving them no rights, benefits, or legal family. ME worked with other children's welfare rights groups to ensure that the benefits to children of civil marriage equality for their parents was evident, and a key reason to support marriage equality.

ME was keenly aware of the need to ensure that its spokespeople were on message, as well as other LGBT and civil society organisations who supported the issue. In the spirit of working towards one goal and objective, namely securing equal civil marriage rights for same-sex couples, and knowing ME could not do it alone, it then looked at sharing messages with key advocates such as the recently formed LGBT Noise, the National Lesbian and Gay Federation (now NXF), BeLonG To, USI (Union of Students in Ireland) and more.

From left: Noel Sutton, Eamon Farrell, Andrew Hyland and Walter Jayawardene at Yes Equality HQ, May 2015.

MEDIA TRAINING

Michelle Thomas was recruited as ME's primary media trainer. A Donegal native, Michelle was passionate about the issue and understood the sensitivity and nervousness of LGBT people speaking to media about their lives. Remember, back in 2008, while there were some celebrities who were out and proud, very few stories appeared featuring 'everyday' LGBT people – school teachers, mums and dads, shop assistants, bank staff and social workers. ME spokespeople were split into two categories. First there were the primary spokespeople who articulated from a professional standpoint in news and current affairs – they were ME's official spokespeople. Moninne Griffith, Director, Gráinne Healy, Chairwoman, and Denise Charlton, then Co-Chair, were most likely to speak on the issue in the media.

Board members including Ailbhe Smyth, Feargha Ní Bhroin, and Ross Golden-Bannon would also step in for print, TV or radio interviews. Michelle and myself ensured staff and Board members were versed in the messages I developed. Learning to rebut opponents' claims, and pivoting arguments back to ME's messaging, our spokespeople were gathering profile and effectiveness. Preparedness was the key to success in media interviews. Other groups, such as the founding members of LGBT Noise, were media-trained by ME, a move that ensured that regardless of whether ME or LGBT Noise were featured in media, the message was the same – that the LGBT community wanted equal marriage rights for same-sex couples, and civil partnership was unequal.

SHARING STORIES WINS HEARTS

A lynchpin of the ME communications strategy was to share stories, specifically stories of regular couples, to win the hearts and minds of the general public. In truth, members of the LGBT community were members of families across Ireland – sons, daughters, grand-children, brothers and sisters. It was essential that this fact penetrated the minds of Irish people. To elaborate on the discrimination which LGBT people, your children and family members, experienced every day, was the core of the sharing-stories strategies. What LGBT stories emphasised was that people simply wanted to be equal, wanted to be treated fairly, the same as everyone else. This was the narrative – simple and uncomplicated. Media training couples was the easy part; finding them was not so easy, especially in the early days. In addition, when couples were identified, often they were fine appearing in a national broadsheet, say *The Irish Times* or *Irish Independent*, but reluctant to share their story with local newspapers in their home towns.

Here, I must pay homage to the couples who put themselves out there in 2008 and shone a light on marriage equality, making it human and tangible. When talking about laws we wanted enacted, it was critical we had a face to the story. Couples such as Orla Howard and Gráinne Courtney, Denise Charlton and Paula Fagan, Linda Cullen and Feargha Ní Bhroin, Eamon Farrell and Steven Mannion, Niamh and Jessica Webbley-O'Gorman, Mark McCarron and Paul Kenny, and Anthony Kinahan and Barry Gardiner. They were

Andrew Hyland (*centre*), Yes Equality Director of Communications, addresses the Yes team and volunteers, May 2015.

courageous and brave, truthful and authentic, and even when faced with a commentator or opponent who was visibly anti-LGBT equality, they held the line calmly with a steely determination and passion. These couples were brave because up until then, same-sex couples were somewhat invisible in Irish society. When Mark and Paul were interviewed on TV3's *Ireland AM* they held hands, and ended up in the newspapers the next day due to the numerous complaints the station received. The complainants contacted the station because Mark and Paul held hands.

Ireland was a different place for LGBT people in 2008. Few put themselves forward for media appearances, and for those who did, even with media training, it was a nerve-wracking experience. It put them front and centre of the debate, and made them very visible and recognisable. Accepting a role as a public face of the campaign left people vulnerable. ME took all measures to protect the couples, and only rarely allowed interviews with the adult children of LGBT parents, never with the younger children. The stories, and the truth and authenticity imbued in the storytellers' words, shone through brightly. Personal stories from real same-sex couples living in Ireland who wanted to marry, made it impossible for people, especially politicians, to ignore the issue. One couple confided in me that they were fearful of potential hate mail or letter bombs when they featured in a local paper. Instead, they were heartened when they received letters of support, love and encouragement from neighbours.

Some of the couples were themselves parents, and their family unit was neither recognised nor protected by the Constitution. The couples were strangers-in-law to their children, meaning their children had no legal right to one of their parents. It was draconian, and sharing these real stories significantly changed the landscape of how LGBT couples, and parents, were viewed across Ireland. As the stories were told, the hearts and minds of the Irish public began to favour civil marriage rights for same-sex couples. Without these couples sharing their true stories, securing equal marriage rights would have been a far more arduous, perhaps impossible, task. The couples made it personal, and showed Ireland what LGBT people were really like, which was just the same as everyone else.

TACTICS

Over the years, and always mirrored against the campaign strategy, ME originated multiple tactics to ensure the agreed narrative reached all sections of Irish society. Employing a dignified but firm tone, the message of inclusion and equality was repeated time and time again, that Irish LGBT people would not settle for less than equal marriage rights, and anything else conferred second-class citizenship, and pushed LGBT people further to the margins of society.

From left: Roisin Boyd, Seamus Dooley and Andrew Hyland listen to the victory speeches at the Ballsbridge Hotel, Dublin, 23 May 2015.

Scene from the RDS count centre, 23 May 2015.

Best ever selfie: Andrew Hyland *(centre)* snaps Brian Sheehan, Gráinne Healy and the crowd at Dublin Castle, 23 May 2015.

CIVIL PARTNERSHIP

The various stages of the Civil Partnership Bill's passage through the Dáil and Seanad provided ME with multiple opportunities to engage with the media. ME was established as a central voice critical of civil partnership, and called for equal marriage rights instead. At this early stage, ME argued that legislators should extend civil marriage rights to same-sex couples. A 2006 paper examining domestic partnerships in Ireland, 'The Colley Report', said of same-sex relationships: 'The introduction of civil marriage for same-sex couples would achieve equality of status with opposite-sex couples and such recognition that would underpin a wider equality for gay and lesbian people.' The report also concluded that civil partnerships could not achieve this.

Aware that ME was not the only opposing voice against civil partnership, a strategy to co-ordinate with other organisations was established. Groups such as LGBT Noise and USI issued press releases in unison. This was effectively a 'bigging up' of the marriage equality news as an issue, and ensuring that at least one group succeeded in getting a story landed on the topic. On a slow news day, a story that may not have landed, or failed to spark an editor's imagination, was elevated because here were two, three or four press releases on the same subject, grabbing a news editor's attention, transforming it into a newsworthy story. Between 2008 and 2011, when civil partnership became law, ME was afforded innumerable opportunities to voice their concerns about civil partnership, and in turn drive the message that only equal marriage rights lead to equality. Indeed, it has been noted publicly that due to our strong opposition to the original civil partnership offering, a more robust Civil Partnership Act was delivered.

MEDIA HANDBOOK

Some of the early adventures in the media spotlight highlighted one fact: that the majority of journalists were not equipped to talk about LGBT issues. A fear existed that they would use a wrong word ('Is it okay to use the word lesbian?'), and there was gross confusion surrounding differences between civil marriage and civil partnership, with some believing civil partnership was 'marriage-like'. ME had to ensure that when the issues were reported on a lack of information by journalists did not damage or undermine our campaign. It was agreed to develop the Marriage Equality Media Handbook, and distribute it to all media. The handbook was an instruction guide to reporting on the issue. It provided clarification when reporting, and included fact-based messages. The handbook was a success and, within weeks of its development, we witnessed an immediate change in how the issue was reported. It was a joy to witness 'gay marriage' used less, and instead being replaced by 'marriage for same-sex couples', in national print and broadcast media. The handbook acted as a means of establishing ME as a serious player on this issue. Our trusted and credible voice was getting noticed.

REPORTS

We put together our first report in 2009, 'It's No Joke: Civil Marriage Rights for Lesbians and Gay Men in Ireland'[2], using findings from the Lansdowne omnibus survey, and profiling two couples and a young lesbian woman, Siobhan McGuire. We also tested some of our newly devised messages. The report concluded:

What ME is calling for, is equal marriage rights for lesbians and gay men. This report clearly shows that the majority of public opinion is in favour of such a move. It is an issue of equality. And for those who cannot have their marriage recognised (who were married elsewhere), or those who wish to get married, it is no joke.

Stephen Connor from Kaph, the café adjacent to the
Yes Equality HQ, Dublin, delivered a special cake
to Andrew Hyland on Monday, 25 May 2015.

Ultimately, the report was well received among media, and generated extensive coverage and exposure for the issue.

Other reports would follow, each developing and reinforcing the narrative and, importantly, attracting respected academics and experts across multiple fields. Spokespeople and independent experts, who publicly voiced their support for ME, provided further opportunity for media exposure. One such report was 'Voices of Children' (Elliott, 2010), flagged as 'Marriage Equality's ground-breaking report on a workshop which documents the experiences of young people growing up in Ireland with lesbian parents.' Never before had the experiences of adult children with LGBT parents been documented in Ireland, but thanks to the research team, Iris Elliott, Celia Keenaghan and Emily Bent, it gave those children an opportunity to be seen and heard. These incredible young people contradicted the position posited by opponents: that being raised by LGBT parents was somehow damaging. These young adults were articulate and incredibly balanced people, and so their media appearances were a success. In fact, some of these young people, Conor Pendergrast and Clare O'Connell, in particular, were to be the key success factors at the Constitutional Convention in 2013.

POSTER POWER

A massive gripe of mine was that so many booklets and reports, and newspapers or magazine features, carried photos of fake couples from America or the UK. No couples were Irish, none were real, this was not good for authenticity or visibility. 'We Are Family' was a national poster campaign, made possible by a grant from The Community Foundation for Ireland, that gave visibility for the first time to real lesbian and gay families living in Ireland. The ground-breaking campaign shattered 'the silence and myths surrounding these families, and called on the government to recognise and protect same-sex couples and their children'. The campaign, while simple, broke the mould of anything that had been undertaken before. Real Irish couples, some with children, in a family-centred national advertising campaign. 'We Are Family' posters depicting real Irish lesbian and gay couples, some with their children, were carried by Dublin Bus and were sent to libraries, family resource centres and community information centres across Ireland.

I enlisted the help of my friend, the production director and photographer, Ronan Healy. The campaign recruited volunteer couples who, with their families, created a suite of four posters. Our Chairwoman, Gráinne Healy, and her partner, Patricia O'Connor with their son Conor; Michael Barron and husband Jaime Nanci; Orla Howard and partner Gráinne

Courtney and daughters Clare and Daire; and husbands David Carroll and Gary Fagan were all used and supported with a media campaign and generated extensive interest and coverage. The families were campaign ambassadors and paved the way for future billboard campaigns, like 'Just Love', which followed in 2011.

Posters being carried by Dublin Bus was an incredible achievement. Some were vandalised, but for the most part feedback was excellent. A few family resource centres refused to carry the posters, due to connections with their local church; others ordered more copies to adorn their walls, the poster of Gráinne with her family and the family dog being particularly popular. Overall, as the first national poster on same-sex family recognition in marriage equality, it was a huge success.

DIGITAL

In 2008, ME was just beginning to see the influence of digital media on the communications landscape in Ireland. Media outlets had crude offerings in comparison to what we see in media now; social media was heavily dominated by Facebook, and Twitter was only used by early adopters. ME's primary digital platform from 2008 was Facebook. It was able to engage directly in dialogue with a primarily young audience, convey messages, promote important events, and relevant media coverage; ME was bringing the story to them. The digital engagement connected ME to a section of youth, who until then, had been disengaged, or maybe disenchanted by LGBT politics. ME's digital footprint expanded quickly, literally connecting to thousands of mainly Irish supporters at first. It would lay the ground for entry into Twitter, and prepare the way for Yes Equality's digital platform supporter base years later.

Probably one of the finest productions for ME, and a viral hit, was Linda Cullen's COCO Television's 2009 short movie, *Sinead's Hand*. It followed a young man, played by Hugh O'Connor, as he knocks from door to door asking for Sinead's hand in marriage (see Linda Cullen's chapter for more detail on this video). The video concludes with the question, 'How would you feel if you had to ask four million people for permission to get married?' The video was a sensational hit, and to date has clocked up almost a million views on YouTube. Amazingly, it remained as relevant in 2015 during the referendum as it was in 2009. More followed, including *Rory's Story* by Fail Safe Films and *Yes to Love* produced for the Constitutional Convention. Years later, Linda Cullen would also produce five more videos for Yes Equality entitled *Marriage and Family Matters*, focusing on the real stories ME had always propounded. The videos featured sports men, parents and grandparents, and an LGBT family. *Sinead's Hand* was the first in a very long line of successful videos for the cause.

Gráinne Healy *(left)*, Minister for Justice Frances Fitzgerald and Andrew Hyland
at the introduction of the Marriage Bill to Dáil Éireann, September 2015.

THE WINDS OF CHANGE

In 2008, when I rang a news desk I'd have to open with something akin to:

> **Me:** Hi, this is Andrew Hyland calling from Marriage Equality, a group campaigning for equal marriage rights for same-sex couples.
> **Journalist:** Marriage for same-sex couples … as in gay couples?
> **Me:** Yes, lesbian couples too.
> **Journalist:** You're serious – marriage? For gays and lesbians? In Ireland?
> **Me:** Yes, and we've launched a new report highlighting that the Irish public are supportive of the government introducing marriage rights for same-sex couples.
> **Journalist:** Not in my lifetime, but send the story on again and I'll see what I can do.

Of course, this was not every journalist's response, but many were stopped in their tracks by ME's mission. It was common that if a story did appear, ME might be called a splinter gay group, or painted as radicals. Crucially, ME always engaged respectfully with friends and foes, and successfully established itself as a trusted and credible voice in Irish society by sticking to the truth. The campaign was a careful balance between fact and emotion, appealing to Irish people's sense of fairness, and a belief that everyone should be equal. This helped to end the reporting of ME as a random splinter group.

Within one year of opening its doors, I was receiving calls directly to my mobile on almost all LGBT issues – from youth and bullying, teen suicide, education, rural isolation and HIV. I was taking as many calls and redirecting them as I was on the issue of marriage equality. As the volumes of calls rose, I knew we were now a serious player on the LGBT landscape.

In September 2010, an independent evaluation of ME as an advocacy group (conducted by Íde O'Carroll and Hibernian Consulting – see O'Carroll's chapter), supported by Atlantic Philanthropies, rated communications for the campaign as 'highly successful'. With the launch of the 'We Are Family' project in June 2010, including posters on Dublin buses, the 'campaign's effectiveness as a communications effort reached historic levels of visibility for Irish lesbian and gay families'. The report also made clear that ME's narrative had been directly adopted by supportive TDs and Senators in the Oireachtas. This was 2010; five more years would pass until the move to a referendum. In January 2015, Frances Fitzgerald TD, Minister for Justice and Equality, announced the wording agreed by the Government for the constitutional amendment on marriage equality. The wording is contained in the Thirty-Fourth Amendment of the Constitution (Marriage Equality) Bill 2015. ME was pleased that the Minister for Justice saw fit to use 'Marriage Equality' as the correct term for the referendum. This was a milestone and reaffirmed the messaging success of the campaign.

OUT TO YOUR TD

ME was a fledgling campaign in 2008, whose influence grew exponentially and was transformed into an influential and dynamic organisation, working to secure equal marriage rights for same-sex couples. It shared a collective vision and passion to transform Ireland into a country that was kind and loving towards its LGBT citizens. It knew this was more than fighting for the rights of same-sex couples marrying. It was about Ireland becoming an inclusive nation, not perfect, but a major advancement on the shameful treatment of LGBT people in the past.

Two women inspired the movement, a group of friends united to create ME, and together with a passionate staff, their dream was finally realised on 23 May 2015. On that day, as our research of November 2008 predicted, 62 per cent of the Irish public said Yes to the proposition that 'Marriage may be contracted in accordance with law by two persons without distinction as to their sex.' ME realised in the early days that the lack of LGBT people presenting to public representatives was an issue to resolve. Politicians were using LGBT invisibility as a reason not to do anything about equality. Creating the campaign, 'Out To Your TD', we asked our supporters to visit their TDs, Senators and local authority counsellors, to make marriage equality an issue – one that would be a vote decider during local, general and European elections. While this was clearly a mobilisation tactic, we fully supported this initiative with communications – photo calls, press releases, print and broadcast interviews. We threw the kitchen sink at it because of the faith we had in the 'Out To Your TD' campaign. Real people were sharing their personal stories with elected officials and asking them to make it an issue in the Oireachtas. It began to work.

Communications, one of the central pillars of ME's strategy to secure its mission, was rooted in deep reflection, expert research, and a clear sense of purpose. Critical, too, was the ability to listen. ME listened to the LGBT community, it heard what they were saying and how they were feeling, and responded with sincerity and a genuine gratitude that they were supporting ME in this gargantuan undertaking. ME listened as carefully to its opponents and critics. It picked apart their arguments and falsehoods, and ensured that spokespeople were empowered, enabled and armed with rebuttals. The strong foundations which all communications' activities were based on guaranteed that ME's voice grew in strength and confidence, secured a place at negotiating tables, and made ME a central player in what would be the Marriage Equality Referendum in 2015.

LEGACY

ME's legacy was to birth a movement that positively transformed Ireland's treatment of its LGBT citizens. As the Director of Communications in the fledgling years, and its Co-Director from 2013, I was able to bring what we had crafted over the years in ME and apply it to the Yes Equality referendum campaign. As a founding member and Director of Communications for Yes Equality, we literally superimposed the ME communications strategy onto this new entity. Supported by a brilliant team, we took the storytelling to new heights, strategically positioned our spokespeople, specifically Gráinne Healy, our main spokesperson, in the hefty debates, and consistently reaffirmed the ME message: that this issue was a simple matter of equality. In other words, the referendum win was the culmination of years of grafting by ME and other groups. It transformed Ireland and, in that process, my life. It was more than a campaign we worked on, it was a vocation into which many of us threw ourselves, heart and soul. We won because we spoke from the heart, and exposed the oppressive treatment against LGBT lives.

Happy campaigners at the final passing of the Marriage Bill, 22 October 2015.
From left: Andrew Hyland, Ann Louise Gilligan, Moninne Griffith, Katherine Zappone, Orla Howard, Ailbhe Smyth, Gráinne Healy and Brian Sheehan.

Andrew Hyland chats to Ailbhe Smyth at Dublin Castle, 23 May 2010.

Ireland isn't perfect, we've a lot to do to achieve equality for all citizens, but at this moment in time, we've a lot to be proud of. Personally, the issue of marriage equality was always more than LGBT people marrying. It was about love and acceptance in its purest form. The campaign was thrilling and exciting. But it was also a mental, physical and emotional slog. Without my family and friends I never could have done it. They are the real Marriage Equality champions.

On 23 May 2015, we began anew. To the 1,201,607 people who voted Yes, thank you.

Íde B. O'Carroll

Across the Pond
Connections to Marriage Equality Ireland

I grew up in grey and white,
in half-tones and undertones ...
(Eavan Boland, *The Lost Land*)

PERSPECTIVES

Despite being located for much of the year over three thousand miles away in Amherst, Massachusetts, there were several strands – professional and personal – to my connection with the Marriage Equality (ME) Ireland campaign. I knew and admired many of the leaders from my experience of conducting research on social change issues in Ireland. When the campaign commissioned me to act as its external evaluator (along with a Dublin-based colleague, Finbar McDonnell), I felt honoured. During a particularly intense year, 2009–10, we piloted an innovative advocacy evaluation approach in the Irish context. While most of our reports were for internal use, we made public 'Marriage Equality: A Case Study', September 2010 (see my website, www.ocainternational.com, to view or to download a copy of the report).

Once the evaluation commission came to an end, my spouse, Annie G. Rogers, and I became financial supporters. We followed the campaign's progress from afar, via social media, right up to that glorious day of celebration in Dublin Castle. However, as a member of Ireland's diaspora, I was deeply disappointed not to be allowed to vote in the historic referendum in May 2015. Nonetheless, our spirits were lifted in June, when the US Supreme Court ruled in favour of marriage equality in America. And then, to crown it all, we marched in Dublin's 2015 Pride Parade alongside campaigners from our former home in Stoneybatter, Dublin. Finally, back in Amherst in September, I discussed the Irish referendum result with Professor Lee Badgett as part of the Amherst Irish Association's Event Series. An internationally respected marriage equality specialist, I'd first met Lee in 2009 when I'd interviewed her for the advocacy evaluation.

Therefore, in the space of just six years, from 2009 to 2015, marriage equality for same-sex couples had become a reality on both sides of the Atlantic.

I take the view, based on my experience, that the ME and Yes Equality campaigns in Ireland used effective advocacy strategies that built on decades of LGBT organising to deliver the successful outcome. I also acknowledge the importance of some American links and lessons that influenced the Irish campaign.

Stoneybatter and Dublin 7 at Pride, 2015.

FOUNDATIONS

From the vantage point of campaign success in 2015, those observing the outcome in Ireland from afar tried to understand how a country for so long considered conservative and Catholic could have delivered such a progressive result – the only nation in the world to secure same-sex marriage by popular vote. This was not something that happened overnight. ME and the later Yes Equality campaigns' advocacy took place in a particular Irish policy context, in a small society (population of just 4.6 million), with significant social networking and a political culture highly attuned to constituency needs. In addition, it built on decades of LGBT community-based projects that facilitated a growing capacity, confidence and visibility, activities that resulted in enhanced public awareness and achievement of a range of incremental human rights.

Not until 1993 was the Victorian legislation criminalising male homosexuality overturned in Ireland, and the presence of lesbians acknowledged by default. That year, I worked on the first national study of lesbians and gays in Ireland, with Eoin Collins, 'Poverty: Lesbians & Gay Men – The Economic and Social Effects of Discrimination' (Combat Poverty/GLEN, 1993). Our research provided ample evidence of numerous forms of prejudice, discrimination, social exclusion and negative health outcomes for Irish lesbians and gay men. People lived in fear and anxiety, were threatened, bullied and beaten up. They lost jobs, left jobs or didn't get jobs for which they were qualified, because of their sexuality. Others were banished from their family of origin, the shame of their sexuality enough to render them exiles. There were serious consequences to being out at home, at school, at work and in Ireland's towns, villages and cities – no wonder people were loath to publicly, or even privately, declare their true sexuality. In 1993, Eoin and I compiled an informal list of people whom we considered as publicly out in Ireland – you could count them on one hand. Compare that with the sea of smiling faces at Dublin Castle in May 2015.

Yet even in the 1990s, things were improving – albeit gradually. A number of community-based activities were building the capacity of Ireland's LGBT communities, work that often took place under the public radar. Again, allow me to draw on my experience here to illustrate the point. A collection of essays by Irish lesbian and gay activists, artists, writers and academics, *Lesbian and Gay Visions of Ireland: Towards the Twenty-First Century* (Cassells, UK, 1995), edited by myself and Eoin Collins, proved the vibrancy of community-based activities in Cork, Limerick, Galway, Dublin and among Ireland's emigrants abroad, in London and New York. The essays also demonstrated the emergence of confident Irish lesbian and gay activists, writers, artists and scholars willing to assume a public presence in that book – people like Joan McCarthy in Cork, Brendí McClenaghan in Belfast, writer

Emma Donoghue in Cambridge, UK, visual artist Louise Walsh in Dublin and academic Eibhear Walshe at University College Cork. In one truly memorable essay from that collection, NYC-based activist, Dubliner Anne Maguire, wrote about the Irish Lesbian and Gay Organisation's battle to include Irish lesbians and gays in New York's St Patrick's day parade, an issue only finally resolved in March 2016!

Significant progress on LGBT rights from 1995 to the 2000s was the cumulative effect of substantial community work, building the capacity of organisations at grass-roots and national levels, as well as strategic policy-related initiatives by organisations. Supports like the telephone help lines – a vital first point of contact for isolated lesbians and gays – were run by local volunteers. Other projects like Lesbians Organising Together, and Outhouse, both in Dublin, or Lesbians in Cork, developed in part because of the support of a range of European Union and State-sponsored measures to promote equality and rights. In addition, strategic initiatives by leaders in organisations like the Gay & Lesbian Equality Network (GLEN), NXF (formerly NLGF, National Lesbian and Gay Federation) and the National Women's Council of Ireland, of which notably Gráinne Healy was Chairwoman for a period, were crucial to building this early equality infrastructure in Ireland. As a result of these various activities, substantial progress was made in relation to LGBT rights. Sexual orientation was listed as one of the nine grounds dealing with discrimination within employment (Employment Equality Acts, 1998, 2004), and in non-employment areas such as education and services (Equal Status Acts, 2000–4).

AMERICAN INFLUENCES

In tandem with the cumulative effect of substantial grassroots and policy-related work on LGBT issues in Ireland over several decades, we can also trace the origins of Ireland's ME campaign to two individuals and to another country, America. American-born Katherine Zappone met Irish-born Anne Louise Gilligan while they were graduate students at the Jesuit-run Boston College, in Massachusetts. When Drs Katherine and Ann Louise returned together to Ireland in 1983, it was as life partners. Almost two decades later, they assumed a very public position as they sought to have their 2004 Canadian marriage recognised. The KAL (Katherine & Ann Louise) Advocacy Initiative was a legal case to establish their right to file joint tax returns as a married couple living and working in the Republic of Ireland.

From 2004 onwards, Ann Louise and Katherine's consistent and persistent public claim to equality in the eyes of the law and their superb media engagements won over many Irish hearts and minds. While the KAL case slowly progressed through the various channels of the Irish legal system, it was nonetheless the main catalyst for the ME campaign, founded in 2008 by Gráinne Healy, Denise Charlton, Ailbhe Smyth and others, to ensure civil marriage for same-sex couples in Ireland.

The ME campaign sought and received funding from The Atlantic Philanthropies, founded by Irish-American Chuck Feeney, a champion of human rights. In its earlier, anonymous funding cycles, The Atlantic Philanthropies, then operating as Tara Consultants, supported a number of community-based lesbian and gay projects in Ireland. Often these initial grants helped to leverage State or European funds that enabled projects to expand, and lesbian and gay groups to grow.

One of ME's first steps was to invite a representative of the Massachusetts Marriage Equality group (Marc Solomon) to conduct a workshop in Ireland in order to share lessons about what worked there. For example, a successful project in Massachusetts involved visits by campaigners to public representatives at their constituency base to advocate for change. That evolved into the 'Out To Your TD' effort in Ireland.

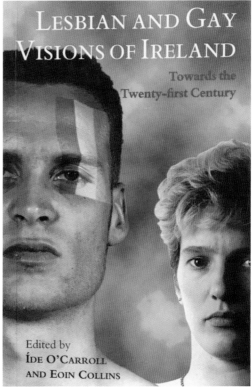

| *Poverty: Lesbians & Gay Men – The Economic & Social Effects of Discrimination*, 1993. | *Lesbian and Gay Visions of Ireland: Towards the Twenty-first Century*, 1995. |

However, just as the ME campaign took off in 2008, Ireland entered a deep economic recession, a time when, unfortunately, much of the government's equality infrastructure had been downsized because of lack of political will and a concern about the growing capacity of civil society organisations in the area.

In addition to these challenges for the ME campaign, a sequence of inter-related legal and political advances from 2006 onwards, with GLEN's Eoin Collins as a main advocacy driver, precipitated the publication by the Irish government of a Civil Partnership Bill in June 2009. The bill sparked some fascinating parliamentary debates in December 2009, and again in January 2010, on the meaning of marriage, family, and politicians' contact with same-sex couples in Ireland. By July 2010, the Civil Partnership and Certain Rights and Obligations of Cohabitants Act 2010 was signed into law, with rights accruing in relation to social welfare, pensions and immigration. For GLEN, in particular, this result was interpreted as a massive victory, based on what was politically feasible at the time, a view shared by its primary funder, The Atlantic Philanthropies. Exhausted by the campaign, my friend Eoin Collins left for New York, where his long-term partner, Josep Adalla, was working after several unsuccessful attempts to establish residency in Ireland.

Since the ME evaluation was happening in 2009 and 2010, side by side with these civil partnership developments, it is important to highlight the ME position. ME was absolutely adamant that civil partnership did not represent the position of the vast majority of lesbian and gay communities' members as it fell short of affording lesbians and gays the same rights as heterosexual citizens. Therefore, at that stage, while GLEN and ME were working towards the ultimate common aim of civil marriage, the two organisations approached the challenge of policy change in different ways. Eventually, GLEN and ME would join forces, along with the ICCL (Irish Council for Civil Liberties), under the Yes Equality banner.

Back in 2011, a year after our work on the ME evaluation came to a close, civil partnership became available in Ireland, the first State recognition of same-sex relationships in Ireland. Yet, of course, the ME campaign continued. Others have written of the steps taken by the ME and Yes Equality campaigns, including an important book by Gráinne Healy, Brian Sheehan and Noel Whelan, *Ireland Says Yes: The Inside Story of How the Vote for Marriage Equality Was Won* (Merrion Press, 2016).

I'd now like to briefly describe why our evaluation approach was innovative, and some of the lessons that emerged. Since much of the information on the analytical framework and evaluation methods used is available in our Final Case Study report, I'll limit my remarks to some process issues and conclusions.

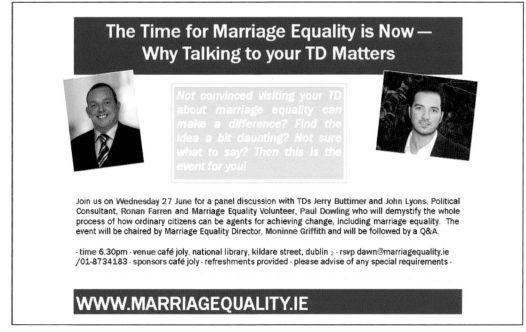

Marriage Equality support material for the 'Out To Your TD' initiative with
Jerry Buttimer TD and John Lyons TD, 2012.

ADVOCACY EVALUATION 2009–10

We piloted an innovative advocacy evaluation framework in the Irish social change context devised in America by leading evaluator Michael Quinn-Patton, in addition to proven advocacy evaluation methods, created by the Harvard Family Research Project. Quinn-Patton applied his framework during an evaluation of a project advocating change in the treatment of juveniles within the US judicial system. The Atlantic Philanthropies funded both the project and the evaluation.

The idea was that a campaign's progress and effectiveness as an advocacy effort could be assessed and continuously improved based on an analysis of six interconnected factors: 1. Strong high-capacity coalitions; 2. Strong national-grassroots co-ordination; 3. Disciplined and focused messages with effective communications; 4. Solid research and knowledge base; 5. Timely, opportunistic lobbying and judicial engagement, and finally, 6. Collaborating funders. Using this framework, along with proven advocacy methods such as bellwethers (gathering data from strategically placed informants who forecast which way the wind is blowing on the issue), and intense-period debriefing (conducting immediate analysis of data following major events to inform future actions), we were able to provide ongoing, real-time analysis of the ME campaign's progress and effectiveness as an advocacy effort.

We gathered a range of data, with the support of the ME team, and completed regular assessments of campaign effectiveness. We then discussed our findings with the ME Board. In that way, the evaluation process informed the actions taken in the following weeks and months. Since the aim was to influence legislation and policy in relation to same-sex civil marriage in Ireland, recommendations for change emerging from the evaluation analysis needed to inform the campaign's activities and facilitate the ME team to adapt to shifts in the wider context.

In the final analysis in September 2010, we were of the view that a constitutional referendum was necessary in order to achieve the ultimate aim. Nonetheless, we concluded that significant gains, and outcomes were achieved by a campaign with an annual grant of €200,000, and with only 2.5 paid team members. Let me end this brief review of the evaluation by listing some key learning points emerging from the process.

Given its modest financial resources, ME relied heavily on volunteers and professionals willing to contribute on a pro bono basis to deliver on its four campaign strategies – political, legal, communications and mobilisation. This, in turn, widened the campaign base and facilitated multiple points of influence on Irish policy-makers and the general public. Activity by ME volunteers throughout Ireland improved the level of lesbian and gay visibility and political engagement, and influenced policy debates.

The campaign's tiny paid team of workers and its active volunteer board were content to slowly build a broad-based coalition of support with members of all political parties and none, with community-based and equality organisations, with Trade Unions, etc. In addition, the advocacy message and method were framed in positive terms, as collaboration rather than control, as doing what was decent and right, as addressing a gap in current provision, and so forth. This approach helped to harvest political capital way beyond ME's 'natural' or immediate allies.

The campaign sparked debate on lesbian and gay issues using findings from international and national research commissioned by the campaign or accessed via its partners, including in relation to families with lesbian or gay parents. In that way, its arguments for rights and equality were substantiated by evidence-based research. With an eye to influencing those in the legal profession in Ireland, ME listed the provisions in other countries to illustrate the growing legal consensus and body of case law on same-sex marriage.

Of course, the campaign didn't always get it right. What project or person ever does? Often the most valuable learning is in relation to the points of weakness. In this case, during the period 2009–10, with only a part-time communications person, the campaign lacked the resources to complete detailed statistical and content analysis of media, to inform its communications strategy. Nonetheless, one of the key strengths of the campaign, we concluded, was its capacity to promote lesbian and gay visibility, especially via the 'Out To Your TD' campaign, and its use of media images of lesbian and gay families. All of these activities helped to counter the idea of a hidden Ireland and communicated the ubiquitous nature of lesbian and gay citizens and families in Ireland.

During the evaluation, we consulted widely in Ireland with community leaders, equality and legal specialists, politicians, journalists and church leaders, those for and against the idea of same-sex marriage equality. It was interesting for us to chart how people were 'evolving' on the issue, politicians, in particular; a trend influenced in no small way by the pressure at constituency level. Since I was living much of the year in America, I also interviewed marriage equality leaders and organisations there as part of the evaluation process. I recall meeting Evan Wolfson in New York, founder of Freedom to Marry, USA. A legal scholar and advocate, he was happy to facilitate the transfer of knowledge from the US experience. He later offered advice to the Irish campaign and was a keynote speaker at an event in Ireland. This was just one example of the enormous goodwill towards Ireland's ME campaign.

Another American connection was M.V. Lee Badgett, Professor of Economics, and Director of the Center for Public Policy and Administration, at the University of Massachusetts, Amherst, and author of *When Gay People Get Married: What Happens When Societies Legalize Same-Sex Marriage* (2010), the first text on the topic. During an initial interview that lasted several hours, I was struck by her capacity to provide an analysis of the European approach to marriage equality advocacy compared to the US approach. It was insightful and compelling, and informed the evaluation. Some years later, in April 2015, just before the referendum, the Yes Equality campaign invited Lee to speak at the Mansion House in Dublin. The event, co-hosted by ME and the EROSS Centre at Dublin City University, was attended by a large number of academics and media.

When the advocacy evaluation came to an end in September 2010 with the delivery of our Case Study Report, it seemed that successful realisation of access to full, equal civil marriage rights for lesbian and gay people in Ireland would require a constitutional referendum that would certainly be contested. And indeed it was. While civil partnership became widely available in 2011, Ireland was heading into a period of further economic difficulty that hurt the campaign's budget and donations from supporters. Nonetheless, as evidenced by the strategic alliance that emerged under the Yes Equality banner – GLEN,

ICCL, and ME – the advocacy effort continued and ultimately succeeded in May 2015, under the astute leadership of Gráinne Healy and Brian Sheehan, in particular.

Regrettably, I was disqualified from voting in the referendum along with other members of the Irish diaspora resident abroad, but I followed events closely on social media. Only those who had emigrated from Ireland in the eighteen months prior to the referendum were technically allowed to vote. I was impressed by younger advocates, savvy social media users, especially recent emigrants who returned in droves, their #hometovote was the number one trending hashtag on Twitter. Impressive too was the 'Call Your Granny' project that initiated a conversation on the issue between the generations. I watched several children of lesbian and gay parents speak with truth and conviction about the quality of their experience growing up in such a household. Theirs was a remarkable media presence.

Other campaign work was conducted outside of the media, but was no less impressive. One friend took six months off work to organise a seriously sophisticated canvassing effort unsurpassed in that Dublin Central constituency. Another travelled the length and breadth of Ireland in the Yes Bus. Massive engagement. Major commitment. Visibility. Public presence. What a contrast to the 1980s and early 1990s!

Of course, the Catholic Church in Ireland sought a No vote and advised its flock accordingly, though in fact many Catholics campaigned and voted for marriage equality. In Amherst one morning, I sat riveted by an NPR radio interview being conducted with Maeve Lewis, Director of One in Four (an Irish organisation which advocates for survivors of sexual abuse). She interpreted the referendum result as a loss by the Catholic Church of its moral authority because of the extent of institutional cover-up of child sexual abuse which she claimed Irish people found simply 'unforgiveable'.

When the Marriage Equality Bill was signed into law on 29 August 2015, I was already back in America, watching proceedings in Ireland from afar. Not all issues were resolved, however, at least for my family. Like Katherine and Ann Louise, I met the love of my life, Annie G. Rogers in Boston, Massachusetts. In our twenty-one years together, the official definition of our relationship has gone from classification as 'domestic partners' in Cambridge, MA, to 'married' in Massachusetts in 2006, and US Federal recognition of our marriage in 2014. In Ireland, however, despite the marriage equality victory, we still encounter a major challenge.

In the past, marriage to an Irish citizen afforded the spouse immediate immigration rights and access to a passport without need for residence in Ireland or naturalisation (1956 Act). This is not the case now. And that is equality, too. Each time Annie enters at Shannon she is quizzed as to her financial resources, the reason for her trip and given a maximum of ninety days to remain. She's had ongoing professional ties with colleagues and projects in Ireland since the 1990s, when she was a Fulbright Scholar at Trinity College, Dublin, and is a member of a Dublin-based psychoanalytic organisation. Yet, only by residing in Ireland for a period of uninterrupted years *might* she access an Irish passport, despite the fact that we have had a home in Lismore, Co. Waterford, for almost twenty years. Unfortunately, despite the success of the marriage equality campaign in Ireland, nothing has changed for my family. Before the win, Annie was allowed to remain in Ireland for ninety days at a time. The same holds true now.

Nonetheless, we remain upbeat about Ireland after the marriage equality win. It will never be the same place. It feels different to arrive into Shannon from America now, as we did in June 2015, holding hands as we walked through the arrivals gate to be greeted by friends wearing Yes Equality badges. I will never forget coming into Lismore, a small town in west Waterford, where one elderly neighbour came over to embrace me, tears in her eyes, and said: 'I voted for ye. We did the right thing.'

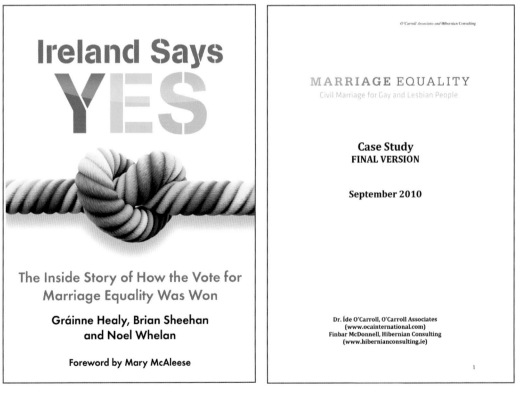

The story of the Yes campaign in *Ireland Says Yes*, 2016.

Marriage Equality: A Case Study, September 2010.

Justine Schönfeld-Quinn

Legal Mobilisation and the Movement for Marriage Equality in Ireland
From Missing Pieces to a Yes Vote

A CAMPAIGN FOR LAW REFORM

The campaign for access to civil marriage for couples in same-sex relationships was first and foremost a campaign for law reform. It began with a legal challenge by Katherine Zappone and Ann Louise Gilligan to the refusal of the Irish State to recognise their Canadian marriage (hereinafter 'the KAL case').[1] This High Court action led to the establishment of Marriage Equality (ME), a social movement founded in 2008 as a successor to that established in support of the KAL case. ME soon became the most prominent organisation in Ireland campaigning for equality in marriage. At the time when ME was founded, couples in same-sex relationships were unable to form legally recognised relationships, much less celebrate legally and constitutionally protected marriages. A mere seven years later, Ireland became the first country in the world to extend access to civil marriage to couples in same-sex relationships by popular vote.[2]

The successful outcome of the referendum on marriage announced on 23 May 2015 made headlines around the world but was, however, far from being the only landmark legal change that year. Just a few short weeks beforehand, legislation was enacted providing a comprehensive reform of family law. The Children and Family Relationships Act 2015 established a legislative framework that addressed parenting by couples in same-sex relationships and made provision for guardianship, adoption and parentage in cases of assisted reproduction in respect of couples in same-sex relationships for the first time in Irish law.[3] Weeks later, in the same year, Ireland enacted gender recognition legislation[4] and also amended section 37(1) of the Employment Equality Act 1998, a provision that had formerly granted bodies with a religious ethos a wide-ranging exception from non-discrimination laws.[5] These legislative reforms, together with the success of the marriage referendum, were the culmination of years of campaigning by ME and others, and of unprecedented social movement mobilisation.

LEGAL MOBILISATION AND MARRIAGE

It is axiomatic that the success of a social movement depends to a great extent on the number of its adherents (Della Porta and Diani, 2009, p. 71) and that referenda succeed or fail based upon the number of supporters they can mobilise at the ballot box. The Irish marriage referendum was no exception. It succeeded because it mattered so much to so many people who were prepared to invest time and energy over many years in campaigning for it. To understand the success of the marriage referendum and the momentum that supported the enactment of so many landmark legislative provisions, it is important to address the process of mobilisation itself and questions such as: what explains the process whereby both the marriage referendum and legislative provision for same-sex parenting commanded such overwhelming political as well as popular support? How did marriage become a goal of the movement? Why were so many people prepared to share their stories with family and friends, to lobby their public representatives, raise funds, and engage in door-to-door campaigning in support of access to civil marriage for couples in same-sex relationships? In addressing the process whereby this mobilisation occurred and how it contributed to political support for legislative change as a lawyer on the ME Board, I had the opportunity to observe how legal frames and arguments were used to foster and sustain social movement and persuade policy-makers and others of the need for legislative change.

To refer to these legal strategies, I use the term 'legal mobilisation' because it embraces the use of law by social movements in pursuance of public policy goals (Paris, 2010; Vanhala, 2010; McCann, 1994). The legal strategies employed by ME were not limited to litigation, but also included the use of legal frames and arguments to foster social movement mobilisation as well as the deployment of legal argumentation in the course of political lobbying. The term 'legal mobilisation' is sufficiently broad to capture all efforts involving the use of law, legal argument or claims about rights in the course of a social struggle (Epp, 1998, p. 18). It therefore encapsulates a wider range of strategies and tactics than litigation, including the use of legal frames and arguments in consciousness-raising and lobbying for law reform (Vanhala, 2012, p. 531).

ME made effective use of legal mobilisation strategies (a) in support of a litigation strategy; (b) to foster and sustain social movement mobilisation; and (c) to engage in political lobbying. The result was a campaign that successfully mobilised Irish people in a way that no other social movement has in Ireland to date. This contributed to rapid changes in public attitudes and ultimately dramatic social and legal change.

THE LITIGATION STRATEGY

The campaign for access to civil marriage for couples in same-sex relationships in Ireland began with the KAL case.[6] At the time when the case was taken, same-sex couples were unable to form legally recognised relationships in the State. The recognition of marriages by couples in same-sex relationships had scarcely featured in Irish public discourse. Although Ireland had made impressive strides in the years after decriminalisation of homosexuality, resulting in the enactment of landmark non-discrimination legislation,[7] it had begun to fall behind other jurisdictions on this issue. Furthermore, marriages by same-sex couples were performed and recognised in only a handful of jurisdictions around the world at that time, including the Netherlands (2001), Belgium (2003), Canada (2005), Spain (2005), South Africa (2006), and in a few states in the United States of America: Vermont (2000), Massachusetts (2003) and Connecticut (2008).

The predominant model of recognition in most jurisdictions at the time was instead that of some form of registered partnership – a status which in many jurisdictions carried less than the full legal rights and duties associated with civil marriage (Boele-Woelki, 2008, p. 1962). The KAL case put the recognition of marriages by same-sex couples on the agenda before the Civil Partnership and Certain Rights and Obligations of Cohabitants Act 2010 was even introduced.[8]

The KAL case was taken against a backdrop of a Constitution that is regarded as having established a constitutional right to marry,[9] and which also guarantees that 'all citizens shall be equal before the law'.[10] This provided a foundation for the legal challenge, the outcome of which was by no means certain at the outset. In particular, the High Court had considerable latitude in addressing the arguments raised by the applicants, in view of the fact that the courts had never before been called upon to address recognition of marriages between couples in same-sex relationships.[11] However, in the KAL judgement, Justice Dunne, while appearing to concede that the Constitution is a 'living instrument',[12] made reference to the understanding of marriage in 1937.[13] To ascertain what that understanding was, the High Court opted for some of the most restrictive judicial interpretations of marriage available. Justice Dunne reached so far back as to consider a nineteenth-century case[14] as an authority on the common law interpretation of marriage, despite the fact that the definition provided therein was no longer an accurate reflection of marriage in Ireland.[15]

In consequence, the term 'marriage', which was not defined in the Constitution, was interpreted as referring to marriage between a man and woman only.[16] The result was a judgment that appeared to defer to legislative action while at the same time narrowing the range of options open to the latter. It was a disappointing judgment, not least of all because many of its key conclusions rested upon questionable assumptions.

A number of passages in the judgment stood out. In particular, the court appeared to conclude that as the applicants were treated in a similar fashion to an unmarried opposite-sex couple for tax purposes, they faced no discrimination on account of the refusal by the State to recognise their marriage.[17] Needless to say, the appropriate comparator would instead have been a couple in the same situation as the applicants, who differed only as to their sex. Given that an opposite-sex couple married under the same Canadian law would have had their marriage recognised in Ireland, it was clear that the applicants did encounter a difference in treatment. The selection of an inappropriate comparator is often a hallmark of poorly reasoned equality cases. Regrettably, the KAL case is far from unique in this regard.[18]

Notwithstanding the acceptance by the High Court that there was no evidence that parenting by couples in same-sex relationships was in any way harmful,[19] Justice Dunne considered that the exclusion of all couples in same-sex relationships from civil marriage could nonetheless be justified on the grounds of child welfare. The High Court had imposed a radically different standard upon same-sex couples as compared to those in opposite-sex relationships. After all, neither capacity to parent nor fitness to do so has ever been a precondition for access to civil marriage.[20] Indeed, an opposite-sex couple serving long sentences of imprisonment was regarded as having a right to marry.[21] Although an invocation of the welfare of children appears at first glance to be protective of children rights, the effect was not to benefit children being raised by couples in same-sex relationships. Instead, the effect was merely to preclude recognition of their families under Article 41. More recently, the Supreme Court of the United States has recognised the economic and social consequences for children that can result from the refusal (in that case by the US federal government) to recognise the marriages of couples in same-sex relationships.[22]

Marriage Equality supporter at the 2011 March for Marriage.

Given the social, economic and legal benefits associated with marriage, it should be no surprise that expert bodies have concluded that children raised by couples in same-sex relationships would benefit if their parents could marry.[23] The reasoning employed by the High Court with regard to child welfare served only to call to mind old tropes regarding gay and lesbian people as a danger to children. In this regard, the judgment was a reflection of prevailing social attitudes in some quarters with regard to same-sex parenting.

In telling their story and mounting a High Court challenge, Katherine Zappone and Ann Louise Gilligan undoubtedly helped to change public attitudes. The KAL case had provided invaluable discursive opportunities as well as opportunities to foster social movement mobilisation. Both ME, and its predecessor organisation KAL, had recognised the impact of litigation outside the courtroom. The High Court action in the KAL case is a good example of legal proceedings that exerted significant influence, notwithstanding the response of the court itself. In consequence, even as the ink on the High Court judgement was drying, social attitudes were changing, in part as a result of the case itself. The case led to increased pressure on the government of the day to introduce legislation providing for the recognition of same-sex relationships. Previous efforts to introduce civil partnership legislation had failed.[24] By 2008, the government was prepared to introduce legislation providing for the first time in Irish law for the legal recognition of same-sex civil partners or cohabitants.

THE MISSING PIECES

I volunteered to work for ME in 2009 while in practice as a barrister in Ireland, having become aware of the work done by the organisation as a result of the KAL case. I joined the ME Board the following year and continued to volunteer legal advice throughout the campaign. The KAL case had raised expectations of legal change with regard to marriage, thereby convincing many, including myself, to become involved in campaigning for it. Although the case had ended in defeat in the High Court, and was then under appeal, legal frames and arguments regarding rights were relied upon in order to foster and sustain social movement mobilisation in support of access to civil marriage for couples in same-sex relationships. Scholarship on legal mobilisation recognises that it is possible 'to capitalise perceptions of entitlements associated with legal rights to initiate and nurture political mobilisation' (Scheingold, 2010, p. 131). This was true of the campaign for access to civil marriage in Ireland. The first step in this process was the identification of gaps in protection arising from the exclusion of couples in same-sex relationships from civil marriage.

My first task as a volunteer was to work on the 'Missing Pieces' research project that identified these differences. This project had been established by ME after the announcement that legislation to provide for the recognition of civil partnerships would be introduced. The identification of benefits accruing to federally recognised marriages have, similarly, featured in campaigns for access to civil marriage in the United States.[25] One of the features of the campaign for marriage equality in Ireland was the involvement of lawyers, often on a voluntary basis, but also as key staff members. By putting their skills to use in furtherance of the goals of a social movement, these lawyers were engaged in what is known as cause lawyering (Scheingold and Sarat, 2004, p. 19). 'Missing Pieces' depended upon the voluntary support of a significant number of legal academics and practitioners.

One such volunteer, Ruth Esther Kelly, a solicitor, had put together a team of researchers to work for ME on the project. A database comprising all of the acts of the Oireachtas and Statutory Instruments conferring rights upon married couples had already been assembled, consisting of more than 1,020 statutory provisions, some of which were no longer in force. Each of the provisions would have to be examined in light of the draft civil partnership bill, in order to ascertain whether a right granted to married couples had been extended to civil partners and, if so, whether the proposed provision conferred the same rights and entitlements. These findings would then have to be updated during the legislative process. It was a mammoth task, ultimately leading to the identification of 169 statutory differences between civil partnership and civil marriage – a figure that would later be widely used in campaigning.

At the start of the 2014 March for Marriage. *From left:* Ronan Healy, Moninne Griffith, Justine Schönfeld-Quinn and Darina Brennan.

The 'Missing Pieces' project played a vital role in articulating a case for marriage. This was vital because there were those even within the gay community at the time that were sceptical of the need to campaign for access to civil marriage and many others who considered that civil partnerships would be sufficient to protect LGBT people and their families. For example, at an event at UCD prior to the enactment of the civil partnership legislation in 2010, some argued that marriage was essentially assimilationist and either unnecessary or even inappropriate to the recognition of same-sex relationships.[26] Marriage did not become a goal of the movement spontaneously but, instead, discussion within the community regarding civil marriage, and the efforts of both ME and LGBT Noise, transformed the issue into one commanding widespread support within the community. By the time of the marriage referendum, the LGBT community was united in support of a Yes vote. The identification of gaps in protection played a key role in this process. It also helped to build and sustain mobilisation both before and after the enactment of the Civil Partnership and Certain Rights and Obligations of Cohabitants Act 2010.

It did so in part by emphasising the differences in treatment of civil partners as compared to married couples. It was clear early on that, although the proposed civil partnership legislation would address some of the differences in treatment resulting from the fact that couples in same-sex relationships could not marry, it could not, nor was it intended to, remedy all of them. One reason for this, evident from statements made in the Oireachtas by Dermot Ahern, then Minister for Justice, was that government legal advisers had formed the view that more equal treatment of civil partners would pose constitutional difficulties.[27] Notwithstanding these admissions, the enthusiastic support for the recognition of same-sex relationships sometimes obscured the reality that the legal status created was not intended to be legally equivalent to marriage. Differences in the messaging employed by both ME and the Gay & Lesbian Equality Network (GLEN), the organisation that campaigned for the introduction of civil partnerships, and which had pursued an incrementalist strategy, sometimes exacerbated tensions between the two organisations.

Below left: Sabrina Schönfeld-Quinn canvasses Dublin 5, 21 May 2015.
Below right: Justine Schönfeld-Quinn at the Dublin count centre, RDS, 23 May 2015.

THE 'OUT TO YOUR TD' CAMPAIGN

The gaps in protection identified in the 'Missing Pieces' audit also featured in the brilliantly conceived 'Out To Your TD' campaign. This campaign directed ME supporters to meet with their public representatives to discuss why marriage mattered to them. The differences between civil partnership and civil marriage were included in the information packs given to supporters, thereby bringing key arguments regarding the 'Missing Pieces' to the attention of public representatives. This contributed to changes in elite attitudes and increased pressure on the government of the day to enact enhanced civil partnership legislation, and in turn raised awareness that civil partnership was by no means a guarantee of full legal equality. I went to visit my TDs, and spoke on behalf of ME at events around the country, encouraging others to do likewise. As part of the campaign, volunteers, led by Board member Carol Armstrong, rang supporters encouraging them to meet with their elected representatives.

The success of this campaign was evident in the Dáil debates on the civil partnership legislation as one TD after another spoke from the heart about the wishes of their constituents, informed by the 'Missing Pieces' report. These debates were characterised by what Dermot Ahern described as 'an unprecedented degree of unity and support within both Houses of the Oireachtas'.[28] Furthermore, although the Civil Partnership Bill was rightly heralded as 'one of the most important pieces of civil rights legislation to be enacted since independence',[29] many TDs acknowledged that the bill did not go far enough and, in particular, that it had failed to protect the children parented by gay and lesbian couples. The reversal in the fortunes of Irish LGBT people embodied in the legislation was mirrored in the fact that whereas those who had opposed the further extension of LGBT rights had remained outside the Dáil early in the evening waving signs and had then gone home, LGBT rights activists and their families, even those who had been reluctant to support civil partnerships unequivocally as they wanted full marriage equality, were by contrast invited to the Dáil bar to celebrate. It was a heartening achievement but there was much work still to be done.

SUSTAINING MOMENTUM FOR MARRIAGE

The euphoria surrounding the enactment of civil partnership legislation and the tortuous pace of the KAL case appeal, given the backlog of cases before the Supreme Court at the time, could easily have undermined the momentum for marriage. However, the launch of the 'Missing Pieces Report' in October 2011 drew attention to the serious gaps in protection remaining after the enactment of the Civil Partnerships and Certain Rights and Obligations of Cohabitants Act 2010.[30] Paula Fagan, who authored the 'Missing Pieces Report' based on the findings of the Missing Pieces audit, did an incredible job of presenting the consequences of some of the most salient differences for individuals and families in a clear and accessible way. The dissemination of Paula's report popularised awareness of the differences between civil partnership and civil marriage beyond the community of legal scholars and activists who were most aware of them. The report included a tabulation of the 169 statutory differences; it emphasised the lack of constitutional standing and the absence of suitable mechanisms to protect family relationships for children parented by couples in same-sex relationships. These findings supported a perception of deprivation relative to others and not only helped to sustain mobilisation over time but also led many others to become active in campaigning.

ME supporters later marched at Dublin Pride wearing T-shirts with the caption 'I'm Marching to Fill in the Missing Pieces' and carrying placards bearing the same message in 2012 and 2013. Key findings within the report soon featured in many of ME's campaign materials and briefing documents. The enactment of legislation providing for civil partnerships was a huge step forward. However, the fact that it was a compromise measure designed to provide basic legal protections while creating a separate and unequal status for same-sex relationships was apparent to many. This was reflected in the language used in campaigning, for example, an LGBT Noise poster campaign for the March for Marriage characterised civil partnerships as 'half measures'.[31]

A similar sentiment was later expressed by US Supreme Court Justice Ruth Bader Ginsburg, in the landmark *US v Windsor* case, who observed that the Defense of Marriage Act, which denied federal recognition to the marriages of couples in same-sex relationships, had resulted in the presence of 'two kinds of marriage; the full marriage, and then this sort of skim-milk marriage'.[32] The fact that people in same-sex relationships were unable to marry the person they loved had become emblematic of the unequal treatment of LGBT people in Irish society more generally. This was reflected in the language used by participants at the Marches for Marriage who held up handmade signs bearing slogans such as 'I didn't raise my daughter to be a second-class citizen'.[33]

The report's findings also influenced the messaging relied upon by ME and LGBT Noise.[34] The dominant framing relied upon by both in mobilising their supporters was equality – a reflection of the recognition that civil partnerships did not represent an equal outcome for couples in same-sex relationships and their families. The annual March for Marriage organised by LGBT Noise brought together supporters of both organisations and others, to create a visible presence in support of the campaign. At these marches, volunteers from

LGBT Noise handed out printed 'Equal' signs and posters advertising the event featured slogans such as 'Be There! Get Equal!' and 'Equality Needs You'.[35]

The gaps in protection identified in the 'Missing Pieces Report' also featured in the emotion-oriented work of ME. The short film *Rory's Story*, for example, produced by Evan Barry's company Fail Safe Films for ME in 2011, took an aspect of the difference in treatment between those in same-sex headed families at a time of crisis (hospitalisation) and dramatised it, thereby illustrating the impact of non-recognition of parent–child relationships with a story to which everyone could relate. Similarly, a poster campaign run by ME featured billboard-sized photographs of real Irish couples, highlighting differences in treatment. The 'Just Love' poster campaign addressed the lack of recognition of the relationship between the non-biological parent and child, featuring a lesbian couple and their daughter with the caption entitled 'The law ignores our little girl, will you?'[36]

Yes Equality HQ team at the arrival of the new Yes Equality sign (behind), 10 April 2015.
From left: Sandra Irwin-Gowran, Paul Boylan, Kathleen Hunt, Yvonne Judge, Craig Dwyer, Gráinne Healy, Moninne Griffith, Lisa Hyland, Sadhbh Turner, Gary O'Reilly, Orla Howard, Ger O'Keeffe, Ross Flanagan, Etain Hobson and Tomislav from Reads Design and Print, Dublin.

THE KAL CASE APPEAL

I joined the legal working group in support of the Supreme Court appeal in the KAL case which was due to be heard by the Supreme Court in 2011. There were a number of weaknesses in the High Court judgement, some of which have been mentioned above. These offered some hope that an appeal might be successful. However, the appeal in the KAL case would face the same challenges as the original High Court action. The Constitution was silent as to whether or not marriage by couples in same-sex relationships could be recognised. However, the provisions of the Constitution on the family have long been interpreted in a restrictive manner. In consequence, Article 41,[37] an Article that intended to protect family life, had instead sometimes legitimated the unequal treatment of different family forms.[38]

In a case heard in the years before the KAL case reached the Supreme Court, Justice Denham expressed the view that the term 'marriage' in the Constitution refers to man–woman marriage only.[39] It was an ominous sign. By the time the KAL case reached the Supreme Court, it was clear, in addition to these above hurdles, that a fatal flaw in the High Court case had become its undoing. Section 2(2)(e) of the Civil Registration Act 2004, which provided that there was an impediment to marry if both parties were of the same sex, had been enacted during the course of the High Court case.[40] This provision enjoyed a presumption of constitutionality as an Act of the Oireachtas; the question of whether this presumption had been rebutted was not addressed in legal argument before the High Court in the KAL case.

The Supreme Court was reluctant to hear the appeal, on grounds that the constitutionality of this provision should have been addressed. It appeared that fresh proceedings might even be required to remedy the defect in the original case. Although a daunting prospect, a referendum on marriage was becoming increasingly likely. The fact that a minority needed to call upon the majority to protect their interests was illustrative of the paradox in the years preceding the marriage referendum whereby legal arguments were more effective outside the courtroom than within it. The video *Sinead's Hand*, made by Linda Cullen of COCO Television for ME, went viral, as it showed the preposterous nature of asking everyone in Ireland for permission to marry.

TOWARDS A CHILDREN AND FAMILY RELATIONSHIPS ACT

A key challenge for ME and civil and children's rights groups was to ensure the recognition of family relationships, in order to ensure that children raised by couples in same-sex relationships would have adequate legal protections. The Civil Partnership and Certain Rights and

Obligations of Cohabitants Act 2010 contained scant reference to children[41] and was rightly criticised for this omission. In failing to address the fact that many couples in same-sex relationships were parents, the legislature had left untouched the legal vulnerabilities created for children, by virtue of the fact that their family relationships were unrecognised.

One consequence of this was that there was no provision for a same-sex civil partner or cohabitant to be recognised as the child's guardian, while their partner was still alive. They could, however, be recognised as a testamentary guardian on the death of their partner but this would only occur if provision had been made for this in the deceased's will.[42] Although gay and lesbian individuals could adopt, only a married couple could do so jointly.[43] Furthermore, as Ireland had not regulated assisted human reproduction, a donor could apply to be appointed as joint guardian with the child's biological mother, while their second social parent would remain a stranger in law. In short, the situation of children raised by parents in same-sex relationships was, from a legal standpoint, precarious.

Marriage Equality is honoured at the 2015 GALAS. *From left:* Gráinne Healy, Patricia O'Connor, Ross Golden-Bannon, Orla Howard, Linda Cullen, Justine Schönfeld-Quinn, Moninne Griffith, Denise Charlton, Ailbhe Smyth, Andrew Hyland and Paula Fagan.

To remedy gaps in protection, a legislative framework would have to be established to protect the rights of children parented by couples in same-sex relationships. The first step was to ensure the upcoming Law Reform Commission Report on the Legal Aspects of Family Relationships included those rights.[44] This was crucial because Law Reform Commission reports are often a precursor to legislation. Judy Walsh, Professor of Law at UCD, and I drafted legal submissions on behalf of ME. Other organisations did likewise. The result was a Commission recommendation that 'legislation be enacted to facilitate the extension of parental responsibility to civil partners and step-parents'.[45] The Minister for Justice, Alan Shatter, later confirmed that a bill to address the rights of children with gay or lesbian parents would soon be forthcoming.

A General Scheme of the Children and Family Relationships Bill became available at the end of January 2014, addressing many of the gaps identified in the 'Missing Pieces Report' in relation to children.[46] This draft legislation was strongly opposed by those who viewed parenting by couples in same-sex relationships unfavourably. It created challenges in ensuring the bill's enactment because the opponents of the legislation tended to regard LGBT people as a threat to the family and children, rather than as people with families in need of protection. In April 2014, when the bill was presented to the Oireachtas Joint Committee on Justice, Defence and Equality, I attended with Moninne Griffith, Director of ME, to answer questions in relation to provisions on same-sex parenting. It had become clear from public debates on the subject that, notwithstanding the fact the bill represented a comprehensive reform of Irish family law as a whole, much of the media and political attention would concentrate on the provision addressing parenting by couples in same-sex relationships. This opposition to the bill resulted in far greater media focus on this aspect of the legislation, with the result that other provisions attracted little public debate.

In consequence, under the new Minister for Justice, Frances Fitzgerald, the more controversial aspects of the draft bill, such as those addressing surrogacy, were dropped. There was a real danger that other provisions of the bill would also be weakened. At a meeting at the Department of Justice, it became clear that this was indeed occurring and that a provision within the General Scheme provided for the recognition of children born as a result of donor insemination, 'whether before or after the commencement of the legislation' was to be removed.[47] In consequence, children born prior to commencement of the act would face a far more complicated path to family recognition.

ME responded quickly by obtaining a legal opinion from two prominent Senior Counsel addressing the implications for children's rights of the non-recognition of their family relationships. The situation was one of immense urgency, not only in view of the risk that the bill's provisions would be watered down, but also because of the perception that further delay with regard to the legislation could undermine the now forthcoming referendum campaign. Notwithstanding these difficulties, ME was successful in ensuring that the Children and Family Relationships Act would, albeit with some amendment, continue to make provision for children born prior to the commencement of the legislation.[48] The Children and Family Relationships Act 2015 was finally passed shortly before the referendum on marriage.

The campaign for marriage equality traversed many of the milestones of my adult life, including both a civil partnership and later marriage. It offered a chance to use legal knowledge gained over many years for a cause that I believed in. In the final weeks of the referendum campaign, hundreds of people canvassed door to door in urban areas. It was an unforgettable experience, particularly in those weeks when my then fiancée finished her final exams and we went door to door in Dublin South Central, surprising our neighbours by asking them if they could make sure to vote Yes on 22 May so that we could marry. The night before the referendum vote, we found ourselves standing along the roadside in Killester, with others from Dublin Bay North, waving banners calling for a Yes vote, heartened by the support of passing motorists. We also gave an interview to the BBC World Service about the referendum on marriage in Ireland. It was a surreal moment because, after so many years, the vote was finally upon us.

We travelled to the RDS count centre in Dublin early on 23 May to help tally votes and were stunned when the opposition conceded so early that day. The atmosphere, both in the RDS and in the city centre, was one of jubilation. Although subsequent legal challenges to the referendum result delayed our marriage, they did not dampen our spirits. We were elated to celebrate both a civil partnership with family and friends on 5 September in Potsdam and later a marriage on 30 November 2015, in Dublin. The fact that our marriage is not recognised in the country where we now live (Germany) is a reminder that full legal equality will only be achieved when LGBT people are equally free and equal in all parts of the world. If Ireland, a country that was the last in Western Europe to decriminalise same-sex intimacy, can become the first country in the world to extend civil marriage to couples by popular vote, there is cause for optimism.

Anna MacCarthy

Making Noise

I had been actively involved with the protest group, LGBT Noise, for a couple of years when I was asked to join the Board of Marriage Equality (ME) in 2010. I was in close contact with ME staff as their organisation got off the ground, and I had volunteered with the group in the early days of their 'Out To Your TD' campaign. I was asked to join the Board in order to bring a younger person's perspective to the organisation, but also to make the sharing of information between ME and LGBT Noise more fluid. I remained, first and foremost, the LGBT Noise representative on the Board between 2010 and 2013.

The very long march towards equal marriage in Ireland was an interesting one, and the stories of the early days are often forgotten in light of the events of 2015 and after. In the wake of the AIDS crisis in the 1980s and decriminalisation in the 1990s, gay rights activism in Ireland seemed to be in a lull. Then, at the turn of the millennium, a handful of European countries began to address the hardship and discrimination being inflicted upon gay and lesbian couples due to the lack of legal recognition for their relationships. However, when the UK introduced Civil Unions in 2004, the debate in Ireland was still very slow to get started. The debates, when they did come, were often dominated by political parties, backroom lobbyists and self-appointed protectors of 'the family'. Rarely did the public hear from ordinary LGBT people and families.[1]

Marriage Equality at the March for Marriage, 2009.

In 2007, when the Fianna Fáil government rejected an opposition Bill on Civil Unions put forward by the Labour Party, frustration at the lack of political will to progress the issue in Ireland began to grow. Young LGBT activists who had been working within the political party system grew increasingly disillusioned with the lack of real progress and support for LGBT rights at party level. It was at this point that a small group of activists decided to form a non-party protest group to unite LGBT people and allies behind the single issue of equal relationship recognition.

This small group of volunteers founded LGBT Noise in 2007 to engage, educate and, most importantly, empower the LGBT community. A core group of seven organisers worked within a non-hierarchical structure. We worked on a consensus basis that, despite much debate, resulted in great consideration being given to the various decisions. From the start there was a focus on how to politicise the LGBT community so that they would then advocate for their own rights. It seems remarkable to think that less than ten years ago, this was a community that was visible to the public only once a year at Pride and, more remarkably, not engaged with by one of the few national gay organisations at the time, the Gay & Lesbian Equality Network (GLEN). GLEN, in lobbying for gay rights, did much of their work in the corridors of power without the knowledge or interest of the vast majority of LGBT people. Noise sought to change this.

LGBT Noise 2011 poster.   Anna MacCarthy speaks at the 2012 March for Marriage.

There was a palpable reticence among people, even among those who attended Pride each year, to speak out about LGBT rights issues or to get involved in what was perceived as a pointless endeavour – to advocate for equal marriage rights. Many LGBT people did not seem to believe that they were deserving of equal rights. Noise knew that to achieve change, LGBT people would have to be visible throughout the year and not just in the standard one-photo coverage of Pride in the national newspapers. Visibility was essential. Noise held brightly coloured and vibrant street events like 'Sing for Civil Marriage' outside the Gaiety Theatre – a choir sang, we took up space, and got the attention of passers-by. Events like these gave Noise volunteers the opportunity to distribute leaflets to the passing public and to put a face on a community that was so often talked about in the abstract. The Noise strategy was to keep the protests light-hearted and accessible for new protesters, and visually appealing for the media.

Noise wanted to have a visible and vibrant presence of LGBT people on the streets of Dublin, in the media, and in the minds of the general public. We wanted to get our message out to the public that LGBT people deserved equal rights. But first we had to convince the LGBT community. We believed that if the people wouldn't engage in the politics, then we would have to bring the politics to the people. A few of us regularly went to bars, night-clubs and community events with flyers about civil partnership, explaining the differences between civil marriage and religious marriage. Civil partnership was a new concept but to many people who were used to religious ceremonies, civil marriage was also a new concept. Noise believed that a separate scheme of relationship recognition available only to same-sex couples and bestowing fewer rights was discriminatory. Helping people to understand the difference was difficult. We were often met with confusion, lack of interest and, on occasion, disdain. Some people felt we were complaining about nothing of worth and drawing unwanted attention to the community. It was certainly difficult to gain traction at first.

Social media platforms were becoming more mainstream at this point and the group realised that we now had the tools to reach more people than with traditional paper leaflets or posters. We could create engaging visual content that referenced decades of activism and bring it into the digital age. Organisers cajoled creative and technically gifted friends to help. Soon we had brilliantly creative graphic designers volunteering to make posters,[2] imagery and videos[3] for us. So many wonderfully talented and dedicated volunteers made Noise what it was. With virtually no funding we called in favours from anywhere we could, and relied on table quizzes to fund our campaigns. Many people up and down the country did extraordinary things to help progress the campaign. We worked with the community bars, Pantibar, The George, the Dragon and the Front Lounge to display posters and videos. In the lead up to our events, short animated videos with facts about civil partnership played on a loop on video screens in the bars. Perhaps patrons were initially a little bemused by the 'gay propaganda' on their dance floors, but numbers at events started to increase slowly through 2008 and into 2009.

Crowds at St Stephen's Green, Dublin, at the 2012 March for Marriage.

Noise formed good relationships with groups like ME and others, but didn't engage in 'respectability politics' and could criticise government for dragging their feet on the issue of marriage equality and LGBT rights. There was a tacit understanding that Noise could say what groups like ME couldn't. Over the years, ME and Noise worked well together, and ME invited Noise organisers to take part in their media-training sessions, which was incredibly useful. We gratefully participated, but overall we pursued our own strategies. Noise forged close links with the Union of Students in Ireland (USI) and with the various LGBT student societies in Ireland. We travelled around the country speaking at student events and educating about LGBT rights generally, and the civil partnership legislation and its pitfalls in particular. As a ME Board member, I often combined these trips and gave presentations on behalf of ME, which usually focused on encouraging young people to visit their TDs to raise the issue as part of their 'Out To Your TD' campaign.

In late 2008, the Fianna Fáil/Green Party government proposed the introduction of a civil partnership scheme. However, the new generation of LGBT activists were not prepared to accept a grudging extension of lesser rights from the government, but it should be noted here that it was welcomed by many older gay people as providing long sought-after protections for same-sex couples. Noise argued that civil partnership was not equality and not acceptable. In response to the proposal of civil partnership, in February 2009 Noise managed to bring 150 or so protesters to demonstrate in front of the Central Bank on Dame Street in Dublin. Rory O'Neill (aka Panti Bliss) was in the crowd that day. Afterwards he wrote a blog post about the event that was to become a game-changer. The post, 'No more Mr. Nice Gay', began 'Dear lazy-arsed queers' and ended with a call to LGBT people to stand up for their rights and to get out and fight for what they deserved. People who had never even considered any of the issues before listened because they knew and respected the formidable character of Panti. Us 'boring' political activists couldn't get their attention but a clever, articulate drag queen, the embodiment of fun, was giving our cause her seal of approval. And people listened.

At the next protest there were hundreds in attendance, and it grew from there to thousands. By June of that year, 2009, Noise had increased its support significantly. I was due to speak at the Dublin Pride post-parade gathering as the Civil Partnership Bill had just been published in a cynical attempt by the then government to benefit from the feel-good factor of Pride. At Dublin Pride I addressed the 8,000-strong crowd at the Civic Offices. It was clear that the community was expected to be grateful for civil partnership but we knew we had to get attention for the fact that it was *not* equality. We needed to grab headlines, and we did. As I tore up a copy of the Civil Partnership Bill on stage, a symbolic act and one of resistance, the media took notice of the cheers of the crowd and of the criticisms of civil partnership voiced by other speakers that day. We had succeeded in altering the narrative around the newly published legislation. Finally, the message that civil partnership was not enough was starting to get through.

Members of GLEN present at Pride subsequently expressed the view that our symbolic scrapping of a few sheets of paper was so violent an act that they felt threatened at the event. Noise was heavily criticised by GLEN for the action, claiming we should have known better because we had 'responsible positions in society in employment terms',[4] a reference to the fact that some of us had what would be considered respectable middle-class careers (I worked as a solicitor at the time). I have no doubt that it was disappointing to them to see the younger generation being uncooperative and unsupportive on the back of their years of work on civil partnership. But Noise was never seeking to upset GLEN or the couples who would ultimately benefit from civil partnership; we were trying to establish a certain rhetoric around the legislation – that it was *not equality* – and it worked. The so-called 'in-fighting' in the community politics that followed was not based wholly on the disagreement around civil partnership versus civil marriage, but rather about power and control slipping from those who had had it for so long.

The disagreements could only be seen as negative if you believed that the community was one homogenous group that was of one view and one voice. Noise has often been described as radical. Noise was not radical. Silvia Rivera and Marsha P. Johnson at the Stonewall riots were radical. Tearing up a few sheets of paper was not radical. It was (mostly) middle-class people seeking media attention to influence the political process in order to achieve a privilege. The fact that it is seen as a radical act illustrates the very conservative nature of politics in Ireland and the attitude of the establishment to grass-roots activism.

Unfortunately, GLEN failed to see the power behind the growing confidence and resolute attitude of the younger generation and our insistence that civil partnership was not equality. Noise believed that our actions and uncompromising stance offered those lobbying for civil partnership leverage in their work. This was often not appreciated. Shortly before the passage of the Civil Partnership Bill, Noise was asked to stop campaigning by GLEN. We were told we compromised the passage of the Civil Partnership Bill. We refused, knowing that the bill had cross-party support in the Oireachtas and that it was imperative to identify its shortcomings. We knew that couples who had waited so long for important protections would be able to avail of them, but equally we knew that the community was getting behind a push for equal marriage.

Making Noise, Marching for Marriage, 2012.

Panti Bliss shapes up to address the crowds at the 2014 March for Marriage.

GLEN had achieved so much for the gay community but it struggled to accept that other organisations now existed in the fight for LGBT rights, among them, ME, Transgender Equality Network Ireland (TENI) and EQUALS, a direct-action LGBT rights organisation. These unseen silencing techniques are, unfortunately, a feature of many political campaigns.[5] This is not just a difficulty for the LGBT community. Other groups advocating for social change in Ireland are still so pitted against each other for both funding and attention that they are afraid to speak the truth about their negative interactions with government or each other.

Noise was always cognisant of the fact that there were different strategies being pursued towards the same goal of equal recognition. The KAL case moved slowly through the courts; GLEN and ME engaged in lobbying in the Oireachtas; ME encouraged voters to visit their TDs; EQUALS took direct action chaining themselves to the gates of Leinster House and were arrested. Noise's strategy was to protest, raise awareness and educate. As primarily a protest group, we sought to occupy public spaces with LGBT people and slogans, and ultimately get images of those events into the media. We wanted to reach the people, especially young people, who had little or no interest or knowledge of politics or civil rights.

When Noise held the first March for Marriage in 2009, we didn't know what to expect but when thousands arrived at City Hall, it was clear that we were making an impact. The march was filled with thousands of hopeful faces with vibrant placards and an unmistakable determination; it was unlike anything the community had seen in years. As the

Crowds gather at the stage, 2014 March for Marriage.

march grew in strength each year, so did the confidence of the community. Noise sought to empower people to speak about their rights and to have the confidence to fight for them. In the following years, Noise held six marches for marriage and, crucially, sought to use the event as a Trojan horse to give space and voice to the many other LGBT rights issues that were important, including: trans rights, gender recognition, removal of Section 37 of the Equality Act, the blood ban on homosexual donors, issues facing LGBT Travellers and asylum seekers, homophobic and transphobic abuse, and international torture and abuse of the LGBT community elsewhere.

These issues were subsequently silenced once the political strategists of the marriage equality referendum campaign took over the narrative. But at these marches, supporters learned about the many issues that faced the community and became equipped to advocate for them. The marches created bright and colourful images of individuals, couples, families and allies that were used time and again in the media as nice antidotes to the stock images of wedding-cake toppers and disembodied hands with wedding rings on them. The profile of those participating in the marches changed over the years, too, with mostly younger people making up the early days and a marked increase in older people, allies and families in the latter years.

Noise ensured that the language used to talk about rights was inclusive and that all identities and family types in our community were recognised and visible. In our weekly meetings, the seven of us would debate at great lengths the language and imagery used. In the early days we made the mistake of championing marriage as an institution but we soon learned that using the language of civil and human rights was more inclusive and in line with the personal politics of many of those involved in Noise.

When the Pantigate controversy broke in February 2014,[6] Noise was ready. We realised that the fallout from the controversy would have serious implications for the referendum but also a potentially stifling effect on public discourse. We had a protest on South King Street outside the Gaiety Theatre in support of Panti. The ability to call hundreds of protesters onto the streets with a couple of days' notice was crucial, as it forced RTÉ news to cover the story that I'm sure RTÉ management wished would go away.

Noise undoubtedly helped to lay some of the groundwork for the work done by the Yes Equality campaign when the time came. The LGBT community was forever changed and the movement for rights was newly invigorated. There were thousands of supporters all over the country who had become well versed in the language of rights and aware of how to counter the arguments from the opposition. These supporters were ready when the time came to get out and join the canvass for the referendum. While many supporters were unhappy with the degrading task of having to beg at the doors of others for legal rights, they became resigned to the fact that this was the *real politik*. I had retired from Noise before the referendum date was announced.

It was clear that Noise's broad-based campaign was considered too inclusive for a single-issue referendum, one that was deemed to require a homogenous community with a nationalistic narrative to appeal to 'middle Ireland'. Having learned from the civil part-nership campaign, Yes Equality seemed keen to ensure there were no disparate voices or divergence from their main narrative. It is arguable whether such a highly conservative campaign was necessary for the referendum campaign to succeed. I think that Ireland was ready at that time for a different and more inclusive type of politics, one that acknowledged the lived realities of many Lesbian, Gay, Bisexual, Transgender, Queer, Intersex (LGBTQI) people's lives, and not only those considered 'appropriate'.

The nearly decade-long fight to achieve marriage equality was a fascinating and hugely enriching experience for me to have lived through. My hope for the future is that marriage will not be at the top of the relationship hierarchy for much longer. Other family and rela-tionship types must be given parity in our laws.

Olivia McEvoy

The National LGBT Federation and Marriage Equality

The National LGBT Federation (now known as NXF) was a founding partner of the marriage equality movement in Ireland. Then known as the National Lesbian and Gay Federation (NLGF), it contributed very significantly to the key early years that framed and shaped the very language, debate and culture of the campaign. Underpinned by a natural alliance with Marriage Equality (ME), that contribution was to continue throughout the lifetime of the transformational campaign for civil marriage equality for LGBT people in Ireland.

NXF POLICY POSITION

The NXF was very clear in its policy position, calling 'on the government to introduce new legislation for full marriage equality to ensure lesbian and gay people are equal under the law as citizens of the country in which they live and to which they contribute'. Its revised policy position paper specifically noted that 'the recent Civil Partnership and Certain Rights and Obligations of Cohabitants Act 2010 does not deliver equality for same-sex couples, most notably failing to protect the children of same-sex parents'. This was based on a number of policy principles, including that

> all loving and committed relationships between consenting adults are of equal moral worth,
> value and esteem. Relationships of this type should be accorded the same status by the

State regardless of the gender of those involved in the relationship. The prohibition against allowing lesbians and gay men to access the institution of civil marriage is discriminatory and contravenes these principles of equal moral worth, value and parity of esteem.

The NXF policy was very deliberate in framing the demand for marriage equality as a human rights and equality issue. As Ailbhe Smyth, Chair of the NXF 1999–2013, said in her opening of the 'Marriage Matters' symposium in 2009:

What we are fighting for when we campaign for civil marriage for lesbian and gay people, is the right to equality. It is not more than that. And it is certainly not less than that. I want to put down a marker at the outset that there is a majority view among LGBT and other equality organisations that the Civil Partnership Bill now before the Dáil is not acceptable. It is not acceptable because it is not enough. It is not enough because it is not equality. Legislating for the right to civil marriage matters to LGBT people, because equality matters to us.

Framing the issue in this broad equality context from the outset would go on to be pivotal to the success of the campaign for marriage equality.

The NLGF is invited to Áras an Uachtaráin, March 2012. *From left:* Ailbhe Smyth, Olivia McEvoy, Sabina Higgins, President Michael D. Higgins, Brian Finnegan and Orla Howard.

Olivia McEvoy addresses the 2015 March for Marriage.

NXF & MARRIAGE EQUALITY: THE EARLY YEARS

The policy position of the NXF made the organisation natural allies of ME, an alliance that would remain steadfast throughout the long campaign. The NXF was represented on the KAL campaign, the precursor to ME, by Ailbhe Smyth. As a result, the NXF became founding members of ME in 2008, first represented by NXF Board members Ailbhe Smyth, Orla Howard and Patrick Lynch. I joined later in 2013 when I was elected Chair of the NXF. Indeed, the NXF was the fiscal agent for ME in those early years, channelling the initial funding from Atlantic Philanthropies as well as lending considerable infrastructural support to the establishment of ME as an organisation.

The National LGBT Federation facilitated some of the earliest debates and discussions on marriage equality, hosting two national symposia with the financial support of the Equality Authority. The first symposium, 'Full and Equal Rights: Lesbian and Gay Marriage and Partnership Rights in Ireland', was held in October 2007. The stated aims of the symposium were to

provide a forum for discussion for LGBT community groups and national organisations, as well as other organisations concerned with the issue of lesbian and gay marriage and civil partnerships. The Symposium will combine a review of the current context in Ireland with insights from international experience and it is intended that the event will provide a platform for these groups to organise strategically to bring about change in this area.

John Fisher, co-Director of ARC International, a Canadian-based international non-profit organisation that strives to develop and assist in the implementation of an international strategic vision regarding LGBT human rights, was the keynote speaker at the event, which was officially opened by the Minister of State for Equality, Sean Power. Other speakers included Judy Walsh, School of Social Justice, UCD; Jan O'Sullivan, TD; Gráinne Healy, then Chair of the KAL Initiative; Rev Chris Hudson, Unitarian Minister; Mark Kelly, ICCL and Eoin Collins, GLEN.

Although the marriage equality fire had only relatively recently been lit, this first symposium was absolutely critical on a number of fronts: it provided information and mapped the legal and legislative landscape for the LGBT community as a whole, encouraging all parties to think strategically about the way forward, towards achieving marriage equality. Most significantly, it put in place the basis for a common platform (a strategic organising structure) comprising a range of interest groups and organisations to enable the achievement of the aim of equality and full citizenship for LGBT people. This would form the basis for the 'Platform for Equality', facilitated by the NXF. Among other objectives, the Platform for Equality was designed to provide a space to discuss dramatic differences in views while laying the foundations for a working relationship between those same parties. A number of meetings under the Platform for Equality were subsequently hosted by the NXF, providing an important mechanism for interested individuals and groups to share information about their campaigns for marriage and partnership rights.

In addition, this 'Full and Equal Rights: Lesbian and Gay Marriage and Partnership Rights in Ireland' symposium put the issue on a level that made policy makers, politicians and ministers take stock, sending an unequivocal message to government and to the Minister for Justice, Equality and Law Reform that 'the issue of marriage and partnership rights was a defining one, not only for lesbian and gay people, but for the very meaning of equality itself in Ireland and that there must be no appeasing LGBT people with second-rate rights and second-class citizenship'.

Following on from the success of this event, a second and much bigger national symposium was staged in 2009, again supported by the Equality Authority, on the topic 'Marriage Matters for Lesbian and Gay People in Ireland'. The aims of this later symposium were slightly more refined, with a view to consider best practice with regard to legislation for same-sex couples in the EU and to review legal and social provisions for same-sex couples in the context of the anticipated introduction of legislation on civil partnership in Ireland. Critically, again, it was also designed to provide a forum for the exchange of information and for dialogue between interested LGBT national organisations, community groups and individuals, as well as legal, equality and human rights professionals and all those advocating for change on the issue of lesbian and gay marriage, subsequent to the introduction of civil partnership legislation. It was an expressed hope that 'such a dialogue, combined with insights from best practice elsewhere, will contribute to creating a strong platform for continuing change within the Irish NGO sector'.

'Marriage Matters' brought together a range of perspectives on the case for marriage for lesbian and gay people. An invitation to Alejandro Alder from FELGTB, a Spanish LGBT organisation that had worked on successfully achieving marriage equality in Spain, underlined the importance of learning from international campaigners, while Patricia Prendiville, former Executive Director of ILGA Europe (International Lesbian and Gay Association), presented a European perspective. The inclusion of Professor Sheila Greene, Director of the Children's Research Centre, TCD, as a speaker, acknowledged the importance of children in the debate and the need to be able to counter any arguments used against marriage equality on this topic, an issue that would dominate the discourse throughout the campaign.

Members of Gloria launch the True Colours fundraiser for Marriage Equality. *From left:* Olivia McEvoy, Richard Deane, Jerry Buttimer TD, Pauline Tracey and Moninne Griffith, June 2012.

The symposium also acknowledged the feminist critique of marriage with specific contributions on that perspective from Gráinne Healy, Chair of the now formed ME, and Peter Tatchell, renowned LGBT activist in the UK. Other speakers included Carol Baxter, Equality Authority; Eamon Gilmore, TD; Brian Sheehan, GLEN; Dr Mark McCarron, LGBT Noise, and a concluding keynote speech from Niall Crowley, former CEO of the Equality Authority.

A series of workshop discussions on strategies for achieving civil marriage at the symposium served to identify many of the key themes and actions that would form the basis of an approach to a unified community campaign. There was a very strong consensus that 'a national alliance of LGBT NGOs is required to advance the campaign for marriage rights' and that 'the coalition should have a clear charter and set of agreed principles and objectives to achieve marriage equality'. It was felt that this coalition should grow out of the Platform for Equality but with a more formal structure to help advance its goals. In truth, despite considerable efforts by the NXF, this coalition largely continued in the form of an informal structure. In addition, the NXF facilitated a number of challenging meetings between organisations that were advocates of civil partnership and those that championed marriage equality. Later in 2015, after a period of dormancy, the organisations that had been involved in the Platform for Equality joined the coalition of organisations that became the Yes partners in the Yes Equality campaign.

The workshop discussions also emphasised the importance of an alliance with civil society and the creation of a 'broad-based coalition for change that would include social partners, schools, universities, sporting, cultural and political organisations' and help 'to identify for politicians, trade unions and social partners the roles that they can play in promoting change in favour of partnership rights for gay and lesbian people in Ireland'. There was also strong support for dialogue with political parties and proponents of equality. More specific processes to achieve marriage equality, such as fundraising events and the need to promote a 'Register to Vote' campaign, were also outlined. A report on the outcomes from the 'Marriage Matters' symposium was published and used by many NGOs to help direct their strategies to achieve marriage rights for lesbian and gay people in Ireland.

In addition to the national symposia that had really served to lend traction to the issue of marriage equality, and the Platform for Equality that had helped to lay the foundations for working relationships within the LGBT community and as part of a broader coalition, the NXF was also involved in a number of other initiatives that greatly contributed to the campaign for marriage equality.

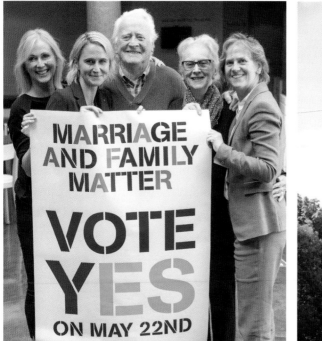

Launching 'Marriage and Family Matter' were *(from left)* Fiona Lavin, Olivia McEvoy, and Paddy and Pat O'Brien with their daughter Joan O'Brien, April 2015.

Yes and No posters in Dublin's city centre, May 2015.

ROLE OF *GCN* IN MARRIAGE EQUALITY DEBATE

The *Gay Community News* (*GCN*), which is published by the NXF, played a very significant part in facilitating debate and discussion on the issue of marriage equality. Multiple *GCN* features and editorials served to inform and engage the LGBT community, keeping the issue current and constantly in focus. Indeed, not only did *GCN* provide a rounded commentary about the work of activist organisations and the community politics involved in the movement, the magazine also gave insight into the political machinations as various governments and parties inched towards marriage equality over the decades. Being the trusted provider of direct information to the LGBT community, *GCN* essentially acted as a media hub for the movement, employed by all of the organisations working towards marriage equality to get their messages across. With an editorial stance that fully advocated and articulated for marriage equality, *GCN* hosted opinion-writing from many of the people who became key players in the Yes Equality movement. It also conducted interviews with many of the country's political leaders, and provided space for well-known commentators to speak directly to the LGBT community.

During the campaign itself, *GCN* provided a commentary that was separate to the mainstream media coverage of the referendum. Coming from an 'insider' perspective, it was a 'safe space' that reflected a strong, confident, active and organised community back to itself. Moreover, it provided a welcome rebuttal to messages from the No campaign unlike other media that were duty-bound to constantly provide what was called 'balance'.

From Katherine Zappone and Ann Louise Gilligan's original court case, to the first civil union in Belfast, the first civil partnership in Ireland and the first equal same-sex marriage in Ireland, *GCN* has published covers that no other media in Ireland did. The issue published immediately after the referendum result was a triple gatefold cover celebrating some of the people who worked on the campaign for marriage equality, including every canvassing group across the country. Ultimately, *GCN* is an archive of the journey that led to Ireland achieving constitutional marriage equality for lesbian and gay couples, from the perspective of the LGBT community.

National LGBT Federation Chairs, Olivia McEvoy *(left)* and Ailbhe Smyth
at the organisation's thirty-fifth birthday celebrations, February 2014.

The first LGBT Platform meeting of the gay community organisations, Dublin City Council Civic Offices, October 2014. *Back, left to right:* Ross Golden-Bannon, ME; Noelle Moran, NXF; Stephen Carroll, Outhouse; Ailbhe Smyth, ME; Kate Moynihan, LINC; Aine Beamish, Outhouse; Aoife Mallon, LGBT Noise; David Carroll, BeLonG To; Mary McDermott and Olivia McEvoy, NXF. *Front, left to right:* Orla Howard, ME; Tiernan Brady, GLEN; Andrew Hyland, ME; Gráinne Healy, ME; Orlaith O'Sullivan, TENI; Oisin O'Reilly, BeLonG To and Mark Kelly, ICCL.

MARRIAGE EQUALITY: A BURNING ISSUE

In Spring 2009, the same year as the 'Marriage Matters' symposium, the NXF conducted what transpired to be the largest national survey of the LGBT community at that time; 'Burning Issues'. One of the central aims of 'Burning Issues' was to collect information on the attitudes of LGBT people to the issue of civil marriage rights, and to gauge the extent to which it was or was not a pressing policy and political priority for the community. The key findings from the quantitative questions posed was that 'securing full and equal access to the institution of civil marriage for LGBT people is the third most important issue of concern' after 'Equal rights at work' and 'Personal security: bullying/violence against LGBT people'. In the open-ended questions, 'gaining the right to access the institution of civil marriage for lesbian and gay people is overwhelmingly the top priority of respondents with a quarter of them designating it as their most pressing priority. On the other hand, civil partnership rights were highlighted as just the twelfth priority of participants in their personal responses.'

Some of the direct responses captured in the survey were also very telling. One respondent, for example, said that the lack of marriage and adoption rights meant they felt they were 'not being recognised as a human being'. For another respondent, marriage equality would significantly improve the rights and wellbeing of LGBT people in many other ways: 'The opening of marriage to same-sex couples will go a long way towards relieving other pressures experienced by LGBT people, such as homophobia, discrimination and negative self-image; same-sex relationships need to be seen as on a par with heterosexual relationships. It will help provide positive role models for younger LGBT people who are coming out'.

The outcomes from the 'Burning Issues' survey were used extensively by ME and countless other organisations in the quest to seek support on the issue of marriage equality among all sectors of society, especially politicians.

GALAS

In another first in 2009, the Gay and Lesbian Awards (GALAS) were set up by the NXF and *GCN* to honour lesbians, gay men, bisexuals and transgender people and organisations for their contributions to Irish society. The awards also honour politicians, employers and others who are committed to advancing equality and social acceptance for LGBT people in Ireland. Most importantly, they promote positive visibility of the LGBT community and the celebration of diversity, both key precepts in building the platform for societal acceptance of the idea of marriage equality. Having grown significantly in stature and status since their inception in 2009, the GALAS also provide important community recognition for many organisations and individuals, often further fuelling the passion, energy and courage to continue in their work.

Yes Equality Dublin 7 says thank you at Dublin Pride, June 2015.

Olivia McEvoy, NXF Chair, at the 2016 GALAS
with Marriage Equality Board member
Justine Schönfeld-Quinn.

ME and their many associates were awarded this community recognition on multiple occasions, including some of the political figures who were important supporters such as David Norris, Ivana Bacik, Jerry Buttimer, Averil Power, Aodhán Ó Ríordáin, Frances Fitzgerald and Mary McAleese. The GALAS have also recognised many of those directly involved in ME itself; Ann Louise Gilligan and Katherine Zappone were the first winners of the prestigious 'Persons of the Year' award in 2009, Gráinne Healy was 'Volunteer of the Year' in 2015 and Ailbhe Smyth won a 'Lifetime Achievement Award' in 2015 for work that included her contribution to ME. ME itself scooped the 'Community Organisation of the Year' in 2011, and also won a 'Lifetime Achievement' Award in 2016.

YES X 10 CAMPAIGN

Well in advance of the referendum on marriage equality, the NXF presented its proposed campaign to colleagues in ME (and other Yes Equality partners) to ensure that the NXF could best complement and support the overall campaign. This merely continued the collegiate partnership that was now cemented between the two organisations. The NXF delivered the 'Yes X 10' campaign, which was based on the premise that while organisations and activists had laid the foundations for the success of the referendum, it was vital that individuals take personal responsibility to ensure that ten people in their personal circle voted Yes on the day. The campaign was directed at supporters who were keen to take further responsibility in securing additional votes. The 'Yes X 10' campaign provided people with branded mechanisms to seek and gather personal support and votes using both printed materials and online campaigning. Launched at the 2015 GALAS, the campaign was widely shared online and was used extensively by canvassers and colleague organisations throughout the referendum campaign.

Civil marriage equality would shape a new Ireland

Olivia McEvoy
Opinion

'Yes' vote in referendum would send message of inclusiveness to LGBT Irish citizens living abroad

With so many pressing time commitments and financial responsibilities facing Irish people, it is not difficult to understand why achieving civil marriage equality for same-sex couples may not quite top their agenda. However, it is important to recognise that the achievement of civil marriage equality for same-sex couples is not simply a minority issue for the lesbian, gay, bisexual and transgender (LGBT) community. The forthcoming referendum on civil marriage equality next spring is a rare opportunity for the electorate to have a meaningful say in shaping the type of Ireland we live in and that we want for young people.

A majority Yes to civil marriage equality in this referendum would mean every child and young person who has yet to "come out" would do so in an Ireland where they would only ever know legislative equality; and all the parents, grandparents, siblings, friends, teachers and others who love and respect them could be assured that they would not be denied equal opportunities in life on the basis of their sexual orientation.

Moreover, legislative equality would help provide a platform on which we could build an Irish culture in which diversity was valued and celebrated and in which people could be their true selves. Legislative equality essentially paves the way for a society that celebrates diverse identities and empowers all citizens of Ireland to live openly and authentically. Building such a culture would greatly help combat the vicious homophobia and transphobia that still exists in many schoolyards, work canteens and on street corners.

Although Ireland is at least on the journey towards social acceptance of LGBT people, homophobic bullying and prejudice, with all of their damaging effects, are still very prevalent in our lives.

Discrimination
It is difficult to accept that in a country whose people have been so damaged by repression and oppression in the past, we are still facilitating a culture in which LGBT people are discriminated against and where anyone perceived as different is bullied and made to feel lesser for that.

Achieving civil marriage equality will also signal to the thousands of LGBT Irish citizens living abroad, many of whom left because they could not live open and honest lives here, that Ireland has joined the extensive and growing number of countries and jurisdictions that afford full equality to LGBT citizens.

Providing protection of and equal status for our relationships and families in the most powerful document in the State, *Bunreacht na hÉireann*, will be a clear statement by Irish people that discrimination of LGBT people, repression and narrow-mindedness have no place in modern Ireland. Indeed, it would finally make good on the promise in the Proclamation to cherish "all the children of the nation equally" just in time for the centenary celebrations of the Rising.

There is every indication that civil marriage equality enjoys overwhelming public support. The most recent *Irish Times*/Ipsos MRBI poll (October 2014) indicates that some 67 per cent would vote in favour of civil marriage equality while 20 per cent would vote against it – (9 per cent had no opinion and 3 per cent refused

There is a danger that because there is such strong public support for civil marriage equality many will assume this referendum will pass easily

to respond). However, this clear readiness to embrace civil marriage equality will count for nothing if it does not translate in the polling booths.

There is a danger that because there is such strong public support for civil marriage equality many will assume this referendum will pass easily. Indeed, there is already an element of fatigue in hearing about the issue because it is erroneously seen as a done deal.

The reality is that unless every person who supports the idea of a more equal Ireland goes to the poll and votes Yes in the referendum on civil marriage equality – and galvanises the support of friends, family and colleagues – the opportunity to shape Ireland for the better will have been lost. And for a very long time.

Opponents of civil marriage equality are well organised and their concerted campaign will motivate and mobilise very significant support for a No vote in the referendum. The campaign for a No vote will likely be extremely well financed, including by people who live outside the country but who see Ireland as a last bastion of "traditional values".

Bruising campaign
As much of the media interpret the McKenna judgment to mean equal time must be given to both sides of the argument in any referendum in order to provide the required balance, the referendum campaign is likely to be bruising in parts, not least for young LGBT people starting out on their journey of self-discovery during this debate.

Indeed, the entire LGBT community will once again be forced to listen to whether our relationships and lives are really of equal value or worth. All this will take its toll on the lives we are living.

What matters most is that we make that toll count for something. So many organisations, activists and LGBT people living openly have laid the foundations needed to win this referendum over many years. We are now relying on the electorate to complete that good work and pass the referendum. In doing so, together as a nation, we can send a powerful message to the world that Ireland is ready to be a country that celebrates diversity and where all of its people live in dignity and as equal citizens.

Olivia McEvoy is chairwoman of the National LGBT Federation

Opinion article by Olivia McEvoy in *The Irish Times*, 3 November 2015.

The marriage equality campaign is rightly lauded as a phenomenal success. It was a campaign that demanded extraordinary vision, tenacity, commitment and strategic effort from a vast range of organisations and individuals. The effort that led to that victory started at least forty years ago with people who had the courage to live open, visible lives in more difficult times and on whose shoulders we stood to be able to achieve what we did in 2015. Founded in 1979, the NXF was able to lend its longstanding history of activism and advocacy as well as its credibility to the campaign.

In addition to the provision of very practical infrastructural support to ME itself, it helped to shape critical aspects of the campaign in the earlier years, most notably framing the debate as a human rights and equality issue, the development of a platform that fostered key working relationships and collective strategic thinking on the campaign, as well as support from a wider coalition of organisations whose backing would prove vital in the latter stages of the campaign. In addition, *GCN*'s constant engagement of the LGBT community, the positive visibility provided by the GALAS and the practical 'Yes X 10' campaign, all made contributions to a campaign waged over many years.

It is a very proud chapter in the long history of the NXF to have played a role in the achievement of civil marriage equality alongside so many fellow activists and organisations, campaigners and canvassers. Together, our efforts have resulted in the most remarkable and defining social change for Ireland.

Ronan Farren

10

The Labour Party and Marriage Equality

In September 2007, I was at a bit of a loose end. I was embarking on a new stage of my career having left my job as a press officer for the Labour Party, based in Leinster House, following that May's General Election. I had worked in politics for over six years at that stage. But, facing the prospect of another term in opposition and with the words of advice of my former boss, Tony Heffernan, to do what he hadn't done and get out of the political bubble, ringing in my ears, I decided to seize the moment and look at some new challenges. That one of those challenges was to be the issue of involvement in marriage equality would never have occurred to me as, quite simply, I had little or no involvement in the issue to that point. But what was in my blood was an upbringing in politics, a knowledge of campaigns, and an interest in liberal issues and debate.

I grew up in a political family in the North during the 1980s and early 1990s. While my home town, Portstewart, on the north coast was more synonymous with ice-creams and retirement homes than bombs and bullets, my father was a reasonably high-profile politician in the area. And while many families understandably turned away from politics at that time, my home was consumed by it. My parents were Southerners who moved to the North in the early 1970s (I know – what were they thinking!) as a result of the opening of the University of Ulster in Coleraine. My father, Sean's, family background in trade union and Labour politics in the South, and my parents' shared commitment to social justice – influenced in no small part by their strong Catholic faith – saw them drawn to civil rights leaders such as John Hume, Austin Currie, Seamus Mallon, and the SDLP. So, my formative years were as much spent canvassing with my father around the Glens of Antrim, dropping leaflets, and joining him at political meetings as they were in the classroom, on the football pitch, or (in my teenage years) in discos or the pub.

I also grew up in a household of strong women. I was the youngest and only boy, with three older sisters, and our politics weren't just handed down to us and accepted. They were debated and interrogated at the dinner table, during car journeys, and on holidays. The more conventional opinions of my parents, who grew up in the Ireland of the 1950s and 1960s, were regularly challenged by my sisters. Never aggressively. Never antagonistically. Never confrontationally. But we were raised to question, to debate, and to lead. And, in a largely female home, I was conscious of gender roles and debates around equality. These were matters that we did discuss and debate. And while I can't really recall any strong discussions about gay rights or sexuality in general, I imagine we would have been quite progressive.

Former Tánaiste Eamon Gilmore watches as the Yes Bus is launched.

Liberty Hall says Yes.

So, how does this background explain my involvement in marriage equality? Well, it doesn't, really. After finishing university, my first full-time job was as a political assistant to Proinsias De Rossa in his role as a Member of the European Parliament for the Labour Party in Dublin. In my eighteen months in that role, the euro, a European Constitution, and the fate of the Nice Treaty were much more live topics than anything to do with same-sex marriage. It was only when I moved to the Labour Party Press Office from 2002 to 2007 that I remember the issue becoming part of the political discourse, and only then very much at the fringes and towards the end of that period.

This was provoked by two things: one, quite frivolous; the second, extremely important and, in my view, extremely important in the journey towards marriage equality. And both happened within one six-month period. In summer 2006, the then Labour Party leader, Pat Rabbitte, attended the annual Pride march in Dublin. Pat is a famously sociable politician, and fully entered into the spirit of the day. Pictures were published in a national newspaper of him having a can of lager with members of the Labour Party's LGBT group and others, enjoying themselves on a hot sunny day. The headline that accompanied the piece castigated Pat for breaking local by-laws by consuming alcohol in a public space. It was one of the most ungenerous, po-faced articles I had ever seen.

Civil partnership meets some opposition, August 2009.

And my boss – the aforementioned Tony Heffernan – memorably gave the journalist who wrote the piece both barrels in a telephone conversation that I overheard. That the newspaper then took Tony to task in print for his defence of Pat only heightened the ridiculousness of the situation. This incident made an impression on me because what was missed in this was how normal and conventional it was for the leader of a mainstream political party to attend the Pride march, and mingle with those attending. That the issue was Pat's drinking rather than his attendance demonstrated a bit of progress.

The second issue that arose only a few months later was the Labour Party's decision to publish a bill to facilitate civil unions. This came not long after the Zappone/Gilligan case had been rejected by the High Court, and was seen by the Labour Party as an effort to make progress on the issue of same-sex marriage in its aftermath. I remember being asked to run the press conference on the day we published the bill, and how much it meant to members of the Labour Party that we were doing so. Of course, it was acknowledged that civil unions did not equate to marriage, but the bill was presented as being as much as could be delivered at that time and was very much viewed as an historic moment for the party. That there had been little or no opposition to taking this step within our parliamentary party – save for one or two more traditional voices – was similarly significant.

Moninne Griffith with An Taoiseach Enda Kenny (*centre*) and Jerry Buttimer TD beside the Yes Bus, May 2015.

All that being said, while the issue was moving more and more on to the political radar, it wasn't really something that I was spending a lot of time thinking about. It didn't feature as an electoral topic during the 2007 General Election, when Bertie Ahern's finances and the vulnerability of the Irish economy dominated political debate.

In the summer of 2007, as I said my farewells to colleagues and friends I had worked with for six years, I did so looking forward to whatever new opportunities would come my way, but with no fixed idea of what those might be. It was at this time that, quite unexpectedly, I got a call from my former colleague Paul Daly, who had himself been asked if he was available to provide some professional support to a new campaign that was in development around the Zappone/Gilligan case. Paul explained to me that a support group – KAL (Katherine and Ann Louise) – had been formed during the case, but that it was now moving into a new phase, having received financial support from Atlantic Philanthropies. The clear remit of the new campaign would be to address the High Court's conclusion that there was no demonstrable public mood for changing the traditional constitutional interpretation of marriage.

As such, a campaign group needed to be established specifically to work towards mobilising public and political opinion in favour of marriage equality. No small task, then. Paul said that as a first step the KAL committee needed to engage someone to create a campaign from scratch. He was already stretched on a number of projects himself, and knowing that I was available, asked if I would be interested. To be honest, I didn't know what to think. This was outside my comfort zone in terms of the subject matter, the people involved, and the task at hand. I hadn't the faintest clue about the likelihood or otherwise of the campaign ever succeeding, nor did I even see myself in anyway invested in its success.

But, in asking myself those initial questions and in speaking to my friends and family about it over the next few days, I very quickly – if not instinctively – came to some obvious conclusions. The issue was right. The cause was right. And, most importantly, the challenge was doable. Not only the immediate task to establish the campaign, but the wider goal of introducing marriage equality in Ireland. Thinking back, I'm not really sure why I thought this. My only conclusion is that perhaps because I was fresh to the issue, and precisely because I hadn't been working on it for years, I saw marriage equality in such simple, straightforward terms.

It was in this spirit that I met with Edel Hackett (who was working on media with KAL at the time), Gráinne Healy and Denise Charlton (co-founders of Marriage Equality (ME)) for an interview about the project. I remember the day before, frantically rereading Dáil debates on Labour's Civil Unions Bill and looking up Wikipedia entries on the status of same-sex marriage in different countries around the world. I knew I was never going to become an expert on the issue overnight, but wanted to at least show some knowledge of the wider context. Whatever bluffing I did, worked. In fact, in meeting Denise and Gráinne, my interest in establishing the campaign increased, and I felt confident enough to say to them at that early stage that I really felt the issue could be won – when, I did not know, but I felt it was achievable. My only issue when they offered me the opportunity to work with them was that this was literally the first thing that had come my way since I started dipping my toe in the jobs market, and I wasn't ready to fully commit while I was still looking at my options. But we compromised on a short-term contract for an initial few months to get the campaign established, and to take things from there.

So, within a matter of weeks, I had gone from barely thinking about same-sex marriage, to being consumed by it. And over that initial period I found that friends, former colleagues, and family were both intrigued by the work I was doing and largely as instinctively supportive as I was. During that period, leading up to the formal launch of the ME campaign in February 2008, a number of incidents and events are noteworthy. I immediately established a positive relationship with Moninne Griffith (Director of ME) who was also working on the campaign, largely concentrating on advocacy, establishing the legal case for marriage equality, and responsible for building support and awareness within the LGBT community. We quickly established clear definitions of each other's work; I concentrated on the nuts and bolts of a campaign – visual identity, political mobilisation and lobbying, communications, online strategy, and, importantly, research into public opinion. There were overlaps between what we were concentrating on, but we immediately hit it off and were able to work together effectively.

An important early input to the shape of the campaign was a three-day visit to Ireland by Marc Solomon, a leading marriage equality campaigner in the USA. Marc was fresh from success in Massachusetts, where his organisation, MassEquality, had repealed a legislative decision to ban same-sex marriage. Marc briefed us extensively on how his campaign group was funded, its messaging, media, and lobbying strategy, and how they went about their work. His key message was to concentrate on the personal, and to bring stories about how the absence of marriage equality impacts peoples' lives directly to legislators and policy-makers. His input helped us shape ME's 'Out To Your TD' campaign, which actively encouraged people to go directly to their public representatives to speak about the need for marriage equality. This actively complemented ME's direct lobbying of relevant ministers, advisers, spokespeople, TDs and Senators. We organised a number of meetings for Marc during his time in Ireland and he remained an important supporter of our work in the following years.

Publishing research results was a key part to Marriage
Equality's communications strategy, October 2011.

'The time has come for gay marriage; it is the civil rights issue of this generation', Tánaiste Eamon Gilmore with ME Chairwoman Gráinne Healy, July 2012.

In those early days, I also had the opportunity to accompany Katherine Zappone and Ann Louise Gilligan on a visit to the European Parliament in Brussels. They attended a meeting organised by a Dutch MEP, Sophie Int'Veld, which brought together campaigners for marriage equality from across Europe. We leveraged the visit to meet directly with Irish MEPs and build awareness of the new campaign. Edel Hackett also arranged a series of media interviews for Katherine and Ann Louise and how they were taking their message to Europe. Over the course of these meetings and interviews, I realised the power their story held. Their simple story of their relationship and their work to achieve full equality was compelling.

Combined with their commitment, their articulacy, and their openness to do whatever it took to achieve their goal, their status as figureheads for the campaign was undoubted.

It would be wrong of me to say that it was all plain sailing. Very quickly I became aware of political tensions within the LGBT community about the issue of same-sex marriage and the establishment of ME as an organisation. In essence, this boiled down to GLEN's support and campaign for civil partnership versus those who saw it as something much less than full equality. To be honest, I could see both sides. But, as someone who was involved in campaigning, I could never understand GLEN's excessively pragmatic position to lobby almost exclusively for civil partnership and leave marriage equality to a later date. While I don't doubt the sincerity of those who adopted this position, their work over many years on behalf of the LGBT community, and recognising that it was easy for me to arrive with all the answers, I thought their support for civil partnership was too enthusiastic and that they were ultimately unambitious in terms of what could be achieved.

There was also suspicion and some hostility towards our own work. As an outsider this was all new territory to me, and I had no baggage either way. But a sense was communicated from some quarters that we were encroaching on other people's turf and subject matter. I largely took this as a compliment. ME was being established deliberately to disrupt and provoke. That some feathers were being ruffled early in the campaign proved that we must have been doing something right.

All this work built towards the formal launch of ME as an organisation on, appropriately enough, Valentine's Day, 14 February 2008, in the Mansion House. Prior to the launch, we had undertaken a significant piece of market research and polling on public attitudes towards same-sex marriage to inform the campaign on positioning and message. The results were extremely interesting. At one level there was little public resistance to the idea of same-sex marriage. The public recognised the inequality. Awareness of the issue and its inherent logic was increasing. People understood the issue in human terms and were much more tolerant and open than many would have believed. In terms of numbers, support for the introduction of same-sex marriage stood somewhere between 60 and 70 per cent – interestingly, this reflected the final outcome of the referendum seven years later.

However, the nature of the debate changed when the issue of children was introduced. There was clearly little awareness that children were already being parented by same-sex couples, and this lack of knowledge fed an instinctive discomfort about the idea among sections of the public. Overcoming this would remain the biggest challenge for marriage equality campaigners right through to the referendum itself. We decided to address this issue from the start. A communications strategy was put in place to begin to do two things.

First, to get LGBT people talking about the need for marriage as opposed to partnership, and, second, to profile LGBT parents and their children to tell their personal stories and dispel myths about same-sex parenting. This would be a long-term strategy and not a challenge to be won overnight. However, the media were largely open to having this debate, and, in those early days, one of the challenges was to find enough LGBT families willing to tell their stories to satisfy media demand.

The formal launch was a success. There was standing room only in the Oak Room and Gráinne Healy delivered an important keynote address outlining the logic for the campaign and how we would undertake our work. She said she believed marriage equality could be delivered and that this campaign was an important part of demonstrating that. She acknowledged two couples whom we had invited to speak at the event. Their compelling contributions of their simple stories were a major part of the event's success. ME as an organisation was up and running: I had achieved my immediate task and the campaign was underway. Reflecting now on that day makes me proud to have been involved. Something new had been established and there was a definite mood that it was timely, necessary, and right. There would be many bumps along the way on the road to achieving success, but I am privileged to say that I was there at the beginning of this stage of the journey.

Over the next few years, my involvement with ME took a number of different forms. Later in 2008 I took up a new position as a consultant with a prominent public relations company in Dublin, where – for a period – I worked with ME specifically on political outreach and lobbying. During that period we engaged directly with representatives from government and opposition, and the message was clear. There was a growing political consensus around the issue but, for the time being, the political establishment was focused on delivering civil partnership before any moves towards marriage. Some parties were more supportive than others, but it was clear that there was much greater awareness of the issue across the political spectrum than only a few years previously.

This became apparent during an analysis I did comparing two separate Dáil debates that were only three years apart. The 2007 discussion on a motion for civil unions saw support for its introduction come largely from Labour, the Green Party, Sinn Féin, Independents, and individual TDs in Fianna Fáil and Fine Gael. Ultimately, the motion was defeated. However, a mere two and a half years later, when the Fianna Fáil/Green Party were passing the legislation to provide for civil partnerships, it was clear that TDs were becoming much more aware of the issues at stake, and the growing mood towards full marriage equality. It was now easier to identify and isolate the opponents of same-sex marriage than to pick out individual supporters, such was the growing consensus. It is difficult to know the extent to which ME's 'Out To Your TD' campaign was part of this, but the fact that more TDs were putting on the record of the Dáil that they had met with gay and lesbian people, their parents, and their friends, and were being asked to legislate for same-sex marriage, demonstrated that it was having some effect.

The election of the new Fine Gael/Labour Party government in 2011 saw the issue move to the heart of the political mainstream. Labour, under Eamon Gilmore, had wholeheartedly committed to holding a referendum to change the Constitution and facilitate same-sex marriage. Fine Gael was much more cautious on the issue. The compromise that was reached in the Programme for Government was to allow for the matter to be discussed and debated by the new Constitutional Convention that was being established to review and update certain aspects of the Constitution. Even getting it this far was an achievement. Back in 2008, I had introduced ME to Mark Garrett, then chief of staff to Eamon Gilmore while Labour was in opposition. Mark was central to the formation of the Labour Party's political strategy and held considerable weight and influence when Labour entered government. Both Mark and Eamon were personally extremely committed to marriage equality and it was they who fought for it to be at the heart of the new government's agenda.

Tánaiste Joan Burton and Senator David Norris on the Yes Bus, May 2015.

Fergus Finlay, Dr Maureen Gaffney and Peter Ward SC address distortions emerging in the debate, 14 May 2015.

Yet even though the Labour Party was leading the campaign within the government to hold a referendum, the need to deal with the public finances, put the economy on the road to recovery, and get people working again were always the primary challenges for the new administration. In doing so, tough choices had to be made, and Labour's popularity, in particular, began to slip in the government's second year. Nevertheless, Mark and Eamon continued to call for a referendum, and Eamon's decision to describe the matter specifically as 'the civil rights issue of this generation' during the summer of 2012, and to say that a referendum should happen sooner rather than later, demonstrated their commitment. However, given the political and economic context of the time, these comments were viewed as slightly frivolous. Eamon came in for some criticism both within and outside the Labour Party, while the Taoiseach was far from wholehearted in his own support, suggesting he had bigger priorities at the time. Despite this, Eamon and Mark continued to pioneer the need for the referendum within the government. Public support for it was growing, too, with the Constitutional Convention overwhelmingly endorsing the holding of a referendum.

By this stage I had returned to work in politics, in a political and communications advisory capacity for the Labour Party. Working alongside Eamon and Mark, I saw how they continued to drive the issue, despite some continued criticisms about the need to focus on other priorities. However, what was clear was that it was now a matter of 'when' and not 'if' a referendum would be held during the lifetime of the government.

The conclusion of the Constitutional Convention forced the hand of Fine Gael, who no longer had any objection to a referendum taking place and who indicated that they would campaign strongly in favour. I believe this was a significant shift. There was now almost total political consensus in favour of a constitutional change, with Fianna Fáil also publicly supporting the issue. The political mainstream had come fully on board, and it was clear that opposition to a change would largely come from traditional conservatives, the Church, and individuals. That was no guarantee of success, but it did clear a major hurdle to holding the referendum.

However, two issues did arise. First, Fine Gael sought to delay the referendum until 2015 to avoid a clash with the Local and European Elections in May 2014. Second, marriage equality lost its biggest champion and advocate at the cabinet table when Eamon Gilmore resigned as Labour Party leader that summer. For a period, there was some uncertainty about the timing of the referendum. Once again, with the government reeling from a major loss of support during those mid-term elections, and its popularity continuing to decline with the introduction of water charges and the subsequent campaign against them, other matters appeared to be taking precedence. Labour Party ministers, under the new leadership of Joan Burton, continued to press the Taoiseach and others about when the vote would take place. Early in 2015 it was then revealed by the Taoiseach in a *Prime Time* interview ahead of a Fine Gael *ard fheis* that it would be on Friday 22 May.

There was some disquiet among my colleagues at the manner in which Fine Gael had sought to use this as a news hook ahead of a tricky conference, and had not fully consulted Labour ministers. This is the type of petty behaviour that happens in politics and coalitions. I sought to see the bigger picture – we now had a date to work back from and we could implement a plan to deliver a successful outcome. I was asked by Joan Burton to co-ordinate the party's referendum campaign alongside my colleague Brian McDowell, the party's general secretary, and Minister Alex White who would be our lead spokesperson during the campaign.

Our immediate challenge was to decide what type of campaign we would run, given that Labour Party members and supporters were 100 per cent in favour of a Yes vote, and that we didn't really need to do much to bring our natural constituency onside. We settled on a strategy of mobilisation. We decided that it was better to actively call on Labour supporters to do practical things to help deliver a Yes vote that was built around discussions with friends, relatives and neighbours, raising money for the campaign, and building support online. We also decided to focus our communications on the middle ground. That meant speaking to middle Ireland, rather than adopting an ultra-liberal tone against conservative groups that we thought would only antagonise the electorate. Indeed, it was a bit of a challenge throughout the campaign to try and temper the more liberal voices in our party – not always to their approval.

Joan Burton also used the campaign to hold a series of public meetings around the country to mobilise members and supporters. We held a major campaign launch in Dublin city centre where we specifically provided a platform for our TD for Kildare South, Jack Wall, to make a compelling speech. Jack was of an older generation and from a traditional, rural, GAA background. He spoke simply and honestly about the issue and his support for marriage equality, and moved everyone in the room.

Johnny Logan drops into the Yes HQ to lend support, April 2015.

The campaign was positive for the Labour Party. It provided a break from day-to-day politics where we were largely on the defensive and the back foot. It was something that we felt would not have been delivered without us in government and that we should actively take as much credit for it as we could. Some thought that we, as a party, could get an electoral boost from the issue. I wasn't so sure. Over time I had seen the issue gain momentum and relevance largely from events outside the political system. Politicians were playing catch-up with the public mood for a change, and I didn't see this as a game-changer for government support. Yes, there was a feel-good factor about the outcome, but I felt that the Labour Party's real achievement was the referendum itself, rather than the result. Without us, we might still be waiting for it to happen.

During the campaign itself, we worked closely with our colleagues in Fine Gael and with the other political parties through Yes Equality. We divided up media slots with Fine Gael so that either they or us were speaking as the voice of government on key debates. They were happy to lead these debates at the start of the campaign, giving way to us for the final major debates in the last week. We had lined up Alex White to do the final *Prime Time* debate, but when we went to confirm this with RTÉ, we were told that the producers had already lined up Leo Varadkar. This appeared to break our agreement with Fine Gael, who, when we contacted them, said they knew nothing about it. It seemed that RTÉ had made their own selection of government people and sought to insert Minister Varadkar into the debate. To his credit, when our agreement was pointed out to him, he had no problem standing aside to facilitate Alex. This time RTÉ weren't happy, to the extent of leaking to the papers that we were seeking to 'block' Leo Varadkar's appearance!

This childishness is, once again, typical of what goes on between politicians and the media. We stuck to our guns and Alex gave a fine, articulate, and strong performance in that debate. Throughout the campaign he was willing to undertake any media engagement or public meeting we asked him to do, even going as far as giving a newspaper interview with his mother and brother Seamus about Seamus's sexuality and why he wanted to deliver a Yes vote. On a visit to the Yes Equality headquarters with Joan Burton following our final press conference, he became emotional when thanking all the volunteers for their work – something that had a powerful impact on all of us gathered in the room.

Over the course of the campaign we also sought to provide a number of media platforms for Eamon Gilmore. Eamon had largely kept out of the public eye since his resignation but, we believed, remained a proud and strong advocate for a Yes vote. For that reason, come results day, we ensured that Eamon attended the main count in the RDS where he was cheered on his arrival. He also received an extremely positive reception from the crowd when he appeared onstage at Dublin Castle.

Labour out in force. *From left:* Billie Sparks, Senator Ivana Bacik and Minister for State Aodhán Ó Ríordáin at St Stephen's Green, Dublin, Thursday 21 May 2013.

A memorable moment for me from that day came slightly later when I accompanied Eamon from the Castle to a Labour Party reception that was taking place in a hotel in Temple Bar. During that walk we melted into the crowd, but a middle-aged man spotted Eamon, approached him, shook his hand and simply said, 'Mr Gilmore, thank you.' Eamon was chuffed and I was glad to be there with him. He had stuck his neck out on marriage equality, driven it within the government, taken flack for doing so, but never wavered. He deserved all the praise he received that day, and I hope he is still basking in the glow.

That evening I went to the Ballsbridge hotel where the main Yes Equality celebrations were taking place. I saw Moninne, Gráinne, Denise, Andrew, and my other friends from ME whom I had got to know well over seven or so years. My involvement with ME over that time had taken a number of guises – paid employee, outside consultant, Board member – it was an organisation I was always extremely proud to be associated with.

And over that time I learned a lot about an issue that I had known next to nothing about. About building campaigns, alliances, and bringing people with you. About creating social change from both outside and inside the centre of power. It was an experience I will cherish deeply and will never forget.

(Left) David Carroll of BeLonG To and Minister of State for New Communities, Culture, Equality and Drugs Strategy Aodhán Ó Ríordáin at the Yes Equality HQ, Dublin, May 2015.

Ross Golden-Bannon

11

The Story of an LGBT Marriage Equality Activist
From Canvassing for Equality to Canvassing for a Yes

We never wanted a referendum and yet, looking back now, we probably wouldn't want it any other way. Not just for us, the LGBT Irish, but for all of Ireland and for the beacon of hope the Yes vote sends to people living in isolation and fear around the world. Those of us who grew up knowing we were different in Ireland in the 1970s and 1980s, and before, know all too well the pain of that isolation. It was morsels of positive news about LGBT progress around the world that often sustained us.

A number of years after I joined the Board of Marriage Equality (ME), around 2008, I remember fellow Board member Ailbhe Smyth saying emphatically that our strategy should be legislative change: the last thing we wanted was a referendum. I was ambivalent, with only a vague memory of the excitement of previous referenda. Ailbhe was insistent that even leaving aside the risk of putting the rights of a minority to the population, the impact on friendships and relationships would be profound. Her words would later come back to haunt us as long friendships were strained to breaking point and indeed some would be irreparably damaged.

For eight years, we worked on the strategy to achieve equality through legislation, with the shadow of a referendum growing ever greater. In a way, it was used as a political stick: 'If you don't accept these watered-down rights we'll have to have a referendum.' But we had exhausted every avenue, the details of which are covered elsewhere in this book, from seeking to amend current law to seeking new rulings to permit marriage equality from successive Attorneys General. But at every move, the political chess masters outmanoeuvred us. They were joined at times by our own, as GLEN (the Gay & Lesbian Equality Network) insisted Ireland was not ready for marriage equality and worked instead towards civil partnership. This was despite the many pieces of research we had done showing a continued rise in support for marriage.

Marriage Equality material explains the differences between
civil partnership and civil marriage, 2012.

CIVIL PARTNERSHIP VERSUS MARRIAGE EQUALITY

When civil partnership legislation was passed, it had over 169 differences between it and civil marriage, so it was by no means 'marriage-like'. Indeed, in an unwitting reflection of GLEN's male-dominated structure, the legislation worked for gay men, who were least likely to have children, and was least helpful to lesbian and gay parents who needed clarity and the equal support of the State. GLEN's stance also reflected their closeness to the political machinery, themselves always some ten years behind the public, rather than the grassroots desire of the LGBT community. Indeed, as the 62 per cent result of the referendum further reflects, some politicians remained behind public opinion right to the end.

Once civil partnership legislation was passed in 2010 we came to realise, and freely acknowledged, that as ceremonies took place across the country, these family celebrations helped normalise the lives of lesbian and gay couples. Civil partnership had become a stepping stone to ME, though it should be stated that I do not consider this was ever the intention of GLEN, as has been retrospectively claimed. I know this from my many conversations with members of GLEN over the years as they dismissed the idea of ME as a group and as a movement. Some were close friends so we agreed never to speak of civil partnership or marriage equality between us in order to save our friendships. The failure of GLEN to take ownership of its previous strategy, which I accept worked to a point, will continue to dog their failure to gain grassroots support for so much of their other superb work. Political chess works well in the Oireachtas, but plays out badly amongst the people.

THE CONSTITUTIONAL CONVENTION – THE FIRST REAL CANVASS

After much hard work, marriage equality was cited in the programme for government in the Fine Gael and Labour coalition of 2011. A new game started and we were put in what some thought was the long grass of the Constitutional Convention. But it turned out that this unique gathering of 100 randomly chosen citizens (sixty citizens and thirty-nine elected representatives, plus a Chairman, Tom Arnold) was in fact an inspired forum to gain support for marriage equality. The Convention was a turning point for the campaign for family equality legislation and for securing the referendum for ME. We had reached out to GLEN, despite the many difficulties we had with them on their failure to support us in the early days. With the help of the Irish Council for Civil Liberties (ICCL), we created a coalition to make a united presentation to the Convention. It wasn't easy but we always presented a publicly united front. I am sure GLEN was as frustrated with us as we were with them, and equally ICCL had a job on their hands managing both.

Messages at Pride, Dublin 2012.

Ross Golden-Bannon with Lord Mayor of Dublin Emer Costello (centre) and
Gráinne Healy at the launch of Marriage Equality's 'Out To Your TD' campaign,
February 2010.

The Convention was an extraordinary experience and, in many ways, our first canvass of a wider vote beyond our bubble. Behind the scenes we met, talked and worked with people we hadn't worked with before. Relationships were built, and though some were not marriages made in heaven, the tactical necessity of them ensured we were publicly united for the battle ahead. The result of the vote of the Convention was heart-warming. From the long grass, the people shot a progressive vote of 79 per cent in favour of holding a referendum on marriage equality, and voted 81 per cent on ensuring legislation that protected same-sex-headed families should be introduced by government.

The Convention was my first taste of talking to people outside my circle about marriage equality. As we left the Grand Hotel in Malahide, where the Convention took place, a very elderly man, part of the Convention, was leaving at the same time. He was so old and infirm he needed to hold the banister as he made his way slowly down the stairs. He reached out and grabbed my arm: 'I voted for you! I voted for you! It's your Constitution too!' I still well up thinking of that. If this elder citizen could cast an equal vote for me at the Convention, perhaps the referendum was not such a bad idea.

It would be another two years before we found ourselves on the doorsteps and even at that there was a sort of phoney war after Christmas 2014 and into January and February 2015. We knew we were having a referendum but didn't know the date. Finally, it was announced for Friday, 22 May 2016 and the Yes Equality campaign had proper timelines to map onto the many strands of our years of work.

Like several ME Board members, I found myself outmanoeuvred from any official role in the Yes Equality committee structures, partly, I suspect, to mollify the uneasy marriage between various groups and partly by missing a key ME Board meeting due to my own work commitments. It was a deeply frustrating time as all our historic knowledge was lost to many enthusiastic but new people whom we saw making the same mistakes we had made. There was also a great loss of practical commercial and political campaigning knowledge that was painfully relearnt. Thankfully, there were enough experienced people at the head of the campaign to bring along the new recruits. Left with nothing to do, and unrecognised by the newbies in Yes Equality HQ on Clarendon Street, I joined the Yes Bus and canvassed in Cavan, Monaghan and beyond. I was hoping I'd be working with Moninne Griffith, who was managing the Yes Bus, but our timetables didn't cross. It did feel odd to me that Moninne, yet another font of enormous knowledge as Co-Director of ME was, in my view, greatly underutilised in the role she was given, important and all as that role was.

I was still feeling out of the loop, wondering when we'd get the go-ahead to start canvassing when I bumped into Senator Averil Power, a long-time supporter of ME. She said she'd been campaigning for weeks. It looked like this would be the best solution: dive into canvassing. I had, after all, done training in Millbank with Alastair Campbell and Peter Mandelson in London on the language of canvassing, so it would be a natural fit. I'd also campaigned in the London Mayoral, Welsh Assembly and Westminster Elections some years earlier, so I had some idea of the messy details of knocking on doors. But I was, like many other people, waiting for a gunshot to go, but, really, Yes Equality HQ wanted each group to take ownership and run with their local campaign. So I set up the Howth-Sutton-Baldoyle Yes Equality group.

With the help of an old friend, James Markey, we secured space at the back of the iconic Summit Inn in Howth for free from the owner Tommy Gaffney. With material and information honed from Yes Equality HQ and Senator Averil Power, we gave a briefing to the twenty-plus supporters who turned up, enough to make it feel like we had a full room. This was really the messaging stage, with material coming from Andrew Hyland, Director of Communications, and regularly updated depending on the national dialogue. Messaging is different from briefing in that it gives people an overall view of what you are trying to do. The research had been done and we knew the sections of the population most likely to vote Yes; most likely to vote No; and those who would be undecided. With limited time and limited resources, it made sense to target the Yes voters to get out and vote, to persuade 'soft Yes' to a hard Yes, and not to allow our time to be taken up by the 'hard No'. It sounds simple, yet in many ways it works against human nature. The temptation is to spend time trying to persuade a No voter. In a way they fascinated us, not always the monsters we thought, just ordinary people. And then a Yes voter, so much more enjoyable to spend time with them, but they had to be a quick chat, too. The people we needed to spend time with were the 'soft Yes' voters, who required an inherently more nuanced conversation.

THE FIRST CANVASS

After a few days canvassing with Averil Power, I launched our first call to canvass for Holy Thursday, 2 April 2015, and our meeting point was the place every large group meets in Sutton: the car park of St Fintan's Church. The irony was not lost on me. I waited and waited and the only person still sitting in a car after the congregation had gone into evening mass was a retired grandmother called Breda Iredale. She'd been a vocal supporter at the first briefing in the Summit Inn but could it be true? The only person canvassing with me on the first night was a senior citizen? She would turn out to be our secret weapon. Her faux little-old-lady act beguiled many a wavering voter.

Messages of support for Katherine Zappone and Ann Louise Gilligan for their 2011 Supreme Court action seeking to amend the Civil Marriage Bill. Ross Golden-Bannon *(left)*, Gráinne Courtney and Orla Howard.

I began the canvass, as agreed with Yes Equality HQ, with a brief on what to say as well as some basic rules on canvassing about closing gates, not walking across lawns and not getting drawn into long debates with fervent No voters. Each week our numbers grew: the biggest barrier being the fear people had about knocking on doors, we created a buddy system. People who'd been canvassing before took newbies with them and they learnt the techniques refined by more experienced volunteers. We had plenty of varied leaflets and carried a selection of faces depending on who answered the door. Interestingly, the leaflets with Gay Byrne's face had amongst the most positive reactions across the Peninsula. In some ways, the evolving design of these leaflets reflected the wider successful cross-communication from the coalface of canvassing to Yes Equality HQ. The first leaflets looked good but were impossible to get into a letterbox. The next batch were duly redesigned. We need older people! Hey presto, the next batch had older faces.

By the third week many other groups had formed and were seeking help. Fellow Board member Orla Howard asked a few of us to help brief and start the Marino group with her and it wasn't long before they were brimming with volunteers, too. I bumped into Dave Farrelly, originally from Trim, at the launch of the Dublin North Bay Yes Equality in Clontarf

Castle. Like me, he'd been waiting for a starter gun and when I said I just set our group up and got everything I needed from Yes Equality HQ, he nearly ran out the door. Within a few days, Yes Equality Trim was active but not without some pain:

> There were a few looks of disgust along the way that were quite hurtful and one particular gentleman, who will always stick in my mind, when he said that voting Yes was 'just a bridge too far for him' with a slight smirk on his face. I always give him a glowing smile when I see him around the town since our sixty-two per cent Yes! (Dave Farrelly, Yes Equality Trim).

But canvassing was not without its fun and camaraderie. Some used pedometers to keep on top of their weight-loss programme, others bagged specific houses to canvass so they could gawp at impressive interiors and, as my old friend Micheál Burke pointed out as he rearranged some garden stone work at a house where we'd got no reply, straight people weren't always equal in taste!

WORKING WITH LOCAL POLITICOS – SOME HAPPY MISTAKES

I contacted all the other politicians' offices and calculated which areas of the Peninsula and beyond had not been covered. Being a logical person, I marked off the areas already canvassed and then we simply started at Sutton Cross and worked our way up the Hill of Howth over the next few weeks. Any canvassing I had done before had been in densely populated, urban areas. I did not factor in the very long drives of the wealthy Sutton and Howth residences. Several local politicians said they just didn't canvass those areas because of the time investment compared to outcomes and they were surprised we'd made the effort. We did change our tactics later but not before a near-100 per cent canvass across Howth Hill. On many evenings, our door count was very low but, as Breda Iredale's daughter Elizabeth proved with her pedometer, our footfall was enormous compared to doors knocked. Still, this worried me as each evening myself and leaders across the country returned the results from our canvass. How many Yes, No, undecided, not at home (a lot of these), as well as the issues coming up on the doorstep. Our door count was regularly a low one yet this would later pay dividends with some of the highest turnouts ever in the area. The feedback to HQ was key, helping them reformulate the daily brief each canvass leader got in the inbox every morning from the redoubtable Andrew Hyland.

As polling day loomed, we became more strategic and, using voter turnout information from both the Labour Party and Senator Averil Power, prioritised roads with higher turnouts for a final recanvass.

At Mulligans, Stoneybatter, Dublin, following a Marriage Equality Board meeting. *From left:* Andrew Hyland, Ross Golden-Bannon, Katherine Zappone, Ann Louise Gilligan and Moninne Griffith.

MESSAGING AND BRIEFING, EARLY PROBLEMS

The daily brief from HQ was vital in briefing the growing numbers of volunteers. The opposition posters had upset a lot of people but they had also acted as a recruitment drive, though much of this was instinctual support. Complicated questions on surrogacy and adoption were frightening to first-time canvassers with little knowledge of LGBT issues let alone the many red herrings the No campaign was throwing into the national debate. These required a nuanced reply and were expertly rebutted at a national level in print and broadcast media by Gráinne Healy and Brian Sheehan but we needed different language and different techniques on the doorsteps.

I reached out to canvass leaders across the country and we created a best-practice rebuttal and script system through email and on the private Yes Equality Facebook page for canvass leaders. It was simple enough; when we got the daily brief, which covered the messaging behind each new issue, we'd reach out and see if anyone across the country had the best one-liner, in pub-talk language, as a rebuttal or an explanation of the issue. One of the most disarming was around the No campaign's 'every child needs a mum and dad/

no to surrogacy' line. It was also a deeply cynical subliminal message that children were not safe with gay men. Many across the country managed not to get drawn into a long debate by simply saying: 'I don't know much about surrogacy or adoption but I do know that Barnardo's and all the major children's charities want a Yes vote for the sake of the children.' That simple response converted a lot of undecided voters to a hard Yes without complicated debating.

By week three, we had something of a script to work with and this was learned by each new volunteer through their canvassing buddy. It sounded simple enough but each short sentence had a purpose depending on who opened the door, right down to how to handle teenagers. Never assume they're not eighteen, if they're not you'll flatter them, if they are eighteen you might annoy them. Yes voters were the quickest, with the important closing line, asking them to canvass their household and wider circle to join them in a Yes vote. We also took the opportunity to dispel the rumour that the Yes vote would be a landslide (as this would mean people wouldn't turn out to vote).

Both sides, May 2015. Senator David Norris speaking from the Yes Bus in Dublin's Ballymun, May 2015.

The key problem many soft-yes voters had was that they were afraid to ask questions in case they were accused of being homophobic, so we always asked if they had any questions or concerns. This gave them the freedom to talk as well as giving us the opportunity to dispel myths. This was key in shifting the large middle ground of soft Yes to hard Yes vote and where we spent most of our energy.

No voters were a quick exchange:

'We're canvassing for a Yes vote in the Marriage Equality Referendum, can we rely on your support?'

'Sorry, I'll be voting No.'

'Thanks for your time anyway.'

Two short sentences and on to the next house. Some people offered the leaflet too in the hope that they might be a soft No, but we didn't get pulled into debates with them.

Yes voters were a temptation as well, as we obviously shared a common view and excitement in what a Yes vote might say about who we are as a people. Some Yes voters had said to me they viewed their vote as taking the Republic back from the Catholic Church. Some volunteers brought this view with them, too.

Volunteer Geraldine Mahony takes up this theme:

> I suppose the reason I got involved was because it was the right thing to do. As a country, I felt the grip of the Catholic Church had finally been loosened. This was our opportunity to find our voice, as a nation. The cause was morally right, we are all equal, so we needed to prove it. As a middle class heterosexual person living in Ireland, I felt that I had a civic duty towards my fellow citizens. I feel it is always 'others' who fight the fight [...] It is easy to do nothing and I felt this was an opportunity to support my fellow citizens and shape our country for the better.

No answer to a doorbell was a concern: on many occasions, we had up to 50 per cent of no answers and I constantly worried that these were all hidden No votes. Yet I knew that many people had changed their views from the early days of the canvass, and indeed over the ten years of the campaign, so perhaps they would be persuaded by the wider national debate on radio and TV. Many canvassers' reasons for volunteering had changed, too. Here's Helen McNamara:

> Not being from the LGBT community myself, I initially was getting involved in the canvassing to help my old friend Ross. At the time I could only imagine how much a Yes vote would mean to him, and I wanted to do all I could to help him achieve this. But as each day passed, and I met more and more positive voters – some of whom shared their own personal stories

with me – the campaign soon became something much more for me. I began to see a Yes vote in the Marriage Equality Referendum as Ireland saying it no longer agreed with the negative and neglectful treatment of, not only the LGBT community but of all minority groups, and that by voting Yes to an all-inclusive and massively more tolerant country, we would be not only creating history, but sending a message to the rest of the world about who we were.

As canvassers and group leaders we sometimes felt like we were in a total bubble, unaware of what was happening with other groups. I worried constantly that others were not following the guidelines from Yes Equality HQ. We had no way of really knowing what people were doing on the doorstep. Then one evening I stumbled across a news report online of a canvass in the West of Ireland. They were saying almost verbatim what we were saying on our doorsteps. A huge sense of relief swept over me along with a feeling of incredible pride in the machinery of Yes Equality HQ on Clarendon Street. Win or lose, we were a beautifully oiled machine.

Canvassing with the Marino Yes Equality group, March 2015.

A PERSONAL TOLL

All the organisations in the world and even the best of briefings could not prepare people for negativity and abuse on the doorstep and sometimes even in the streets. Part of the training for canvass leaders from Yes Equality HQ was the important role a debrief should play in every canvass. It was an opportunity to offload negative experiences as well as share positive ones. This was met with some bemused looks from seasoned party political members: though they understood conceptually the difficulties posed by homophobia, they were perhaps unaware of the terrible toll homophobia can have on our emotional lives and mental health.

There were essentially two types of experiences: those who were LGBT or had close LGBT relatives; and those who were heterosexual and had a moral belief in supporting the cause. For LGBT people, every knock on a door was like coming out again. One evening, when the Raheny area called out for support, a few of us joined them and I met two older gay men. They were strong-willed, organised and hugely supportive of all the younger gays. It was only in a private conversation with them afterwards they told me they cried at night when they were on their own.

The experience of Anne Cooney, another Howth-Sutton-Baldoyle volunteer, speaks of similar pain:

> I have two daughters, one of whom is gay, and saw no reason why my gay daughter should not, if she wished, be able to marry in her own country as her sister could. I have also worked with LOOK, a support group for parents of gay children, and knew of their wishes for equality and fairness for their children.
>
> Canvassing was, at times, harrowing and exhausting; there were evenings when I poured a glass of wine and wept for every person who had to ask to be seen as equal to the person opening the door to them.
>
> But for all of the negatives, it was also such a comforting, uplifting, unforgettable experience; to have had the camaraderie and fun with the other canvassers and the encouragement of most people we canvassed, young and old. They were indeed with us, and it did come to pass! YES!

Anne had been verbally abused by a man in Sutton Park as she tried to canvass him to vote Yes for her daughter. She was very shook, as we all were, but she continued nonetheless and knocked on the next door only to crumble in the face of a Yes vote. The stranger hugged her, saying, 'We're with you, don't worry, it will be passed.'

For other straight allies the canvass was as much about today's Ireland as its future. Here's David Soffe:

My reasons for canvassing were simple. I had a lot of gay friends and I wanted to do every-thing I could to ensure we got the right result in the vote. I didn't want the wrong result to come through and regret not being involved. Secondly, I wanted to make sure the Ireland my children grew up in afforded every child the same possibilities, gay or straight.

Interestingly, David Soffe was one of many straight allies in our group. For the vast majority of the campaign I was the only gay in the village. It made for some curious exchanges. Many straight men were not so comfortable sharing negative experiences to the group in the debrief and yet they had their own challenges. The assumption was made that all the men canvassing were gay. But in our group it couldn't have been further from the truth; for the first time in their lives they had a taste of what it was like to be gay. And it wasn't good. One straight ally quietly approached me after the debrief and asked if I was often shouted at in the street. I said less so now that I am older but certainly it was not unusual. I asked if anything had happened to him that night. It turned out that kids on one street had been shouting homophobic abuse at him. He'd decided not to say he was straight and kept walking. That story was repeated several times in our group but what really struck me was that they all, to a man, did not try and defend themselves with their heterosexuality.

As our group grew, we were joined by a young lesbian woman. Conversely, she seemed invisible to many voters. When she knocked on one door, the man who answered it talked about lesbians in the abstract before it dawned on him in horror that he had one on the doorstep. She took it with good grace and laughed it off, but responses such as that were deeply hurtful.

But for others, even seasoned politicos and canvassers, it brought up the difficult issue of canvassing friends and family. This is Lisa-Anne Dwyer, another volunteer from the Howth-Sutton-Baldoyle group:

> Having been brought up in a household where canvassing for radical changes for equality for all society was the norm, there was no doubt I wanted to be involved in the marriage equality referendum to ensure the same rights I was entitled to were extended to all my family and friends.
>
> I was lucky the people I encountered whilst canvassing and in general were either in favour of the changes or politely told me they hadn't decided yet. The biggest struggle I experienced was the realisation that a key member of my family was going to vote No even though support for marriage equality had been an integral part of our family.

For the wider population, the very canvass itself had become a national phenomenon. Nobody could miss the distinctive Yes Equality branding and by now hordes of people were out in the streets canvassing. Party politicians confided in private that they had never seen anything like the mass mobilisation before. As referendum day drew nearer, our group had grown to near unwieldy numbers requiring splits into smaller groups. Finally, I had to make the decision that new people had to commit to at least three canvasses as more seasoned volunteers were wasting valuable time training people who came for one night and didn't come back. It seemed that canvassing for a Yes vote had become the latest fashion statement.

Yes Buns, May 2015.

THE HAPPY ENDING

With the final days in sight, cracks were beginning to show in me, though I didn't know it. I'd taken three weeks' leave to campaign and I'd been flat out for a month or more before that, too. I lived, slept and breathed the campaign. I felt that every moment should be filled with something campaign-related. For ten years before that, it was a constant presence in my life and now it would all end in a single day. I am not sure if I ever really slept as I just drifted into mashed-up images and words of the campaign. Finally, a particularly sneering

No voter got to me on an evening canvass. I went home and broke the rules of canvassing with a Facebook update on what it really felt like. 'So long, and thanks for all the Nos' struck a chord with many people and was shared many thousands of times, reprinted in the UK *Independent* newspaper, translated into German and even shared and commented on by none other than eighties pop star, Holly Johnson, one of the few positive role models I had as a teenager. I felt a sense of relief and was lifted by the huge wave of support I got from the post which invigorated me for the final two days.

A core group of the Howth-Sutton-Baldoyle Yes Equality volunteers went to the count centre in the RDS. We located our area right down to the box numbers of the streets where we grew up or lived. We quickly picked up the entirely different skills of tallying: counting the Yes and No votes as the boxes were emptied and sorted. We'd heard a rumour that one box from the north inner city of Dublin was 100 per cent Yes. We didn't get that high but we did get some of the highest turnouts, which was a direct result of our dogged canvassing rule of knocking on every single door. We also bucked the national trend with the road where I grew up voting 69 per cent Yes.

Moninne Griffith and Denise Charlton listen to the victory speeches at the Ballsbridge Hotel, Dublin, 23 May 2015.

And when I was in the count centre on that most historic day and it became apparent that it was going to be a massive YES, I felt such a surge of pride that we as a nation were going to move forward together, and that we were no longer embarrassed or ashamed of who any of us were.

But perhaps we should conclude with Breda Iredale. In direct contrast to many older voters, this retired grandmother not only voted Yes, but solidly campaigned through wind and rain for some eight weeks to persuade others to vote Yes too. She'd even temporarily dipped her toe into 'that Facebook thing'. This was her parting shot after the historic win:

> It's been a wonderful seven weeks. I have met some lovely people on the canvass and also at doors. It's only since I started canvassing that I realised what gay people have been through. One bad comment made me fearful and wondering if I could continue going from door to door as a senior citizen, so God knows what this must have been like for lots of you. I am proud I stood up and was counted. Well done to all I met and please share or what ever you do as I have no friends on Facebook. I am now officially signing off Facebook so Ross can't put up photos of me any more. Stand tall and be proud.

Kate Moynihan

Lesbians in Cork (LINC) and Marriage Equality

The journey to equal marriage for Lesbians in Cork (LINC) cannot be discussed without first looking at the history of LINC and membership of the organisation. Lesbian activism has had a long history in Cork, from small underground gatherings in the 1970s to today, with Cork the only city in the Republic with an organisation that works exclusively with lesbians, bisexual women and their families, not only from Cork but also from many other parts of the country. Since the early 1980s, there has been a community in Cork; the Women's Place in the Quay Co-op, the established Lesbian Line, The Other Place, Cairde Chorcaí and LINC. Set up in 1999, LINC is the result of decades of lesbian and bisexual women organising and supporting each other, and the vision of those who followed their dream of having their own community resource centre.

LINC aims to improve the quality of life, health and well-being of all women who identify as lesbian or bisexual in Ireland. The objectives of the organisation are:

- To build a safe, accessible and vibrant community centre (actual and virtual) for lesbian and bisexual (LB) women;
- To provide information and support for LB women and their families;
- To promote the mental, physical, emotional and sexual health of LB women;

- To inform and contribute to relevant policy development at local, regional and national level;
- To be a model of best practice rooted in feminist, social justice and community development principles.

From its early days, LINC has been rooted in feminist ideals. As such, it was a challenge for many members of our community to endorse a campaign that was promoting what they saw as the patriarchal institution that marriage represents. For many others, it was considered the most appropriate way to have their families recognised and acknowledged in law. We were well aware that the women in the community were divided over the issue. LINC has always been for the community, by the community; as such no policy adoption or change is taken without first consulting with the community. This process is through bi-annual community meetings where such issues are discussed and debated. LINC's position on civil partnership and marriage was no different, and many discussions and debates took place at community and board level.

Among the many women who have been involved in LINC over the years, a large majority have been parents, and families and children have been an important concern for LINC. The lesbian parenting group set up in the early 2000s was one of the most dynamic groups within LINC, offering support to each other and their families. The dominant narrative in society was and still is that 'family' referred only to heterosexual-headed families. Lesbian parents challenged this view and were often, as a result, seen as unfit parents. Over the years this was reflected in court battles, where lesbians considered to be 'unsuitable' as parents were refused custody of their children.

In an attempt to inform themselves and educate the relevant services, LINC, on behalf of the parenting group, invited Professor Susan Golombok to Cork in June 2003. Professor Golombok had undertaken extensive research on children of lesbian parents and was invited to deliver two seminars, one to the group themselves and the other to legal and social professionals involved in child welfare. This was an important step for LINC and put the rights of children and their parents, biological and non-biological, to the fore of our work.

March 2006 saw the establishment of a Working Group on Domestic Partnership by the then Minister for Justice, Equality and Law Reform, Michael McDowell. The working group, chaired by Anne Colley, was tasked with the job of producing an options paper on Domestic Partnership. Angela O'Connell, on behalf of LINC, made a submission to the Working Group detailing LINC's stance on the subject. It was no surprise that the main focus of the submission was again on families and children. O'Connell stated that 'the status of illegitimacy was banished from our statutes almost two decades ago, but the children of same-sex parents still await an avenue to claim the parentage of both of the adults who planned them and raised them in love and hope for a better future'. She went on to say further that 'the introduction of domestic partnerships for same-sex couples should allow the children of these families to receive basic protections currently afforded only to those children born into families based on marriage'.[1] And so the journey for LINC, from seeking to protect our children and families, to lobbying for domestic partnership and, ultimately, marriage, had begun.

Cork Action poster, 2011.

Kate Moynihan *(left)* with Jo-Anne Ticker, Chairperson of LINC, Cork Pride, 2015.

When the conference on the 'Legal Status of Cohabitants and Same Sex Couples', organised by the Colley Working Group, the Gay & Lesbian Equality Network (GLEN) and the Equality Authority, was held in Dublin in May 2006, some members of LINC staff and steering group attended. Several international speakers informed the conference of the situation in their countries, including Spain, which had introduced marriage the previous year. LINC participants came away believing that full civil marriage rights had to be the goal and that settling for some form of civil union would amount to us remaining second-class citizens. On a different note, one of the abiding memories of that day is Minister Michael McDowell, who opened the conference, being the target when a copy of the Constitution was thrown at him by members of the Ancient Order of Hibernians.

In March 2008, LINC organised a conference, 'Marriage and Lesbian and Gay Families', which was chaired by Ailbhe Smyth and took place in the beautiful surroundings of the

Custom House Board Room in the Port of Cork. Some of the reflections on the day came from a gay father and a lesbian mother. Dr Fergus Ryan spoke about children's rights in the context of LGB parenting. However, it was the speech made by a seventeen-year-old Ailbhe Egan that best portrayed the need for formal recognition of LGBT-headed families. Ailbhe, the daughter of a lesbian couple, ensured that no one in the room left without knowing the importance of both her mothers and how her family unit was no different to any heterosexual family grouping, except that they were not legally recognised as such. She also explained that because of her age, legal recognition was not going to happen for her family, but her concern was for her young cousin and his family whose parents were also lesbian. Again, family, family, family!

The Civil Partnership Act 2010 was recognised as a major advancement for our community. For relationships where one person was a foreign national, as several of our members were, it was particularly important and gave them access to a possible solution for overcoming difficulties with residency and work permits. However, it was also a disappointment that families were excluded. The exclusion of children and non-biological parents from the legal bond to each other has caused much fear and pain for families over the years, and this was not ameliorated by civil partnership.

The dissatisfaction felt with civil partnership is not to take away from the work that was done to achieve it or from those of our community who officially celebrated their relationships through it. The many days of celebratory joy up and down the country brought newfound confidence for many and helped bring much needed visibility to our relationships. However, it also emphasised that more work needed to be done to achieve equality of recognition for our families. This inequality LINC consistently highlighted in delivery of our awareness training programmes.

LINC's submission to the Constitutional Convention on Same Sex Marriage in March 2013 again addressed the absence of 'family' from previous civil partnership legislation, stating that failure 'subjects same-sex couples and their children to inequality, discrimination and prejudice'. Support for women with concerns for their families continues to be a key element of LINC's work. The Children and Family Relationship's Act 2015 was welcomed and when commenced in its entirety will help address many of these concerns.

From the consultation and work done over the years to when it was announced in late 2013 that the government was accepting the recommendation of the Constitutional Convention to hold a referendum, LINC has been committed to playing a role in achieving success.

Ailbhe Smyth at the Yes Equality press conference held after the referendum, 24 May 2015.

PERSONAL

If Carlsberg did jobs ... well, I landed into the equivalent when I was appointed LINC co-or-dinator in October 2013. I had been involved with LINC in a voluntary capacity for many years as a service user, steering group member, Director and company secretary, so I was delighted when I was appointed to the role. The announcement came a month later that the government was accepting the recommendation of the Constitutional Convention to hold a referendum. I was co-ordinator of the only lesbian and bisexual women's organisation in the republic: what was there not to love!

My own conversion on the road to marriage equality, for many years, was one foot in, one foot out. While I had been an activist for most of my lesbian life, I wasn't sure that this was where I wanted to direct my activism and there were times when I was sure it wasn't. I listened to arguments and debates for and against marriage and civil partnership when developing my own position. By the time I became co-ordinator of LINC, my mind was clear and I was committed to playing my part in a referendum campaign. It had come down to two things for me. Firstly, it was an equality issue; the LGBT community was deprived of a right that was only available to the heterosexual majority. This excluded a large minority in society, being both discriminatory and unjust in the process.

Secondly, while the argument was made that the referendum had nothing to do with children, I believed it had everything to do with them. It was about two different groupings of children; the LGB children and the young people who were beginning to realise they were different to their classmates, that they were gay or lesbian and struggling to come to terms with that because of how they would be viewed by society, fearful of being bullied and the reaction of their families and society. Also, those who had come out and knew that opportunities for them were not equal, that they were treated as second-class citizens. The success of the referendum was essential for them whether they ever decided to marry in the future or not, as it was essential that another generation would not grow up feeling the rejection that had been part of many of our lives. To that other group of children, those children of LGBT couples, being told that your family is not a family; your mother is not really your mother. Parenting is about giving a child love, warmth, care and protection and the ability to provide that is not gender-specific. The success of the referendum would send a loud message of acceptance and equality to those children and their families.

As for all successful campaigns, much of the work is developed prior to any public visibility. This was also the situation for the grouping that would go on to form Yes Equality Cork. Many hours were spent meeting and discussing the future campaign. The committee was made up of LGBT and straight, male and female, young and not so young, activists, seasoned campaigners and those who had never campaigned before. What was clear was that everyone was totally committed to one goal and that was inspiring. Ah but now I'm starting to tell the story of Yes Equality Cork and that's a story for another day!

Anthony Kinahan

Marriage Equality
Champion Volunteers

Saturday, 17 February 2007 was a crisp clear spring day, and Barry and I were nervous. We hadn't really been affectionate in front of our family and friends before, and now … we were going to have to kiss and dance in front of them. It preoccupied our minds. That day, Barry and I were joined as civil partners in Belfast City Hall.

We were thrilled.

We thought ourselves lucky that we were able to make such a public declaration, because when we initially got engaged in 2004, there was no such thing as civil partnerships … never mind the opportunity of being able to avail of one just up the road from where we lived. We were delighted that, even if it wasn't our home country, at least in some jurisdiction we were recognised as a couple of some sort.

The day went perfectly and when it came down to it, we didn't mind kissing and dancing in front of people, as they were all there to support us. Barry and I were making this commitment to each other eight years after we first got together. We met through friends of friends. The Dundalk Outcomers ran a once-a-month gay disco in a function room in the Westcourt Hotel in Drogheda. I went with my best friend and it was our first LGBT social night. We were running late. Barry was there on his own waiting for us. It was his first LGBT social night too and he was feeling really awkward, standing in a dark corner afraid of being spotted by the wrong person. When we didn't turn up, he left. He stopped to tie his shoelace.

We came walking down the street and caught him before he went home. We went back to the disco. Later in the night, I asked Barry out to dance and that was it … it just felt right. That was February 1999. And all because Barry stopped to tie his shoelace.

In 2004, after living together for a couple of years, I realised that I didn't see my future without Barry. I decided to propose to him. He said yes. There was no civil partnership then, so we were making a life commitment to each other. It meant a lot to us.

Coming out is never easy, but we've been lucky. Our family and friends have never been anything but supportive of our relationship. We have never been treated any differently by them. Our nieces and nephews have grown up never knowing anything different. It's just natural to them. We have never hidden our relationship, but, in the early years we certainly wouldn't have been shouting about it from the rooftops. We had to make our adjustments to our new life. We became accustomed to not walking down the street hand in hand, or kissing in public. We came to the grim acceptance that because we were gay, we'd have to be careful in public. We'd never be able to have kids. We'd never be able to marry. We'd never be considered a 'real family'.

This sober deprecation of yourself certainly takes its psychological effect. As an LGBT person in Ireland, one is forced to accept that society ranks one as second-class, at best, and subversive at worst. Both Barry and I have suffered from depression at one stage or another, in part because of the effect this has on your self-esteem.

We decided to move to London in the autumn of 2007. By that stage, civil partnerships were accessible through the UK, so, we decided to enter into a civil partnership in Belfast before making the move to London.

While in London, we got a taste of what it was like to live in a country where our relationship was legally recognised. The simple things like filling out forms and being able to tick the civil partnership box were unspeakably self-affirming. In London, other possibilities opened up to us. At that time in the UK, couples in a civil partnership were eligible to apply to be adoptive parents. We've always been quite paternal and we were finally able to consider that having a family of our own might be in our future after all. We made some tentative enquiries and attended some meetings. However, in early 2010, reality was dawning on us. While we were eligible to apply to adopt, it would take us a couple of years to get our finances in order before we could even consider applying. It was also about this time that we were feeling homesick and wanted to move back to our family and friends in Ireland.

So we were faced with a dilemma. We could stay in London for the long haul and hopefully adopt at some stage, or go back to Ireland to be with our family and friends, but, back to a country where our relationship wasn't recognised, giving up our eligibility to adopt.

With aching souls, we moved back to Ireland in March 2010. The lack of opportunity to parent became somewhat of a sore point for us. We couldn't talk about it with each other. It was too raw. It became taboo.

Eventually, we accepted the fact that we were home. Civil partnership in Ireland was to be enacted in the following January, but it wasn't enough. Still only married couples and single people could apply to adopt. We became convinced of the fact that if we wanted equal rights, we were going to have to fight for them. So fight we did!

After doing some research, we got in touch with the Marriage Equality (ME) organisation. We marched with them for the first time in Pride 2010. It snowballed from there. We marched with them in every Pride and every subsequent March for Marriage. We became involved in the 'Out To Your TD' campaign. We lobbied all the Louth candidates for the 2011 general election, making sure they all knew that marriage equality was an issue that meant something to people in Louth. It was slow progress, but eventually over the years we became quite well known to our local elected representatives.

Barry Gardiner (*left*) and Anthony Kinahan at Dublin Pride, July 2011.

Barry Gardiner *(left)*, Dawn Quinn and Anthony Kinahan celebrate the Constitutional Convention results, April 2013.

As an actor, I am not afraid of public speaking, so I knew I had a specific skill that that could help the campaign. The campaign was cultivating personal stories to make the abstract idea of marriage equality a more personal and concrete issue to which people could relate – putting faces to the cause.

I suggested to Barry that we might make ourselves available as media representatives to the campaign, so we would be some of the voices creating visibility about the issue. Barry was reluctant. He wasn't adept at public speaking and he certainly wouldn't have been used to being 'out there' with our relationship. Also, Barry was concerned that our visibility as a gay couple might have adverse consequences for his job as a Special Needs Assistant in a secondary school. With a bit of coaxing, Barry pushed himself out of his comfort zone and agreed to my suggestion. Through ME, we received media training and we have been so glad we did. We are one of the lucky LGBT couples with a solid, supportive foundation of family and friends and we felt we were safe and secure enough to be public about our relationship without fearing negative fallout from our nearest and dearest. We were able to tell our personal story about what marriage equality would mean to us in the media, which personalised the issue for some undecideds or previously uninformed people.

We started doing radio and print interviews, mostly in the local area in Louth. At the same time, we were still lobbying our local elected representatives and attending as many ME events as we could. After an 'Out To Your TD' seminar held by ME in the National Library during Pride Week 2012, Barry and I had an idea. While the ME campaign was a national campaign, it was difficult to make people outside of Dublin realise that this issue was important to couples in their local community. We suggested to ME HQ that we wanted to set up a regional ME group in Louth to create awareness about the campaign in our community and provide information to local supportive activists. In July 2012, with the support of ME HQ, and our friend Rachel Matthews-McKay, Marriage Equality Louth was born – the first regional group of its kind. We informed our local elected representatives and with the help of Dundalk Outcomers, we arranged information nights about how people could get involved in the campaign at the local level. In October 2012, ME Louth helped local Sinn Féin councillors to secure a motion of support for ME from Louth County Council. With social media, we were able to establish a growing local group of interested activists.

It was during this time that a shift occurred in our minds about parenting. Before now, we had just been thinking about having a child to call our own, because *we wanted* to parent. Eventually, we considered the idea of becoming foster parents. It became less about what we wanted and more about the fact that we had space in our lives and space in our homes for a child who needed it. We made some investigations and decided to apply to be foster carers in January 2012. After a very thorough application process, Barry and I were approved as the first same-sex foster carers in Louth in November 2012. We have had a number of placements through our doors over the years, which has given us a lot of experience, and we have learned a lot from these young people. However, from a civil rights perspective, the contradiction inherent in our position as foster carers was frustrating. The law allowed us to be foster carers and to temporarily care for vulnerable children, but it didn't allow us as a couple to apply to adopt them. The law was not in the best interest of any of the parties involved. By this stage, we weren't just involved in the campaign so we could have the right to apply to adopt as a couple. While that had been our initial impetus to get involved, we were very much involved now on the principle of equal rights and justice.

We continued to be involved in media interviews, telling our personal story about how marriage equality would change our lives. Pieces on us appeared in *The Irish Times* and the *Irish Independent*, as well as appearances on the Ray D'Arcy radio show and various local radio and print pieces. We also started volunteering on the telephones in ME HQ (which was not always easy at times due to us living in Drogheda). We were helping to encourage supporters to contact their local elected representatives. We also volunteered for the *Yes to*

Love video that was to be shown at the Constitutional Convention about marriage equality. We were delighted to be part of this and the video was very effective at the Convention. The Constitutional Convention voted 79 per cent in favour of holding a referendum on marriage equality. We were just thrilled to have been a little part of this.

We also were happy to have our experiences included in different academic studies about the fight for equality in Ireland. One of the most significant pieces of research we were included in was an LGBT Parenting study by Iris Elliott 'Voices of Children'. This was launched in January 2014, with figures such as Alan Shatter, TD and Minister for Justice, and Geoffrey Shannon, Chairman of the Adoption Authority and Special Rapporteur on Children, in attendance. It was here the bourgeoning Children and Family Relationships Bill was outlined in detail by Minister Shatter. I was honoured to be asked to speak at the conference about my experiences of being a gay parent in Ireland. As a result of this, RTÉ News also did a feature on us and we were part of a panel for *Morning Edition* on RTÉ.

We submitted a chapter for the book *To Have and To Hold: Stories & Reflections from LGBT people, their families & friends* (editors Patricia Devlin and Brian Glennon), which was published in April 2015. This chapter was all about how being second-class in the eyes of the law affected us, and what marriage equality would mean to us.

We also had our first experience of canvassing when we helped a 'Pledge to Vote' drive with the then formative Yes Equality Team at Electric Picnic 2014. That was a really positive experience and lots of fun. In the run-up to the referendum in 2015, local media interest intensified and we did a number of interviews for local papers and radio.

Yes Equality Louth volunteers and talliers on results day at the Louth count centre, Dundalk, 23 May 2015.

Karl Hayden *(right)* chats with An Taoiseach Enda Kenny, with Claire Farrell in the background, Grafton Street, Dublin, May 2015.

In September 2014, ME Louth, along with Dundalk Outcomers, had our first regional meeting with Yes Equality in preparation for the referendum campaign. Local Equality groups started popping up all around the country. We had a head start, with ME Louth having been established for a couple of years already. But nothing could prepare us for what was to come!

From January 2015, the campaign became very full-on. We attended national meetings. We boosted our social media presence in an attempt to gather more supporters. We started our local 'Register to Vote' drive. We started our fundraising efforts.

In March 2015, ME Louth partnered with Dundalk Outcomers to form Yes Equality Louth. We knew canvassing (as well as all the other madness) was coming down the line … and even though we tried to prepare ourselves for it, nothing compared to being out there and doing it. The atmosphere in the whole country became stifling. Every time we turned on the TV we had a panel of people discussing our future. No campaigners were telling the country how we shouldn't be able to marry or, in more extreme circumstances, how we shouldn't be parents. It felt the discussion in the media was largely dictated by the irrational sensationalism of the No side with the debates rarely sticking to the actual question that the nation was going to be asked on 22 May.

I also remember my first day going to Dublin after the No posters had come out. It caught my breath. Every second lamp post from Drumcondra down to Dorset Street in Dublin had a No poster on it, telling people that 'Two Men Can't Replace a Mother's Love'. That felt really overwhelming and oppressive.

Meanwhile, Barry and I were co-ordinating Yes Equality Louth. We were organising events and trying to get canvassers trained in both Dundalk and Drogheda. It was a lot of hard graft. Most days it would mean the whole day on the laptop, before going out canvassing that evening, then coming home and posting items of interest out on social media at night, while also trying to work and parent and have a life at the same time. We hosted the Yes Bus on its first day of operation and we ran a successful 'I'm Voting Yes. Ask Me Why' event on 6 May in D'Vine restaurant in Drogheda, chaired by John Hamill from Vennetics. We had speakers at Yes Equality Louth group from all different walks of life and perspectives, though the audience took full advantage of the open mic. It was well attended by local politicians, which helped with the publicity.

Canvassing was a unique and surreal experience. The majority of us had never canvassed before. Barry and I were for a long time well versed in the issues of marriage equality; however, we had to make sure the whole canvassing team we gathered were on the same page. I attended the Canvassing Training Sessions organised by Yes Equality with Senator Averil Power and learned a lot of useful techniques that we passed on to our canvassers. On 16 April 2015, we started our first door-to-door canvassing in Drogheda. It was an exhilarating experience.

On the whole, we received overwhelming positivity from voters through our canvassing. It was this positivity that kept us going through the tough times. Our canvassing figures were very representative of the final result. On average, about two out of every three doors we went to were a hard Yes, which was always very encouraging to hear, and a relief!

Through the canvassing, we learned not to judge a book by its cover. There were a number of occasions, I would knock on a door and an elderly woman would answer. I would spot the crucifix on the wall and my heart would sink, expecting a No. But then, the lovely woman would surprise me with 'Of course, I'll be voting Yes, sure love is love. Why would I get in the way', or other comments like that. These surprises would melt my heart and send me skipping down the road.

There would also be that rare moment where you would turn a hard No voter into a Yes vote and that was always a great feeling. Those situations would often be perfect examples of how personal stories and putting a face on an abstract issue really swung it for us. After hearing our personal stories, people would rethink their whole opinion. Times like that were very heartening.

Yes Bus in Co. Louth, May 2015.

However, the most extreme and dramatic moments that are rooted in my memory are negative moments, unfortunately. Barry and I have been very lucky. In all the sixteen years we had been together, we never really experienced any direct homophobia (we are now together nearly eighteen years!). We naively thought that homophobia may not really exist in Drogheda. We were wrong. During the campaign, we were told that we were 'sick and wrong' and we should be ashamed of ourselves; we've been called 'abominations' and 'faggots'; we've been run off property; we've been called 'disgusting and offensive people'; we've been told 'No! Ye have enough [rights] already. Marriage, you're not having it.' Some of these incidences shook us and rattled our sense of ourselves.

Some people took the opportunity to offload on us. To some people, the idea of me being able to marry my partner and have equal rights was so upsetting and distressing that they would lose the run of themselves. I did not think these people *really* existed in real life and, if they did, I didn't think they lived in my town. We were exhausted from the whole campaign, but negative instances like this really tired us out. Barry couldn't face canvassing for about a week after one particularly negative experience. We were left hardened and on high alert to protect ourselves against the next unforeseen onslaught. Furthermore, as we got nearer to the voting day, some voters were becoming increasingly confused and frustrated by the misdirections of the No side and were irate with referendum fatigue. By the week of the referendum, I had pretty much had my fill of people telling me, 'No, you can't marry the love of your life.' Frankly, I don't think I could have taken it for much longer.

A couple of weeks before the referendum, we got my parents to do a #VoteWithUs video, which was very well received. The next week, Barry and I did our own #VoteWithUs video. We found this quite emotional and cathartic.

Finally, 22 May arrived. We decided to do a silent canvass on the day. We had Yes Equality posters as sandwich boards and we stood on the three main bridges in Drogheda. We got lots of beeps of support. However, we did get the odd bit of abuse. Drive-by homophobia! (People can be very brave when they're in their cars.) I was on my own at one stage and I got one guy who told me to 'jump in the river'.

Later, when I was on my own again, I got this guy who stopped in a black pick-up (with his daughter in the back seat) and told me how 'sick and wrong' we 'faggots' were and that the thought of us having kids was 'disgusting' – yet there he was, cursing and being abusive to somebody with his daughter in the back seat. Later, when I was with a middle-aged female volunteer, the same guy pulled up and told her to suck his cock (he still had his daughter in the back seat). The sad and disgusting irony! We finished up the canvass that evening and then we hit the social media, pushing people to get out to vote. Then, at 10 pm, we sat there, at the laptop staring at the screen, incredulous that there was nothing left to do. Everything that could have been done was done. We had done our best.

We didn't know what to do with ourselves. It was in the hands of the gods now.

After a fitful night's sleep, we got up early and went to the Dundalk Count Centre. Within forty-five minutes of the boxes being opened, we had a clear indication that Yes was going to win. It was surreal. Everything we had fought so hard for, for years, was now coming to fruition. But we were so tired and so focused on what we were doing that it didn't really sink in until later in the day. We were so happy and relieved that it went through. We partied well into the night with our Yes Equality Louth crew. It was very emotional and rewarding.

For us, *the* most positive thing to have come out of the whole struggle and campaign is that we were lucky enough to make some lifelong friends. Between the ME organisation and the Yes Equality Louth group, we have met some truly inspiring people who give us faith in humanity. To see people, young and old, straight and gay, political and non-political, stand up for what they believe in, and do something to try and make their corner of the world a better place, was truly a beautiful and moving thing to behold.

Anthony Kinahan *(left)* and Barry Gardiner appear in the *Yes to Love* video created by Marriage Equality Board member Linda Cullen, and shown at the Constitutional Convention, April 2013.

After the vote, we didn't know what to do with ourselves. We had spent so much time and energy on the campaign that when it was all over we were a little bit lost. We got back to working and parenting and having a life. We partied at Pride in Dublin and Dundalk. We attended the Seanad on the last day of the Marriage Bill passing the Houses of the Oireachtas; we were interviewed by RTÉ News on that occasion, also. We were commended by the Mayor of Drogheda with an award for our work on the ME campaign, both locally and nationally. Then we started preparations for our wedding – what this whole fight was about.

Saturday, 16 April 2016 was a crisp clear spring day, and Barry and I were nervous. We weren't nervous about kissing or dancing in front of anybody – those times were long gone. We were nervous that the day would run smoothly. We were nervous that all the people we had invited who'd helped us get here would have a good time. We were nervously excited that after all this time, after all the fighting for it, we were finally going to be able to make this declaration of love and commitment in our home country. That night, Barry and I were married in a humanist ceremony. It went perfectly. It was the happiest night of our lives. We are proud. We are finally equal!

Carol Armstrong

14

Leading the Marriage Equality Volunteer Team

There are so many wonderful causes, political, charitable and community-based: the list is as long as it is varied. Sometimes it can be difficult to decide where to give your time and energy but in 2008, my choice was clear. I had spent a few years working with Dublin Pride but wanted a new challenge. Pride is more a celebration of LGBT culture than anything else nowadays, but originally it was a political movement. These marches through city streets served as demonstrations for empowerment in both social and political change. For me, this led to thinking about what I could do to create change within Ireland.

At that time, Norway had passed a Marriage Bill, Nepal too, Barack Obama had just labelled Proposition 8 in California as 'unnecessary' and it seemed Marriage Equality (ME) was really starting to gain a foothold in people's consciousness. February 2008 saw our very own ME group in Ireland formed and so I decided that was the place for me.

The first person I met in the Baggot Street offices was Dawn Quinn, officially the team administrator but it quickly became clear that Dawn did about a million different things a minute and was very passionate about the role volunteers played in the 'Out To Your TD' campaign. This campaign involved calling ME supporters and asking them if they'd be willing to visit their local TD (member of parliament) to discuss why the issue of marriage equality was important to them. I signed on and was on the phones the very next week. I was extremely nervous about calling people at first. It's an intimidating prospect to pick up the phone and try to talk to strangers about what they can do to bring about significant change. The first thing I noticed was how open and motivated our supporters were, and this gave me the confidence I needed to move forward.

I quickly learned that our supporters really wanted to talk to their TDs but were intimidated by the process. A lot of our work was in facilitating them by answering questions so that they felt they had the necessary tools to start that conversation. I, of course, contacted my own TDs and had a wonderful experience when I went to the Dáil to see John Lyons. He was called to the chamber for a vote during my visit and he kindly invited me to watch from the public gallery as the Taoiseach spoke on the issue of the Magdalene Laundries. Afterwards we had a great conversation and I knew that the TD campaign was going to bear fruit if we, the volunteers, could stay motivated and keep going.

What we asked our supporters to speak to their TDs about, changed over the years. Initially, we hoped to prevent a two-tier system of relationship recognition, with the proposed introduction of civil partnership. After that bill passed, we looked to encourage our supporters to speak to their representatives who were on the Constitutional Convention, to make sure they supported full marriage rights and then, as time passed, we were eventually asking supporters to vote Yes to marriage themselves at the referendum and to encourage their loved ones to do the same. At each and every step I was deeply moved by the support and the desire for change I encountered.

Some supporters reported back that the TD they spoke to hadn't put much thought into marriage equality; some said their TD was amazed it was important to so many people. It became very clear that in time we could see TDs change their outlook on the issue and this was critical to moving the campaign forward. With each visit came a deeper understanding for TDs of the importance of this issue and with that we knew we could eventually bring about change. The telephone conversations of the 'Out To Your TD' campaign were the opening conversations for the strategy that led to the win in May 2015.

ME moved offices to Outhouse in Capel Street and, as this office was bigger, the group of volunteers expanded and changed and new people brought with them even more motivation and enthusiasm. Every volunteer made a difference in helping our supporters get our messages across to the government and to their own families and friends. I had the pleasure of meeting new people: volunteers like Laura Sheehan and Michelle Malone had been there even longer than I had, and others joined to bring their own unique skills set; it was a fun office!

Celebrating after the Constitutional Convention, April 2013, at the Panti Bar, Dublin Marriage Equality volunteers *(from left)* Barry Gardiner, Anthony Kinahan, Michelle Malone, Paul Dowling, Carol Armstrong and Laura Sheehan.

Marching for marriage at the 2012 LGBT Noise march were *(from left)* Danielle Thompson, long time Marriage Equality Volunteer Barbara Hughes, Suzy Falvey, Grainne Sheridan and Roisin Farrell, August 2012.

Running for Marriage Equality. *From left*: Kirsten Killoran, Carol Armstrong and Andrea Bonnie, 2011.

On being invited to join the Board of ME with the volunteer perspective, I met and spoke to people at various events like Family Days and I attended the Ard Fheisenna of many political parties over the years, constantly having my own mind opened by all the different viewpoints and wonderful conversations that arise when you are surrounded by well-informed and curious minds.

We took part in many of the LGBT Noise-organised Marches for Marriage and I remember during Pride 2011 we were walking with our ME banner when the news came through that New York had signed their Marriage Equality Bill into law. It was a wonderful moment to share it with our entire community.

We had some inspirational evenings where we got all the volunteers together and heard from people such as Senator Katherine Zappone, and her wife, Ann Louise Gilligan. There was also a memorable evening with Freedom To Marry president Evan Wolfson. Volunteers asked questions about where Evan felt the US got things right and where they felt they could improve. We listened eagerly for lessons for the Irish case. All of these evenings made us feel that we had the tools and the will to bring about change in Ireland and it was inspiring to be a part of it.

Carol Armstrong *(foreground)* with other Yes Equality volunteers including *(from left)* Jeanne McDonagh, John Lyons TD, Ross Golden-Bannon and Ger Philpott at the Yes HQ, 21 May 2015.

Every year we had to keep an eye on fundraising, but it was good fun. People ran marathons, others had cake sales, we had a large, annual raffle and volunteers tried to get supporters to sell tickets, as well as selling as many tickets as we could ourselves. My mother won first prize once and we went to New York; to this day I think that was her favourite thing about my volunteering!

The year 2012 saw Barack Obama make his famous evolution quote, ultimately saying, 'I think same-sex couples should be able to get married', as well as Proposition 8 finally being put to bed; progress was being made overseas, and in 2013, ME made our submission to the Constitutional Convention. This meant the volunteers talking to people about making sure all of the TDs and Senators in that room in the Grand Hotel in Malahide were informed. This was incredibly motivational and our supporters were never so enthused about getting involved; volunteers could point to the rest of the world and ask people if they wanted Ireland to be part of this wonderful forward momentum, and supporters responded. You could feel the movement shift and we knew that this was our chance.

Once the referendum was called for May 2015, ME joined forces with the Gay & Lesbian Equality Network (GLEN) and the Irish Council for Civil Liberties (ICCL) to became Yes

Equality, and we knew our goal was coming closer. I'll never forget leaving work to go to lunch with my friends and walking through the streets of Dublin in the weeks leading up to the vote. Everywhere I looked I could see rainbow flags in shop windows, posters of support and nearly every passer-by was wearing a Yes badge. It was magnificent to know that what we were involved with for so long was now firmly in the public consciousness and it is one of the greatest examples of democracy in action that I have ever witnessed. It became clear that a small group of people can change the political and social landscape and that the public will get behind an issue, if people are willing to give them a platform to do so.

Canvassing houses and speaking to people on their doorsteps, I was nervous about getting bad reactions but the worst I got was a very polite 'Go away'. Most people were enthusiastic in their support and some even shed a tear while relating the story of their gay son or lesbian sister. I never felt so proud to be Irish or as optimistic about society as I did then.

On polling day I was in the Yes Equality Office calling supporters to remind them every vote counts, when people started to talk about the #hometovote twitter sensation. It was incredible; people tweeting pictures of themselves at airports and on ferries on their way home to vote. All the volunteers in the office were overjoyed and emotional and the feeling was one of cautious optimism.

Marriage Equality with LGBT Noise outside Dáil Éireann, August 2014.

I was in the RDS in Dublin on 23 May to see the ballet boxes emptied and the counting begin and it was obvious within a very short space of time that we had won. All of those evenings in the ME offices after work were worth it and I celebrated with my fellow volunteers, the people who had spent years on the phones bringing us to this point. It was a humbling experience and one I will never forget.

It was a strange feeling to wake up the next day and know the campaign was over. We had done it but now there was a strange void left behind. I remember going into work the next Monday and everyone congratulating me but then getting on with their normal day. I wanted to shout that it wasn't a normal day, that everything had changed for the better, that we had done it. As a single person I suppose I also felt a little removed from it; most of the other volunteers had their weddings to arrange but I could happily settle for knowing Ireland is a fairer and more just society thanks to what we achieved.

When I look back on volunteering with ME, the first thing I feel is happiness at all the people I spent time with and got to know. Then I am overcome with pride at playing a small role in changing the Constitution of Ireland. We might be a small country but we are one with a deep sense of fairness, and I think that is what won out in the end.

Darina Brennan

15

Raising Funds for Marriage Equality

I was standing at the side of the stage when the singing waiters broke into the most beautiful operatic singing. I looked over at Gráinne Healy and Katherine Zappone, who were both standing observing 350 people waving their linen napkins and singing 'Ireland's Call' at the top of their voices, opera-style: 'Ireland, Ireland together standing tall, shoulder to shoulder we'll answer Ireland's call.'

I walked over to them both, all three of us had tears welling in our eyes, we had a hug, looked up and felt the emotion in the room, and for a few very brief seconds we dared hope that we might just get this marriage equality over the line. The date was 6 February 2015, and 22 May was looming fast. It was coming to the end of a very challenging few years – a personal struggle that would see me, with the help and support of amazing friends, family, and business colleagues, raise a significant amount of money for Marriage Equality (ME).

It all started back in early 2008; my good friend Andrew Hyland (later Co-Director of ME) sold me the dream of equal marriage rights. At that stage, civil partnership was already on the government's agenda. I thought, 'Well this is good enough for us, we will never get full marriage rights in my lifetime'. I debated it in my head and with friends and family for several months and in the end decided, 'Why should I settle for second best?' Civil partnership? I wanted to marry my partner just like my parents, siblings and friends. My question was, why are people cherry-picking my civil rights? Why are LGBT people being treated completely different in the eyes of the law? The choice for me was simple in the end. I didn't want to get civil-partnered, I wanted to marry the person I love, with all the protections and rights that it brings.

The release of the ME video *Sinead's Hand* in August 2009 was a pivotal moment for me. It spurred many of us on our journey with the campaign. The challenge ahead was really mirrored in that video, in that we were literally going to have to knock on every door in Ireland to ask permission for the right to marry the person we love. It seemed crazy but it was very true. To date that video has received over 668,400 hits on YouTube. With an army of volunteers, we knocked on all those doors and thankfully the rest is now history. We did it. We achieved marriage equality in Ireland.

I got directly involved with ME in 2008, initially helping with fundraising lunches in Fire Restaurant.[1] I then became a volunteer on the ME phone lines, working with our database to get our supporters to start lobbying their local TDs to get the marriage equality issue on the political agenda, in the first instance. Cold-calling was probably my worst nightmare, I was nervous and shy. I was probably the worst volunteer on the phones!

Darina Brennan behind the scenes, 'Art for Marriage Equality', November 2011.

Every Tuesday evening a team of us got together in a cramped little office on Baggot Street, using our small network of supporters to ask their local TDs to pledge their support. Ireland was at the beginning of the global economic meltdown: marriage equality was not an issue that concerned the nation at that point in time. People were too busy worrying about the collapsed economy and how it was affecting their daily lives. It was our job to raise people's consciousness to the unfairness of our situation, and it was also vital that we kept it as a live issue in the minds of our legislators.

I was honoured to be asked to join the Board of ME to head up the fundraising side of the campaign. I was much more comfortable with this role, as over the years, working in hospitality, I had built up a lot of relevant contacts and supporters. I generally work fifty to sixty hours a week, also, which meant burning the midnight oil for as long as this was going to take.

We initially started with a couple of fundraising lunches in Fire Restaurant, where I was then Executive Head Chef. These were quite small to begin with, mainly supported by our core group. Creating awareness and building some momentum was really our main goal then, years before we knew there would be a referendum on the issue!

My first fundraising venture was organising 'Art for Marriage Equality'. The idea was to approach Irish artists and ask them to donate a piece for a fundraising auction. A small group of us met on Monday nights in Outhouse on Capel Street in Dublin, where ME had offices for a time, to plan and strategise. We started with nothing except high aspirations and a determination to make it work. Artists Steven Mannion-Farrell, Will St Ledger and Jim Fitzpatrick, and sculptor Ann Meldon-Hugh, were first to lend their support in donating their work. Claire Noon, the ceramicist, not only donated a beautiful piece, she also volunteered to hang and present all the work when we found a suitable venue for the auction. Steven Mannion explained why he supported the event and got involved:

> When my husband and I got married, we had to travel to Canada to do it. I didn't believe that civil partnership was an option, because Eamon asked me to marry him, he didn't ask me to civil partner him! When I said I wanted to be with him for the rest of my life, I didn't mean as a legally recognised, cohabiting, same-sex, civil partner – I meant as his husband. That's why my husband and I, our family and friends supported Marriage Equality and the team who worked so tirelessly to achieve it.

Ann Meldon-Hugh added:

> I believe this is an extremely important cause to support. All Irish people should be treated as equal, and all Irish families and children should be given equal rights. Families, human

relationships and the interactions of the individual with the environment around them is central to much of my work, so it seems fitting that I should give a piece to a cause that works to improve and stabilise the Irish legal environment for the families of gay and lesbian people in Ireland.

The initial generosity was quickly followed by others: Pauline Bewick (donation) Terry Bradley (donation) Gabhann Dunne, Mary Burke, Diane Copperwhite, Mark P. Cullen, Hugh Fitzgerald Ryan, Loretto Cooney, Annmarie Greevy, Aine Macken, Odile Hendricks, Clinton Kirkpatrick, Marc Matthews, Sarah K. Ryan, Claudette Mathews, Maria Magee, Louise Walsh, Selma Cormack, Dave Daly, Stephen Cullen, Bernie Masterson and Rachel Mathews-McKay. Milliner Tootsie Royale created a stunning 'Just Love' head piece, reflecting the 'Just Love' theme then adopted by ME to show that the right to marry was about the right to have love recognised.

Eamon O'Connor, Director of Adams Auctioneers, kindly offered his time and services to run the auction. I was desperately trying to find a venue that would allow us to hang work on the walls and have an auction. It needed to be a city-centre venue. I was feeling completely out of my depth and comfort zone at this stage; I wasn't sure I could 'pull this off' and not let everyone down. Getting a venue was easy enough but getting permission to hang pieces on walls was another matter.

Padraic O'Kane, Managing Director of Fire Restaurant and Venue, came to my rescue, and we managed to secure premises. A stunning Georgian House steeped in history on St Stephen's Green was an ideal location and had also been used for previous art auctions, and so hanging work was not an issue, thankfully! My suppliers came up trumps and kindly donated red and white wine, glasses and cheese for the event. My family and friends and ME staff and their partners jumped in and poured wine, took coats and sold raffle tickets.

It took us twelve hours of long hard slog to hang, label and price the pieces. We got some excellent publicity in the lead up to the event; we were mentioned, with pictures, in *The Irish Times*, *Sunday Independent*, *Irish Independent*, national magazines and online. Radio interviews were conducted and interviews and quotes from some of our amazing artists followed.

The pieces were on display for two days in advance of auction night in late November 2011. The nerves were palpable, it suddenly occurred to me that we might not sell all of this beautiful work, as we only had about ninety guests attending on the night. But we sold every single piece. Some guests bought two! It was a huge relief for everyone and we were on a roll. I felt a ground swell of support – suddenly anything seemed possible for ME.

Publicity shot for 'Art for Marriage Equality', St Stephen's Green, Dublin, November 2011.

I took a break after the auction from ME, as it was coming into Christmas and work was pretty hectic. Spring 2012 came upon us very quickly and I had to come up with the next fundraiser idea. Confidence was high after the auction. As Board members, we were constantly discussing ways to engage the public and get as many 'celebrities' and well-known faces to lend us their support. I managed to secure the Round Room at the Mansion House, the perfect place to host an event. I had a venue but no solid plan. I put the feelers out about possibly holding a concert of some description and 'Just Love', a gig for marriage equality, was born. Again, business colleagues came to the rescue, and donated their time and expertise free of charge. We adopted the same principal as the art auction: get as much publicity as possible, and raise as much money as possible. Royseven, The Heathers, Brian Kennedy, X Factor boy band Element, and the Dublin Gospel Choir were the first acts to confirm their involvement, followed quickly by Gloria Choir, This Club, Bitches with Wolves, Shaz Oye, Tadgh Cooke and a host of DJs spinning away while the band changeovers were happening.

We received excellent print and social media coverage in the run up to the event. All the major radio stations got behind us. The place was packed! This is what some of the acts had to say about getting involved with the gig. Singer and *Voice of Ireland* judge Brian Kennedy: 'I am a supporter of Marriage Equality, because the clue is in the title. Civil partnership is anything but equal and a loving couple, be it two women or two men deserve the right to marry if they wish. It's a basic human right as far as I'm concerned.' Lead singer of Royseven, Paul Walsh: 'At its core it must be remembered that the Marriage Equality movement is about the importance of living in a world where all humans are considered equal. We are all different, so let's treat each other the same.'

We rocked, danced and sang the night away. We were starting to really build momentum and support. Worthy of a special mention is Irish supreme musical legend Finbar Furey, who was not available to perform on the night, but donated his prize tin whistle (that he had from the age of fourteen) and a letter of support for us to auction. Finbar immediately backed our campaign without question, well before most others got on board. This meant a huge amount to us because in the past, ME had found it hard to get people with a public profile to support the cause.

Long-time Marriage Equality supporters Karl Broderick *(left)*, Brian Kennedy and Alan Hughes pose for 'Just Love', November 2012.

Brian Kennedy at the Marriage Equality tent at Electric Picnic, August 2014.

The overwhelmingly positive Constitutional Convention result baked into a cake by Darina Brennan and her team at Fire Restaurant, 2013.

I took a career break in the second half of 2013. I had my first Christmas off that year ever. For the first time in twenty years I wasn't asleep at the Christmas dinner table. I started my current role with Dalata Hotel group in the beginning of 2014 in the Ballsbridge Hotel. Hotels are quite different to restaurants as they are a 24/7 business and operation. I knuckled down for the first six months and then started to plan the next event for ME.

I was thinking of late November 2014, but with a busy hotel and Christmas ahead, we took a risk and pushed back the date for the next fundraiser to early February 2015. We were running out of funding fast, just when we needed it most. I don't think any of us on the Board got a full night's sleep from February until May. To be frank, we were seriously desperate for finances, but obviously couldn't say that publicly. We all felt that we were on the cusp of something great and final, but we needed one last push, and again, funding was the key to spreading the message of equality and running a successful campaign. This was a very frustrating time as the No side contended that we were financed by Atlantic Philanthropies; in reality, that funding source had dried up two years before. I don't think the public really understood that ME was being run by a small army of volunteers on a tiny budget and a serious belief that we could change the status quo.

Des McCann, my new boss, was fantastic and also a great marriage equality supporter. Des kindly made the newly refurbished ballroom available for the next ME event. I settled on a fundraising lunch and auction on 6 February. I had suddenly turned into an event organiser! To be honest, I would prefer to be in a kitchen any day of the week. I got a great piece of advice from Des Doris from Alchemy Events: 'Darina, you have to be like a swan, graceful and unruffled on the surface, looking cool, calm and collected, no one will know that you are manically paddling below the surface!' That advice will stay with me in all aspects of my life forever.

At this point we were four months away from the vote. Suddenly we were popular! This was the first fundraising event for which I didn't have to beg, borrow and steal. The Marriage Equality Referendum was firmly in focus and finally on the agenda of many people. My only thought at the time was why we couldn't have had this level of support five years before. But that is how these things happen. Nothing in life, as we all know, is ever that simple. As I was writing the menu, I found it strange that I would not be in the kitchen for this event. I would, in fact, be working the floor. My kitchen team played a blinder pulling out all the stops and creating an incredible lunch. The nerves were beginning to get to me. My team politely asked me to remove myself from the kitchen as they were in control.

Eamon O'Connor did the honours again, spearheading the auction on the day. We managed to get some amazing prizes. Mary McKenna, Managing Director of Tour America, was a huge supporter of ME from the outset. Tour America donated a five-star, seven-day Caribbean cruise with flights for the auction. I found myself inundated with works of art (mainly personal donations from supporters), top-restaurant vouchers, ten pairs of sold-out

Karl Hayden takes some instructions from Darina Brennan at the hugely successful Marriage Equality fundraiser, Ballsbridge Hotel, Dublin, February 2015.

concert tickets, and a vast array of books signed by their authors. Marco Pierre White organised a meet-and-greet with himself, dinner and wine and a signed copy of his latest cookbook for auction. The response overall was incredible. Even on the day, people were handing me vouchers as they walked in. My boss Des rang around the hotels in the group and organised ten weekends away around the country. It allowed us not only to auction but also to offer great prizes for a raffle. Every single cent we could raise counted and mattered.

I got in touch with Alan Hughes and his now husband Karl Broderick. I had cooked for them for their civil partnership reception in Fire. As I listened to their speeches opening the event, the tears were streaming down my face with joy and sadness. Alan offered to MC for the day, Karl organised the singing waiters, an ice-cream van for later in the evening, and many prizes. Alan had actually tried to plug the gig for us but was silenced, not by TV3, but by the Broadcasting Authority of Ireland rules which meant that broadcast media were curtailed with how they mentioned either side in the referendum. It was very frustrating. Alan kept things moving along on the day, his sense of humour and wit entertaining everyone.

Brian Kennedy again selflessly gave up his time to sing after the lunch. Brian's voice in that ballroom on that day set the tone. We also had 'Mario and the singing waiters' who masqueraded as real staff throughout lunch service, they were so convincing that they had fooled my mother entirely. Mum kept calling me over to her table to complain about them and tell me the service from them was dreadful as they kept loudly dropping plates. I did not want to ruin the surprise for what happened next. They broke into the most tear-jerking aria that brought the house down.

It was a great day and we raised a large amount of money. We knew everyone in the room was going to keep this momentum going until 22 May 2015. We needed people to reach out to their friends and families and simply talk about why they were voting Yes.

As I have been writing this piece, going through the archives and my own notes, I still cannot believe it has happened. We are now equal citizens in this beloved country of ours. Initially, I honestly thought I would be in my twilight years when it finally would happen for us.

I have many, many people to thank for the help and support I was given over the years. My family, friends and work colleagues. To you all, a huge thank you. I could never in a million years have pulled those events off without you. Take a bow, all of you, as you have played your part in changing Irish history, Irish law, and have afforded all of our citizens an equal right to marry.

Finally, to Laura, the love of my life and the woman I get to walk down the aisle with this year (2017). Thank you.

Denise Charlton *(left)* and Paula Fagan

Our Families and Our Children for Marriage Equality

Letter to the Editor

The Irish Times

16 May 2015

Our son told us yesterday, that most people were voting Yes in the Marriage Referendum. He is eight years old. We asked how did he know? He replied with great confidence, how could they not vote Yes, because our family is the same as other families. We should be treated the same. Sensing a doubt in us, he assured us that all his class were voting Yes.

As parents we are full of awe of his confidence and belief in the Irish people. However, in darker moments, we as parents have a 'what if' dread. What if he is wrong? How will this shatter his positive perception of the world? How will we support him and his brother with the level of rejection that a No vote will bring? In our brighter moments, we think he is right, that Irish people will be persuaded, as we are, of the views of the children's organisations. Organisations that have worked with the children of Ireland for generations. The same organisations that advocate for children to feel cherished and valued, that they must be treated equally regardless of their sexual orientation or the sexual orientation of members of their household.

I hope my sons' faith in humanity will be confirmed and celebrated as people go to the polls on May 22nd. Children do matter so please vote Yes for their equality.

Yours etc.

Denise Charlton and Paula Fagan

'Missing Pieces' report 2011.

Dr Jane Pillinger and Paula Fagan prepare to present their research at the LGBT Parenting Conference, January 2014.

People fought the marriage referendum for many reasons. For some, it was about access to marriage and legal recognition of their relationships. For others, it was more for general recognition and acceptance. For us, it was about our children, our family, having the same rights as other families. So that our children would have the same constitutional protections and rights as other children. If marriage was a positive environment for children, why would a state withhold these advantages from our family?

At the first Marriage Equality (ME) fundraising lunch in November 2005, we had just found out that we were going to become parents, after many years of trying to conceive. We were ecstatic and realised that day that this was no longer about supporting others in getting legal recognition for their relationships, no longer about our partnership, but about the rights for our family and most importantly, our son (and later sons) to live in a country that treated them equally.

Many of those on the Board of ME had children, or were hoping to have children, and this was a huge motivating factor. To us it seemed very clear, that only access to the full constitutional protections of marriage would suffice, and this was what our children deserved. We were only too aware of the social and legal consequences resulting from the absence of essential rights for both ourselves and future generations of LGBT families. We wanted to argue for the benefits of legal recognition which would include legal stability, relationship stability, and security and reduced stigma for our children.

Marriage Equality's 'Voices of Children' launched by Moninne Griffith, Minister of State Ciaran Cuffe and Gráinne Healy, October, 2010.

The ME campaign was born in The Shanty, home to Katherine Zappone and Ann Louise Gilligan. Mark Solomon, from Freedom to Marry in the US, came to work with us as supporters of Katherine and Ann Louise's High Court case for marriage equality. We realised then that we needed to broaden the campaign to include other couples and families, in order to continue to win public hearts and minds and accelerate the campaign. Judge Dunne in her judgement in Katherine and Ann Louise's case had said that their right to marry was not a case of public interest, nor an issue for which she could see much demand. We needed to demonstrate otherwise. We had to encourage others to join with Katherine and Ann Louise in the fight for equal marriage.

Mark shared some of the strategies that had resulted in legal 'wins' in the US. He demonstrated the need for greater visibility for LGBT families. We realised the need to show how ordinary we are, with the same needs and challenges as other families, but different in relation to the rights and protections to which our children were entitled. We needed to encourage people to understand the impact of the lack of legal rights on our families and the positive impact that affording those rights would have.

Denise Charlton speaks from the Yes Bus, 20 May 2015.

Social-media image used to promote the 'Share the Love' fundraiser, devised by Denise Charlton and Paula Fagan, February 2015.

Dalkey canvas with the Yes Bus, 10 May 2015.

The first public opinion poll that ME commissioned found that those polled believed there were no issues for LGBT families; in fact, many thought there was already legal recognition for same-sex couples. The poll also highlighted that lesbians had limited visibility. This highlighted for us that LGBT families were invisible and the discussion around them theoretical and full of misinformation. There was no knowledge of the lack of rights LGBTI families experienced legally. Any limited knowledge of LGBTI families indicated that participants in the poll were uncomfortable with the possible 'harm' to children within the same-sex headed family structure. It was clear to us then, ready or not, that Ireland had a duty to our families and we needed to make them visible in order to persuade legislators to reflect this in future legislation; and that marriage equality would provide us with protections afforded to other families.

When ME conducted an additional poll some years later, and the question was posed in the context of children's rights, people answered positively that children should have a legal right to both parents – over 56 per cent of those surveyed said so. We knew very early on that we needed to make our families visible and communicate the impact of the legislative inequalities from a child's perspective. We were also pretty sure, from work on other campaigns and in other countries, that our children would become the battleground in any future referendum campaign on marriage equality.

With the introduction of civil partnership, no additional rights or recognition for our families and children was included. This was a fundamental omission in the civil partnership legislation, resulting in some leading political and legal figures entering into the debate on the need for legal rights for children of LGBT families. This included the then Ombudsman for Children, Emily Logan, who, on reviewing the proposed Civil Partnership Bill stated, 'The omission of robust protections for children of civil partners will have real consequences for the young people concerned and it is in their interests that the law reflect and provide for the reality of their lives.'[1]

These interventions succeeded in amplifying the debate; however, negative narrative by the opposing side about our families and children was a real challenge. We knew that to counter their unfounded or misinformed arguments that same-sex parenting was flawed, second-rate, or inherently damaging, we had to communicate widely about the reality of our lives. Our children were young, so we made the decision to be one of the public families in the debate. We participated in many media interviews, trying to add value to the debate and highlight the impact of lack of legal protections on our family. We wanted to provide real faces of families who would benefit by marriage equality. We did magazine photo shoots at home, and spoke on radio and TV about what marriage would mean to our family. We wanted our family to be respected and celebrated like other families. On one occasion, friends and family joined us for an hour-long programme, and again we appreciated their unwavering support. Our aim was to show that our families were not theoretical and that our children existed and were being reared in loving households, with support from extended family and friends around them. We knew from other campaigns of the need to tell our stories but to tell them strategically and effectively.

However, at that stage there was a still a crucial voice missing from the debate, one that would prove to be key throughout the campaign but particularly during the Constitutional Convention on Marriage Equality – the voices of the children from LGBTI families. Up to this point, we and other families had spoken out, but as our children were young, we were speaking on their behalf, from the perspective of being their parents. A key milestone for the campaign came through a conversation that one young adult called Evan Barry had with one of his mums. During this conversation, Evan described how he felt very angry and upset about the way his family was being portrayed in the media, reflecting that 'Everyone talks about us, but no one ASKS US!'

This conversation sparked ME to embark on a project to do exactly that. To ask adult children who were born to LGBT families about their experiences. Thus the 'Voices of Children' project was born; a groundbreaking report on a workshop which documented the experiences of young people growing up in Ireland with LGBT parents. 'Voices of Children' focused on the realities of children of LGBT parents in Ireland and the impact of the lack of legal protection for them and their families. It was a small-scale qualitative study, with a simple intent: to provide a space for children to meet, discuss and interpret their experiences, and identify ways in which Irish society could engage with them. The lack of legal and social recognition for their families emerged as a key issue, as did the young people's commitment to building networks of solidarity with other children of LGBT parents, and effecting social change so that future generations experienced a positive, secure future.

The report was a huge milestone in supporting the reality of children from LGBT families and their experiences. It highlighted the impact of the lack of legal recognition for their families and the State's role in affording those legal rights and protections. It concluded with highlighting the role of the law in combating homophobia. Young people who participated in the project took to the airwaves and were persuasive and generous in the sharing of their experiences and making LGBT families visible. The report and its findings was supported by a strong body of international responses which challenged the unfounded claims that LGBT people were unfit, and communicated this to the Irish State and into the public discourse. In the Constitutional Convention, tasked with deciding whether Ireland should have a referendum on extending marriage in the future, two of the presenters, Conor Pendergrast and Clare O'Connell, articulately argued (and persuaded many) on why their family should have legal rights and how they wanted their mums to be able to marry, like any other parents. They demonstrated that they were ordinary children, even though many of them proved to be extraordinary. Thus Evan Barry's question was answered and the answers were powerful when the children in same-sex-headed families spoke.

Leeson Street says Yes: offices of Gearóidín Charlton and Corry McMahon, May 2015.

ME then launched its 'Just Love'[2] campaign which included a ground-breaking report, 'Missing Pieces',[3] revealing 169 legal differences between civil marriage and civil partnership. The report highlighted the discrimination that same-sex couples experienced as a result of the differences between civil partnership and civil marriage. It was accompanied by a first-of-its-kind 48-sheet poster campaign, with posters depicting real couples and their children.[4] *Rory's Story*[5] was also part of the campaign, a video story[6] about a young boy discriminated against because of the sexuality of his parents, when one of his mums was battling a life-threatening illness. *Rory's Story* was made by Evan Barry's company, Fail Safe, another testimony to the contribution that 'Voices of Children' and the participants were making in the debate and for a positive outcome in the campaign.

At this point the children's organisations began to support the principle of children being treated equally and supported marriage equality as being good for children. A coalition of groups working with young people and children advocated strongly that this was an important right for children and young people who were LGBT themselves or who were from LGBT families. This was crucial in the debate. The groups advocated that while the Marriage Equality Referendum was solely focused on the issue of marriage and did not directly impact on parenting rights or responsibilities, that marriage equality was, and is, an issue that directly affects children and young people.

Marriage Equality happy campers. *From left:* Katherine Zappone, Ann Louise Gilligan, Moninne Griffith with her daughter Edie, Andrew Hyland, Ross Golden-Bannon, Orla Howard, Gráinne Healy, Ailbhe Smyth and Denise Charlton, 22 October 2015.

Many of the children's services' organisations highlighted their experience of how children who contacted them were directly and adversely impacted by a system in which the right to marry is restricted to heterosexual couples. The groups provided evidence and demonstrated that children who are LGBT often feel excluded, isolated and undervalued. They advocated that the referendum gave an opportunity to send a clear message to all children that they are valued and that treating them differently because of their sexuality – or the sexuality of someone in their household – was unacceptable. They advocated, in their various roles, to ensure that children are afforded equal rights as citizens. They called for Ireland to support children's ability to grow up, form relationships and have those relationships recognised equally by the State. They wanted to make it clear that children and young people across Ireland were valued equally, irrespective of their sexual orientation.

The then Minister for Justice, Alan Shatter, became convinced by the arguments and began to draft legislation (the Children and Family and Relationships Bill) that would provide the provisions required for LGBT families, and others.

Post the Constitutional Convention of 2013, when ME joined forces with ICCL (the Irish Council for Civil Liberties) and GLEN (the Gay & Lesbian Equality Network) for the referendum campaign, the visibility of families remained a crucial strategy promoted by ME. Initially, it was thought that the issues would be resolved through the Children and Family Relationships Bill and would ensure that children and LGBT families would no longer be part of the referendum debate.

However, the No side knew that this is where people were unsure and they tried to shift the debate on the national airwaves to surrogacy and other issues of possible concern related to our children. One of the No posters had a picture of a toddler under a bold headline about surrogacy. This was part of consistent attempts to divert the debate away from the central issue of extending the freedom to marry to gay and lesbian couples. They attached the issue of surrogacy to same-sex marriages despite the fact that surrogacy, like all forms of assisted human reproduction, is largely availed of by heterosexual couples, who for medical reasons are unable to have children. Constitutional lawyers were quick to counter this position, confirming that the Oireachtas, not the referendum, would decide laws on surrogacy.

However, it was truly countered with many brave families and family members coming out to discuss their stories and how they wanted equality for all their children, siblings, nieces and nephews, mums and dads. One of the most powerful mums was former President Mary McAleese, arguing for the need for all children to grow up with the aspiration of marriage and having a family. She was so powerful talking about her son Justin with such pride and she appealed to the nation to provide equality to all Ireland's young people and outlined the positive impact of this. A mum of nine children spoke about her desire for all her children and grandchildren to be equal. Many spoke about their deep faith and how they believed that marriage equality was not contradictory to these beliefs.

The No side had another poster, our least favourite being the one that stated 'Every child deserves a father and a mother'. This was their central message, that two biological parents of opposite sex are the ideal form of family. We were so worried about the long-term impact of these posters on our children. But, actually, the message angered many of our friends and families, who came out in droves to support us. Our parents, our children, our sisters, brothers, nieces and nephews became champions for marriage equality. Our families were warriors, campaigning constantly, canvassing door to door, hosting and attending fundraisers, arguing with people into the 'wee' hours, and persuaded many a voter to vote positively. One of my Dad's last votes was for the referendum, coming from his sick bed, in his light-pink jumper. To this day, we don't know as a family if the jumper was symbolic or a fashion error! But his, and our families' support, for us and the boys, was unwavering, and we will never forget it. All around the country people went public about being lesbian or gay or came out in relation to a family member, to say why they were voting Yes and asking others to join them. Their bravery and honesty moved many a vote and resulted in the resounding Yes vote on 22 May.

During the campaign, Thalia Zepatos from the US organisation Freedom to Marry came to support the national Yes Equality team to share some of the learning from their work in the United States. One of the examples she suggested was moving the visibility of lesbian and gay couples into a wider family context. Based on this advice, visual resources including posters and films were produced capturing images of LGBT couples with their extended families. The result of this shift in focus was the production of happy and diverse family images where LGBT couples were often indistinguishable from other family members. Reinforcing the message that LGBT people do not exist in isolation but rather live ordinary lives, surrounded by their families and friends, and again showing loving families, supported a positive outcome on 22 May.

Gráinne Healy and Denise Charlton at the Road to Equality Summer School, Killiney, Dublin, July 2016.

People ask often what the referendum outcome meant and means for our family. There are many things. Mostly we saw our children grow in confidence about their family structure and the support and affirmation they received during the campaign. The support given by our extended families and friends meant that they grew confident, despite the efforts of the No side. They now talk about their mums as a couple. They and their friends explore the possibilities of people marrying – boy to girl, boy to boy and girl to girl. And mostly, we hear their friends asking if their mums are getting married, just before they ask if there are chips for tea …

Richard O'Leary

Faith in Marriage Equality and the Pilgrimage for Yes

Standing outside the gates of a Dublin office, the nameplate behind us reads 'Registration of civil marriage and civil partnership'. There's irony in the locked gates. Umpteen couples came here to get married when Ireland's Church authorities opposed their Catholic–Protestant mixed marriages. Fortunately for these couples at the Registration Office, they were able to have a civil marriage without distinction as to their religion.

We take a photo for the launch of our campaign group Faith in Marriage Equality. The seven of us in turn step up to the video camera to make our appeals to the people of Ireland. Looking into the camera, I say: 'We of Faith in Marriage Equality have come together from a variety of faith backgrounds. We support those loving, committed, same-sex couples who wish to enter civil marriage regardless of their gender.' Next, the Reverend Stella Jones, wearing her clerical collar, tells us of marriage that 'I believe we should have one equal right for absolutely everyone.' Patricia Devlin then speaks as a Catholic and a grandmother, followed by Brendan Butler, Ciaran Ó Mathuna, Brian Glennon and Hugh Denard. We are not alone. We have the backing of our Catholic allies in 'We are Church Ireland' and 'Gay Catholic Voice Ireland', plus the Church of Ireland group 'Changing Attitude Ireland'. Moninne Griffith of Marriage Equality advises us on strategy; Michelle Thomas advises us on communications. Stephen Spillane in Cork, adept in social media, joins us to share our message.

Faith in Marriage Equality is launched on 12 February 2015 outside the Dublin Marriage Registry Offices. *From left:* Brendan Butler, Hugh Denard, Rev. Stella Jones, Richard O'Leary, Patricia Devlin, Ciaran Ó Mathuna and Brian Glennon.

Our message is one of civil and religious liberty, contained in our four-point Charter. As we disperse, we set about disseminating our 'Faith for Yes' message in letters to the papers, through press statements and interviews on local radio. Already the 'Faith for No' groups – the Catholic bishops and conservative Christian organisations are spreading their message, claiming that all religions are against same-sex marriage. We know this is not true.

THE RELIGIOUS CASE FOR YES

We need to organise a high-profile public event to challenge the No campaign's near monopoly of the faith voice in the debate. What would help is a prominent Catholic, Protestant and Jew for Yes to help us. Linda Hogan, leading theologian, Catholic and Vice-Provost of Trinity College Dublin, answers our call. She provides Trinity as the venue on Saturday, 11 April 2015, for a conference co-hosted with the Irish School of Ecumenics, called 'Marriage Equality: The Religious Case for a Yes Vote'. In her address she declares that, 'Theologically speaking, there are no impediments to gay and lesbian people marrying in a civil ceremony.' Professor Hogan is joined on the platform by the Church of Ireland Bishop of Cashel, Ferns and Ossory, Michael Burrows. He announces that he too is supporting a Yes vote. He says same-sex marriage would contribute 'to a fairer and more truly equal Ireland'. In doing so he joins the Church of Ireland Bishop of Cork, Paul Colton, who had also declared for Yes.

Ireland has few Jews, but at the time of the conference there is a visiting scholar and rabbi at Trinity, Professor Kris McDaniel-Miccio. She joins the coalition of faith speakers for Yes. The event is a great success and garners publicity. Professor Hogan is quoted in the press saying that 'This debate is being framed as religious people being no voters with everyone else voting Yes. This couldn't be further from the truth. People of all faiths support sharing the freedom to marry with gay and lesbian couples.'

GO WEST

It was one thing to establish the idea of 'Faith for Yes'. The bigger challenge was to make that idea more widely known. After canvassing in Monaghan with the Yes Equality bus during the Yes Equality campaign, it was apparent to me that we had not yet won over a majority in rural Ireland. Faith in Marriage Equality resolved to redirect its effort to that part of the country that might be considered the stoniest ground for the 'Yes' message – the West of Ireland.

Coincidentally, I came across a Bus Éireann[1] travel brochure inviting me to 'Experience the wild Atlantic Way ... an epic journey of Ireland's stunning western seaboard from Donegal to Cork ... rugged, liberating ... a journey of inspiration'. I answered the call: 'Go West, young man' or, in my case, 'Go West, middle-aged man', and so I took the bus to Donegal to start a pilgrimage for Yes.

Faith in Marriage Equality comes to Monaghan town, 5 May 2015. *From left:* Richard O' Leary, Canon Charles Kenny, Church of Ireland, and Ross Golden-Bannon.

Response from a Yes activist to the No posters, April 2015.

Building in O'Connell Street, Dublin, wrapped in a Yes poster, May 2015.

PILGRIMAGE FOR YES

The pilgrimage began on the first day of May at the 10 am mass at St Eunan's Cathedral, Letterkenny. As soon as the mass ended, I slipped out the door, taking up a position outside the church. It was very quiet on the street and there was a nip in the air as I waited for the mass-goers to emerge. Clutching my 'Faith for Yes' leaflets I wondered, anxiously, how we would be received. 'Good morning, here's something to read on the marriage referendum,' I said as I pressed my leaflet into passing hands. The mainly older congregation took my leaflets, passively. Some of them clearly assumed I was campaigning for No. Gradually it sank in who we were and what we were for. One woman said, 'You've some cheek canvassing outside a Catholic church.' 'I'm just sharing an alternative view,' I answered.

Another woman interjected, 'I'm really glad you're here.' She added that 'they have leaflets from the No side inside the cathedral'. I replied that 'People of faith on both sides and not just the conservative side should be heard.'

The conversations continued and it was encouraging to discover that there was a diversity of opinion among these church attenders. The good news was that so many were open to being persuaded to vote Yes, contrary to the instructions of their bishops. Once the small crowd had dispersed a woman, who had been at the mass, came up to me and said 'My own son is gay. He had to leave Donegal but I'm voting Yes.'

Having completed my morning's work, I looked wistfully at the Bus Éireann timetable. Have I mentioned that I had declared that I would do this pilgrimage by public transport? It seemed like a good idea when I announced the tour a fortnight earlier. It had indeed helped garner media publicity. Unfortunately, the news headline on RTÉ radio on Friday, 1 May was: 'A two-day bus strike due to cause disruption to hundreds of thousands of commuters nationwide has begun, following the breakdown of talks at the Labour Relations Commission'. Not a one-day strike, but a two-day strike. Would you blame me for suspecting some conspiracy to halt the pilgrimage for Yes on its first day? Fortunately, Noel Sharkey of Yes Equality Donegal was on hand to drive me from Letterkenny to our next event that night in Donegal town.

LOUGH DERG

The following morning I didn't hang about to sample the delights of Donegal town. I got up early and enquired about getting to the nearby pilgrimage site of Lough Derg. This holy island is best known for its retreats of fasting and prayer. There is a tradition of pilgrims to the island and writing petitions about their everyday concerns, such as good health, success in exams or getting married. A driver, who was herself heading to Lough Derg, gave me a lift. Realising she was a devout Catholic, I thought to myself, she's probably a No voter, maybe even a No campaigner.

'So what brings you to Lough Derg?' she asked.

'I'm actually taking a break from campaigning for Yes in the marriage referendum,' I said.

She didn't flinch. She said to me that 'Lough Derg is a place where no one is judged, everyone is welcome to come as they are.' 'Sounds like my sort of place,' I said. 'Maybe I'll even make a prayer petition that I too might be allowed to get married.' We both laughed. She kindly helped me to arrange a lift later, on a Lough Derg pilgrim bus, onwards to Sligo town.

That afternoon at four o'clock I'm sitting on the ferry boat, waiting for it to make the return crossing from the island to the mainland, when the Prior of Lough Derg steps aboard. The Prior announces that he has been asked by pilgrims to bless the souvenirs that passengers have bought at the island gift shop. He says a short prayer and then proceeds to walk down the central aisle, sprinkling holy water over the luggage. Large drops of holy water land on my suitcase – a suitcase packed with leaflets of 'Faith for Yes' to marriage equality.

Later that Saturday night in Sligo town, outside the cathedral of the Immaculate Conception, a campaigner from Yes Equality Sligo helps me to distribute these same leaflets to people after mass. I refrain from telling them that these leaflets had, unknowingly, been blessed by the Prior of Lough Derg.

KNOCK

The following morning, Sunday, 3 May, and the end of the bus strike means I can take the early bus from Sligo to Knock. On hearing that Knock was on the itinerary one 'Yes' supporter gasped, 'You're intending to canvass in Knock?'

'Yes, why not?' I replied.

'You do know it's the conservative Catholic heartland of Ireland?' he added.

'I know,' I answered, 'but there shouldn't be any "no-go" areas for vote Yes.'

According to the Knock Visitor's Guide:

> The story of Knock began in August 1879 when fifteen people from Knock village witnessed an apparition at the gable wall of the Parish Church … a heavenly vision consisting of Our Lady, St Joseph and St John the Evangelist … Saint John Paul II visited Knock shrine in 1979 … and people still come today in search of healing, reconciliation and peace.

In the village I was joined by three supporters from Yes Equality Mayo. Two of them took up a position in front of the general store while two of us headed for the parish church. Inside the church, I noticed a stack of colourful No leaflets. These were invitations to join in a special prayer, a nine-Day Novena from 14 May until Voting Day. The text asked that we 'please continue to pray that Ireland will uphold the Sanctity of Marriage between a man and a woman in the upcoming Referendum'. With all these Novenas for a No vote, I felt we were outnumbered.

Walking slowly down the main street, I'd like to be able to report that I felt like a confident evangelist carrying a message of love and inclusion. To be honest, I felt more like a wary Doc Holliday, in the film *Gunfight at the O.K. Corral*. We reached the Basilica of Our Lady of Knock, Queen of Ireland. Here in this enormous church there are frequent daily masses and when we arrived, mass was already in progress. I took up a position in the peaceful square outside the main exit. As the mass ended, a steady stream of pilgrims poured out from the church. I thrust into their passing hands our 'Faith for Yes' leaflet. 'Good morning, here's something to read on the marriage referendum,' I said.

The pilgrims accepted the leaflets calmly as they ambled leisurely across the square. I'd handed out dozens and had paused to reload when suddenly a figure appeared in front of me. At first I couldn't make out what he was saying, that is because he was shouting, shouting at me.

'This is wrong,' he screamed, 'you're promoting sodomy.'

'We're promoting the wider availability of civil marriage,' I countered.

'It's against the teaching of the Church!' he shouted.

'Two Church of Ireland Bishops support Yes,' I responded.

'They're heretics,' he replied.

I was stunned. His face was red and bursting with fury. Then he turned and ran wildly after people who had passed me, snatching my leaflets from their hands and tearing them up in a frenzy. Was it frightening? Yes, a bit. My fellow campaigner heard the shouting and recognised that I was under fire. She hurried over and managed to draw him away. Afterwards, a man emerged from the basilica and told me and my fellow campaigner to clear off.

As I walked back to the bus stop I recalled the tourist brochure. It had invited me to 'Experience the Wild Atlantic Way … liberating … a journey of inspiration'. I don't think this was the 'wild experience' they had in mind. Nor is everyone open to being 'liberated' or 'inspired'.

Mary McDermott (*left*), Yes Equality, with Canon Marie Rowley-Brooke, recently retired Rector of Nenagh Union of Parishes, with the Yes Bus in Tipperary, May 2015.

AFTERNOON TEA

Apart from Knock, the subsequent canvasses in Galway, Ennis, Limerick and Killarney were not confrontational. There was even time for a side trip to carry out a special canvass. A supporter from Yes Equality Clare collected me at the bus station in Ennis and drove me deep into the Burren national park. We followed the narrow, twisted roads until we reached our destination. Craggy Island. Suddenly, it loomed in the distance: Father Ted's house.[2] I recognised it all; the long driveway up to the large grey parochial house, the vast lawn, even the sheep.

When booking in advance for afternoon tea I hadn't mentioned that I was on a pilgrimage for Yes. After all, this was Craggy Island and for all I knew the new Mrs Doyle might be a No supporter. I needn't have worried. Cheryl, the owner, was lovely and she made the most delicious scones I have ever tasted. I was delighted to discover that she was already a firm Yes supporter. She even let me take some photos to upload to our Facebook page for Faith in Marriage Equality. I was sure that Father Ted was a Yes supporter. Father Dougal would ask, 'What is gay?'. Father Jack would be too drunk to know there even was a referendum. As for Bishop Brennan? 'That would be an ecumenical matter' is what I guessed he would say.

HOME TOWN

The cup of tea at Father Ted's helped steel me for my arrival in my childhood home town of Cork. The previous week I had a letter published in the *Irish Examiner*:

> *Dear Editor*
>
> *I was disappointed to read the pastoral statement by Bishop John Buckley on marriage and the family. I am surprised that the Bishop only understands marriage in terms of biological reproduction given that more than 10 per cent of heterosexual couples are infertile. I had the wonderful experience of a loving, faithful same-sex relationship with my partner Mervyn for twenty-five years until I was widowed in 2013. I will be returning to my home-town of Cork on Wednesday next at the conclusion of an Atlantic Way 'Pilgrimage for Yes'. Bishop Buckley taught me thirty-five years ago. I am available to meet him to help him to understand same-sex couples are family too.*
>
> *Dr Richard O'Leary,*
> *Faith in Marriage Equality.*

On Wednesday, 6 May, during the mass at St Mary's Cathedral, Cork, I recalled that this was the same church where, as a twelve-year-old, I had been confirmed as a member of the Catholic Church. Now, decades later, as an openly gay man, I was handing out leaflets for marriage equality.

After our canvass outside the cathedral, we walked the hundred yards to the nearby St Ann's Church, Shandon, where we were warmly received by the Church of Ireland rector. Later, on the Sunday before the referendum, Yes Equality Cork followed up our work with the distribution of 'Faith for Yes' leaflets outside masses throughout Cork.

YESVENA

Two days before the referendum and both sides were throwing everything they had into the campaign. The Novena for a No vote was reaching its culmination. Our Faith in Marriage Equality held its own 'Faith Witness for Yes'. This was affectionately called the 'Yesvena'.

We held our Yesvena at Parnell Square, Dublin, at the premises of the Irish Congress of Trade Unions. We deliberately held it at a non-religious venue to emphasise that this referendum was about civil not religious marriage. Six persons of faith gave public 'witness' statements of why they would be voting Yes. Among them was Senator David Norris, who explained that as a committed Christian he thought that 'Jesus Christ would be in the Yes camp'.

Two days later, by a large majority, the Irish electorate voted Yes to marriage equality. Maybe my prayer petition at Lough Derg had been answered? Maybe the Yesvena played its part? The following month, at St Audoen's Church in Dublin, Faith in Marriage Equality held a Service of Thanksgiving for the outpouring of love and generosity shown by the people of Ireland.

Richard O'Leary enjoys a cup of tea at Father Ted's
house, Kilfenora, Co. Clare, May 2015.

Orla Howard

Challenges of the Personal and the Political

By the time I arrived at my mid-thirties, the very grim Ireland of the eighties and nineties was ending, leading into an early Celtic Tiger Ireland that seemed more hopeful for people like me. I was one of many who felt that LGBT people were nowhere on the radar, and that decriminalisation of homosexuality in 1993 was as good as it was going to get. However, this was the start of the new millennium and little chinks of light started to break through the grey skies. This was the time when our equality legislation had made Ireland the envy of Europe and things were looking better for Irish women: Mary Robinson had been a great president, followed by another great woman, Mary McAleese; and *The Irish Times* had a female editor.

This was a time of hope, although it was still a tough place to be a lesbian. At that point I had been involved in gay community activism as a board member of the National Lesbian and Gay Federation (NLGF, now NFX). The NLGF had long campaigned on equality issues for LGBT people, and along with its campaigning work, its focus at that time was keeping *Gay Community News* (*GCN*) financially viable, and ensuring that the Irish Queer Archive was housed somewhere safe and kept intact.

It was around then that I met Gráinne Courtney, my partner. Within minutes of us getting together I knew that I wanted to marry her. Of course, the idea of marriage was impossible. We were lesbian, after all – there would be no marriage for us.

NewsFeatures

Families come out for gay marriage

Same-sex parents hope that talking to TDs about civil union in advance of next month's Heads of Bill will have an impact, writes **Róisín Ingle**

Seventeen-year-old Clare O'Connell knew exactly the message she wanted to get across to her local TDs when she and her family met them to discuss the issue of same-sex marriage in Leinster House earlier this week.

"We go to school and play basketball and listen to music. We eat pasta and do our homework. It's not radical, we don't live in a hippy commune and the only dif-

The family's story, like that of many Irish families, is not straightforward. Clare and Daire are the natural children of Courtney from a previous marriage. Their father has since remarried, a right they are hoping might be afforded to their mother. The girls were bridesmaids for their father and stepmother last August and say they'd like to perform the same role for their mother one day.

From left: Orla Howard, Daire Courtney, Gráinne Courtney and Clare O'Connell visit their TDs as part of Marriage Equality's 'Out To Your TD' campaign, *The Irish Times*, 16 February 2008.

PROPOSALS

I proposed to Gráinne frequently, but I knew it was something that wasn't going to happen. Gráinne, on the other hand, wasn't so hot on the idea, mostly because at that point she was still legally married to her now ex-husband. She knew she was safe to answer 'yes' to my many proposals because our relationship would never have that legal standing. What was more pressing and life-changing for me was that Gráinne's two daughters, Clare and Daire, had also come into my life.

I had always wanted to be a parent, and had wanted to have children of my own. Along with the notion of marriage, the possibility of having children as gay or lesbian people at that time was for many of us remote. My biological clock bellowed at me loudly through my late twenties and thirties, and though I explored various means of having children, it was not to be. So, this new love in my life brought with her eleven-year-old Clare, and eight-year-old Daire.

With two small children, life required much adjustment and I (gradually) realised that, if I was taking on a parenting role, I could not hop off instantly to the movies/activism meeting/fundraiser/gig. My domestic life changed quite dramatically at that time but it felt like other things were changing, too; that the quest for equality for LGBT people was moving into a different gear.

When Katherine Zappone and Ann Louise Gilligan first took their case against the Revenue Commissioners in 2004, they started something. They were two married women seeking to be taxed like other married people. Could they ever have imagined how this action would trigger such major events in the following decade, ultimately involving the whole nation in a discussion, and a referendum on equality?

KAL

Initially a small group of supporters came together to help with the case and this group became known as KAL (for Katherine and Ann Louise). The NLGF would go on to help with the KAL case, and three of the NLGF board: myself, Ailbhe Smyth and Patrick Lynch, joined the KAL group in 2007. Funding had been secured from Atlantic Philanthropies to set up an organisation to bring the KAL issue to a broader social and political audience, and in spring of 2008, Marriage Equality (ME) was launched.

Our kids were always engaged with the issue of ME and the topic was frequently discussed at meal times. During some of the more difficult times, I took great comfort from the simplicity of the kids' logic, and their simple conviction of what is right and what is wrong. Children see the obvious while adults allow themselves to develop 'scales in their eyes' and complicate what is often very simple. I remember a ten-year-old Daire ardently protesting that it 'just isn't fair! You are not treated equally and that is not right!' Both girls became important spokespersons for ME, and contributed often from their perspective as the children of gay parents.

Daire and Clare's first public appearance was in *The Irish Times* in February 2008. A feature article appeared to coincide with the formal launch of the new ME organisation. The headline read 'Families come out for gay marriage' and it was an account of our family visiting our TDs, as part of ME's 'Out To Your TD' campaign. It was well written by Róisín Ingle, who accompanied us to meet our constituency TDs in Leinster House. We had requested meetings with three TDs: Sean Haughey (Fianna Fáil), Richard Bruton (Fine Gael) and Finian McGrath (Independent). The girls, Clare aged seventeen and Daire aged thirteen, argued with Richard Bruton, who introduced himself saying 'it is not my area of expertise'. He viewed civil partnership as being the means to solve our problem and when the kids applied their simple logic (it's not the same so it's NOT equal!), he excused himself to rush to another meeting. Finian McGrath gave us much of his time and was very supportive, while Sean Haughey declined to meet us.

The girls enjoyed the process, but we were all a little anxious about such a public telling of our story. That was the first time we had done anything of this nature, and as time went on, it got a little easier, but we were always anxious about the reaction or possible backlash from our stories being made so public, particularly for the girls. Gráinne and I were heartened when they received genuinely positive feedback from that first *Irish Times* story from their family, and in their school – both from their teachers and their friends.

Throughout the years of the campaign, it was difficult to get spokespeople to come forward publicly, and even more difficult to get couples with children. As a result, Clare and Daire featured regularly in many of the campaigns and interviews. Neither experienced any negativity around being the children of gay parents and they got positive feedback to their campaigning, that is, until the lead into the marriage referendum, when both the girls participated from the audience in the TV debates.

Prior to ME's launch, the NLGF ran the first of two symposia on the topic of marriage. The discussion began to grow and the term 'marriage equality' could be heard more frequently, both in the media and in political discussions. It also began to emerge that there was a difference of opinion within the gay community on what would be the best way to achieve marriage equality.

From left: Clare O'Connell, Orla Howard and Conor Pendergrast at the Constitutional Convention, April 2013.

THE STRATEGY VERSUS THE OBJECTIVE

Throughout my time as an LGBT activist, and also in my real-life career (the paid-for job), I've frequently encountered groups of people who share the same goal (or objective) but had devised different strategies on how to achieve that goal. In theory, having different strategies is important and positive: if you are aware that one strategy is not working, another can be used or adapted and all the effort continues to be focused on achieving the goal. That is the theory.

So if the theory is so simple, then why is it so hard in practice? Well, bring in the 'human' factor – which will include any number of variables, including different personalities, different size of organisations, each with varying strengths and weaknesses, different egos, different access to influential groups, etc. – and the 'strategy' tends to overtake the objective in its level of importance. Then, people (and organisations) become so attached to their strategy that they allow the objective to slip out of sight and defending or maintaining the strategy becomes the goal. Statements like 'this is the only way we can get this to happen'; 'we believe that only this strategy will deliver what we want'; or 'our strategy is the best', became the entrenched and much defended positions.

Of course, this happens in every walk of life, but in our small LGBT community it became apparent that different strategies (or positions) were being taken: ME believed in achieving nothing short of equal marriage while the Gay & Lesbian Equality Network (GLEN) believed in an incremental approach, starting with civil partnership. A rift developed between these two organisations and was also evident within the LGBT community.

Representatives from GLEN spoke about the importance of civil partnership at every opportunity and on every public occasion. This really irritated the hell out of many others and it was not obvious to ME, or to the other LGBT community groups, that GLEN's objective was, in fact, the same as everyone else's. In fact, their approach seemed to say that GLEN was unilaterally deciding on behalf of everyone else that civil partnership was as good as it was going to be, with no effort to explain the rationale of its (later stated) strategy of civil partnership first, marriage equality second. The rift widened. This was a major obstacle to any possibility of collaboration between the two organisations. Much later, following the Constitutional Convention, Gráinne Healy, Chairwoman of ME, invited GLEN and ICCL (the Irish Council for Civil Liberties) to a (very tense) meeting where each organisation clarified its objectives. This became one of the milestones that, in time, would allow both organisations begin to consider working together in the ensuing Yes campaign.

New York Wedding Day, May 2013.

Doctors for Yes launch, *front from left:* Gráinne Courtney, Fiona Lyons, Veronica O Keane, Minister for Health Leo Varadkar, Aodhán Ó Ríordáin, Des Crowley, Susan Smith, Brian Sheehan and Noel Sharkey, May 2015.

RIFT

For me, this rift presented the most difficult obstacle I encountered throughout the journey to equal marriage. I didn't buy into the GLEN idea that civil partnership was a stepping stone, and as a Board member of ME, the policy of pushing for marriage was at odds with the GLEN strategy. The personal issue for me was that my lifetime friendship with GLEN Director Brian Sheehan was under severe strain. We had been friends since childhood, growing up within 100 metres of each other in the small west Clare town of Kilrush. As the rift became more obvious, Brian and I agreed not to talk about it. We knew that neither would persuade the other to change position, so, at the time, that seemed like the best solution.

At my most non-partisan moments, I believed, and would broadcast to anyone who would listen, that achieving equal marriage *was* everyone's objective and nobody would care how we got there, so long as we got there. There were to be many difficult moments in the coming years, and my own personal strategy was to keep a firm hold on that objective.

Several attempts were made to join the LGBT community groups into a united effort. Following the 2009 'Marriage Matters Symposium', the NLGF tried to encourage the main campaign groups, ME, GLEN, LGBT Noise (who had formed the previous year to campaign for equal marriage) and NLGF to join forces and create a 'Platform for Equality'. It wasn't entirely successful at that time because GLEN was disinclined to participate. GLEN pursued their strategy of achieving civil partnership first, and it was enacted in January 2011. ME got on with the groundwork of recruiting volunteers, assembling allies and forging relationships with civil society groups to pursue marriage. Huge work by ME, in particular, along with LGBT Noise and other LGBT organisations, went into civil society-oriented campaigns and political-party linkages, punctuating the time and building to the referendum in 2015. There were many highlights, and low lights (as well as difficult friendship moments) throughout this time.

HUMAN RIGHTS ISSUE OF OUR TIME

Moving on to the summer of 2012, the Labour Party leader, Eamon Gilmore, pronounced that the time had come for gay marriage and went on to add that it was 'the human rights issue of our time'. His comments, along with the growing momentum generated by ME, LGBT Noise, NLGF, GLEN and others, led to the issue being included in the Constitutional Convention in April 2013. By this time, I had resigned from the NLGF board and was allocating more and more time as Deputy Chair of ME. Aside from the tremendous and positive result (79 per cent of the delegates voted in favour of calling for a referendum to amend the Constitution in favour of same-sex marriage), I saw the event as a pivotal moment for the eventual campaign for civil marriage for three reasons:

- The Convention decided the format for its events including who would speak (giving a total of only thirty minutes for the LGBT input, inviting ME, GLEN and ICCL to address the delegates);
- A positive result had to be achieved – anything else would set back gay rights in Ireland for decades;
- It was clear that the social and political establishment saw ME and GLEN as the principal LGBT organisations, so, if we could not find a way of working together, civil marriage would not happen.

The time limitation of thirty minutes imposed for presenting to the Constitutional Convention resulted in some tricky negotiations between ME and GLEN; however, a sensible format was agreed. At ME's suggestion, a chunk of the precious time was allocated for two children of LGBT parents to address the Convention, with extraordinary effect. Our daughter Clare addressed the Convention along with Conor Pendergrast, who, with his brother, has two lesbian mums. They were both brilliant. Clare told her story confidently and elegantly and both of them made a critical impression on the ninety-nine delegates.[1] Afterwards many of the delegates cited their input as being of the greatest impact of the Convention process. My part at the Convention was looking after the technicalities for the presentation slideshow, so I got to attend the otherwise closed sessions. Watching Clare and Conor speak so well will be forever a precious memory.

NEW YORK

The comprehensive result from the Constitutional Convention meant that, like it or not, we were now heading for a referendum. Efforts to persuade the government to legislate for marriage were no longer entertained. The previous winter my efforts to persuade Gráinne Courtney to marry me had, finally, borne a positive result and we had decided to go to a country where we could legally marry. As we headed off with the kids to our New York wedding in May 2013, we had no idea that a referendum would be announced and voted on by a landslide in just two years. Had we known, we might have waited to marry in Ireland. We did have an unofficial little ceremony at a big family party in Dublin when we returned, during which I promised not to make Gráinne marry me again (I would live to regret this when marriage was finally legalised in November 2015. Before I could even suggest another wedding, Gráinne firmly rejected it – alas, no more weddings for me).

In late 2013, the embryonic Yes Equality group revisited the idea of the need for an LGBT Platform and so it was resurrected and the LGBT groups began to assemble to be involved

A rainbow appears for the Marino Yes Equality canvass group, 20 May 2015.

Dáil Éireann passes the Marriage Bill. *From left:* Orla Howard, Karl Hayden, Moninne Griffith and Andrew Hyland, 30 September 2015.

in the thinking and planning for the forthcoming referendum. At this stage, there was no definite date, though it was hinted it might be late 2014 or spring 2015. The association born of the tripartite work at the Convention between ME, GLEN and ICCL continued into a more structured relationship, with the three organisations meeting regularly. The rift between GLEN and ME was still raw, but for pragmatic reasons (including GLEN clarifying their commitment to marriage), it was now apparent that a good working relationship was needed to face into a unified referendum campaign. The ICCL played an essential role in mediating the 'troika', as it was initially called, keeping an objective perspective and nudging the process along. Nobody liked the 'troika' tag and the group soon became known as the coalition.

UNIFYING

By summer 2014, the Taoiseach, Enda Kenny, stated that the referendum would take place early in 2015, and our biggest fear of it moving later into the year towards the summer was the possibility of the college term being over and not having the student vote. The date of 22 May was pushing it – the youth vote was going to be critical. Meanwhile, work was underway on research, focus groups, marketing and branding plans, regional networking, fundraising and many other areas, all being carried out by staff from the three organisations – much of it a continuation of the work which had been started by ME in the previous decade. As the year drew to a close, LGBT people all over the country were asking, 'What should I be doing?' There have been many accounts of the next five months and the decision that Brian Sheehan of GLEN and Gráinne Healy of ME should jointly lead the Yes Campaign. That the two heads of these organisations would agree to join forces was a big surprise, even to me.

Orla's niece, Amy Howard (aged 7), with her poster for the Yes Campaign, April 2015.

However, the pairing of these two turned out to be an inspired idea, and they went on to become the architects of the Yes campaign. The 'official' joining forces of ME and GLEN was a great personal moment for me, and a relief to the unspoken tension that almost hijacked my friendship with Brian. For the campaign, it was a unifying moment that was essential to get a Yes vote, and while it might have seemed inevitable to some, it was never a given, and it is still commendable.

Yes Equality was launched early in 2015 and the process took on its own life force, like a steam train powering to its destination. All those LGBT people asking what they should do went canvassing, fundraising, distributing leaflets and badges and, most importantly, talked to people. People jumped on the fast-moving train and it gathered speed. The Yes HQ provided materials and information and all across the country the message was disseminated.

There were many nervous moments. The awful No posters; the bear-pit TV debates; the dreadful, persistent, badly informed commentary in the media about surrogacy. But, there were many good moments, too. The train had gathered many volunteers, each bringing vital skills to the campaign. My professional background is in advertising and marketing, so I was able to bring some of this expertise to the Yes Equality campaign. I took five weeks leave from my day job and worked at the campaign HQ on advertising and fundraising. The family did a lot of media work: interviews and articles, and the extended family did one of the Yes Equality campaign videos. Clare participated from a panel on *The Late Late Show* and Daire spoke from the audience in the Claire Byrne RTÉ TV debate. Some of these debates were hostile, negative, divisive and deeply personalised. We worried how much we should ask of the girls as the referendum drew closer, and, after the Claire Byrne show, we decided that they had done more than enough and it was time for them to stop.

Gráinne and I, along with a fantastic group, spent the evenings canvassing sections of the Dublin North Bay constituency. It gave me great heart to hear that Richard Bruton TD launched the constituency canvassing campaign and had spoken passionately about civil marriage equality. He had come a (commendably) long way from that conversation our family had with him for *The Irish Times* back in 2008.

ADRENALIN

For those last few weeks I was waking at 5 am, mind racing, adrenalin flying. Although I felt safe in the knowledge that the campaign was being carefully and expertly directed by Gráinne and Brian (or 'Bráinne' as they were known by then), I worried if I was doing *everything* I could, so as not to wake up on 23 May and regret I hadn't done more. I know now that many other LGBT people had the same feeling. A standout moment from those last weeks was in Kilrush, my hometown. I had taken a few days to go down and organise a leaflet drop of the west Clare area and this dovetailed with the arrival of the Yes Equality Bus to Kilrush. The bus drew into the town square and a bunch gathered to greet it, which included my elderly mum. Even for an Irish May it was cold and blustery, and I suggested to my mother that she need not come to meet the bus. 'Of course I'll come! I'll stand by you, Orla,' she said. It was a big physical effort for her to be there and a moment I will forever cherish.

The Yes Equality campaign train steamed along to polling day. The tens of thousands of people who were involved ensured its success. No one organisation or person can claim the credit – this was about LGBT people, their families, friends and colleagues standing up to decide what kind of a country we wanted to live in. As Vincent Browne said on the TV3 coverage from The George during the count, 'I get it now, it was never just about marriage ... it was about acceptance.' Vincent wasn't the only one to 'get it'; in a landslide vote, 62 per cent of the Irish electorate said Yes to equality, publicly affirming its LGBT people. Of course, there is a long way to go to achieve full equality for all of us, but this campaign and its result was a standout moment.

BBC website announces same-sex marriage is legal
in Ireland, 16 November 2015.

Objective achieved: Brian Sheehan *(back left)* and Orla Howard *(back right, in pink)* celebrate the Yes result, Ballsbridge Hotel, Dublin, 23 May 2015.

On 25 May, the Monday morning after that fantastic weekend of love, celebration and rainbows, I went into the Yes HQ to clear my desk. The big open-plan office that had housed the dozens of campaign volunteers, materials, fruit boxes, flags, T-shirts, posters and badges was deserted. People were taking a well-earned break. Only Gráinne Healy and Brian Sheehan were still working away in the media room next door, giving interviews to international broadcasters who were enchanted and delighted with the Irish result. The office phone rang in the big, empty room. I hesitated before answering it because the Yes HQ regularly received truly outrageous crank phone calls, easily distinguishable in the crowded open plan space. Sandra Irwin-Gowran, Kathleen Hunt and Lisa Hyland (Yes HQ Staff during the campaign) would handle many of these calls with grace and patience, never being short or angry and sometimes even getting a round of applause from the rest of us.

I took a deep breath and answered the phone. A woman who sounded like she was in her older years spoke. 'I just wanted to ring and tell you that I voted No, and I'm sorry.' I waited, a little surprised and not sure what to say to her. 'I voted No because I was afraid, and now I know I was wrong.' I was still unsure what to say so I just thanked her for calling. She was one of the 38 per cent who voted No, and I have no doubt that many of those would vote differently now.

Being part of the ME organisation and its journey has been an honour for me and I'm glad that my family, Clare and Daire in particular, got to play a part in making Ireland a better place and is now a part of our history. It was often difficult, time consuming, thankless, contentious and severely tested some friendships. But ultimately it was fabulous and wonderful. And, didn't we keep a firm hold of that objective?

Linda Cullen

Making Short Films for Marriage Equality

I became involved in the Marriage Equality (ME) campaign in the very early days. Denise Charlton asked me to join the newly formed ME Board and, at first, my response was poor. I told her I wasn't much interested in marriage. I didn't necessarily see it as something the lesbian and gay community wanted. It was a patriarchal institution. My own mother didn't think much of it, it hadn't served her well. Denise responded, asking, 'What's that got to do with the fact that others might want it and are not allowed have it?' Well, she had me there, it was a bit of a slam dunk.

It was true, what did it matter if I didn't personally want to avail of marriage. In truth, my argument was a little more complex than I am making out, but my reasons for becoming involved did boil down to the fact that others might want to get married and why the hell shouldn't they?

Oddly, it's a big enough leap for lesbian and gay people to make – certainly for those who grew up in the 1960s, 1970s, 1980s and even 1990s. We were a seriously marginalised group. Our visibility was poor. Our fears were great, and well founded. So the notion of us having access to the great and treasured societal institution of marriage seemed impossible. And, if I am being perfectly honest (which I am), I didn't think we would achieve marriage for at least another twenty years. Or more.

In fact, I only began to think we might make it on 22 May 2015 when I cried my way through the day; from going to the polling station to vote with my partner, Feargha Ní Bhroin, and our twin daughters and obsessively viewing the #hometovote feed. Only then did it seem possible, really possible. During the final weeks of the campaign I was worried that we were living in a bit of a bubble. I kept replaying in my mind some of the more difficult and aggressive recent debates that had been on national television. And then, of course, I would ask myself, what would we do, what could we do if we lost? Because this referendum had become about so much more than marriage. We had asked the question and had to prepare ourselves for the answer. We asked the whole country if they accepted us, their lesbian and gay brothers, sisters, friends, aunts, uncles, sons and daughters. Do you accept us, do you love us and value us, really? Once it was out it couldn't be taken back and it was terrifying. Absolutely terrifying.

I didn't sleep at all on the night of 22 May. I doubt if any campaigners did, so that's a lot of sleepless households. We received an email at about 2 am from a friend of Feargha's in Africa who'd just seen the front page of *The Irish Times* (how it gets to Africa first I don't know), and a few hours later we were able to see it for ourselves. And it was probably the first time I thought we just may win this referendum. The fact that *The Irish Times* used such a particular picture of an LGBT family on its front page before a single ballot box was opened said something to me. That it was a picture of my own family was another thing altogether.

On the ME Board in the early days of 2007/2008, I was involved in discussions and decisions. I gave my tuppence worth when I could. I had strong opinions about certain things and none about others. My mother died early in 2007, too young, after a long battle with cancer, and Feargha and I had decided to start trying for a family. Feargha's brother died just months before the referendum. I only say this to remind myself that everyone on the campaign had all their own stuff going on all the time. There was much parental loss, illness and tragic events ongoing in the background of the fight to win marriage equality in Ireland. Too many to mention but some particular snapshots come to mind, when I think of Una Mullally and her cancer during the Yes campaign and how she wore a bumbag of chemo drugs that were literally being administered into her system as she appeared on a live debate on RTÉ. I picture too Ann Louise Gilligan, who became extremely ill in 2014 and still managed to engage and follow through on all she committed to in the campaign. And of Denise Charlton's dad (a great supporter from the beginning of ME) who hauled himself down to the polling station in his beautiful pink jumper, always so handsome, even then as he was dying from lung cancer to vote for the very last time in his life, to vote Yes.

Tess and Rosa Cullen Byrne hold their 'equality' signs at the March for Marriage with their parents, August 2014.

Linda Cullen canvasses with the Yes Bus, Dublin, 10 May 2015.

My involvement, other than being a Board member, was to make certain visual content at key times. I was well placed to do that given that my day job as Head of Television in COCO Television, the independent production company I co-own and run with my business partner, Stuart Switzer. I've been a camerawoman, director and writer in the past and was currently producing lots of content, mostly for television. I was delighted to do something concrete and practical that would last and be useful.

I was prepared to gather the people and resources to make something of significance and there was a lot of discussion at the Board as to what that particular thing would be. What was the message we wanted to share and how did we want to share it? At that time, social media was new and its use had not yet been fully explored; this campaign went on to use it most successfully in Ireland for the very first time.

It's interesting to remember that in 2008/2009, much of the general population were still confused about what civil marriage was. Many still thought it was something to do with the Church, so strong has the hand of the Church been in this country. And, indeed, much of the gay community was still not convinced that they wanted marriage at all. The Gay & Lesbian Equality Network (GLEN) was pushing hard, behind the scenes, for civil partnership, but we were never going to accept such a second-class proposition. So, when we were looking at a number of marriage equality messages made in the US, we hit on one and thought it encapsulated the reality of what the hoped-for change was about for us, on a personal level. And that's what became *Sinead's Hand*. The film that went viral within a few weeks (over 668,400 hits as I write), which far exceeded our expectation for its reach. The film depicts a young man who is knocking on doors all across Ireland, asking for permission to have 'Sinead's hand in marriage' – an activity that, ironically, all those who campaigned in the Yes Equality referendum actually *did* have to do when canvassing for a Yes vote in 2015. But at the time of its original launch, it seemed an extraordinary thing that gay people, unlike our straight brothers and sisters, should have to ask everyone in Ireland, strangers and friends, if we could have the right to marry the person we love. The purpose of the film was to show the absurdity and unfairness of such a proposition and push legislators to simply legislate to introduce civil marriage equality for same-sex couples in Ireland. The video is still getting lots of views and has garnered a lot of positive reviews from international media.

Numbers holding up: *Irish Times*/IPSOS MRBI poll, October 2014.

It was difficult to decide what message we wanted to give, who we needed to address it to and in what manner. We spent a lot of time and energy formulating what our message should be and how it should be disseminated. We took days to decide on the wording at the end of this short film: 'How would you feel if you had to ask 4 million people for permission to get married?' Similar to the US film that inspired *Sinead's Hand*, this message was clear and simple and obviously intended for straight people, those who *could* marry. It was intended to appeal to a sense of fairness, a sense of justice. And it's a powerful message. The final line stated 'Lesbians and gay men are denied access to civil marriage in Ireland'. And this was a very simple point of information. There was so much confusion about civil marriage as opposed to getting married in a church, we were constantly clarifying that this was our messaging.

The film was also made in a very particular way so it could be shared with absolutely anyone, parents, friends, siblings, grandparents. It was non-combative in its approach; it was sweet and fun. We asked the very kind and gentle-looking Hugh O'Connor to be the lead actor (any mother would love her daughter or son to bring him home). He played a very unthreatening, fresh-faced, slightly comical, straight guy who went from door to door asking for Sinead's hand in marriage. The people answering the doors were mostly friends and colleagues of mine, but again a mix of people, men and women, with a Gaeilgeoir (Irish speaker) thrown in for good measure. And we chose a wonderful piece of Lisa Hannigan's music that fit perfectly with the piece, and got a lot of positive comments in its own right. Lisa Hannigan, Hugh O'Connor, all the team who made this video (onscreen and off), all gave their time and expertise free of charge (special shout out to Peter Murphy, director; Nicola Ronaghan, producer; Colm Wheelan, DOP; and Joe McElwaine, editor).

In 2009, ME was not looking for a referendum, it was a terrifying notion. However, the message worked really well in terms of people's sense of justice: 'How would *you* feel if you had to ask four million people for permission to get married?' We are not a nation that feels we should have to ask permission for anything. That we ended up doing exactly that is another matter and, in fact, became arguably a stronger way for us to gain access to marriage and equality, than by a mere change in legislation; rather we got a change in the Irish Constitution – but it was by no means an easy route.

Feargha[1] and I took a break from ME in 2010 after our daughters were born. Two little five-pound babies demanded every moment from us, so we were out of the loop for the next couple of years. Tentatively, I came back before the Constitutional Convention in 2013 to help prepare for that, and again to use video to convey the marriage equality message. This time the film had a very specific purpose. To show the participants of the Convention lesbian and gay couples. We had to remember that the sixty-six ordinary citizens participating may not have known any gay people; may not have been aware of any lesbian or gay couples and it was crucial that they heard from them, from people who were not going to be accused of 'having an agenda', whose only 'agenda' was living their lives as best they could, in equality.

So again I reached out to my friends and colleagues and we went about making this video for the Convention. At first there was a feeling within the ME group and staff that we should be making this to put it online and for every possible outlet. This was an understandable mistake often made when producing visual material and film. It can be so expensive to produce that you want it to be all things to all people. It became clear to me after many discussions with the director, Martin Gaughan, that we couldn't be all things to all people. Martin wanted to include straight couples to show how couples were just couples, whether gay or straight. and we all wanted the same things. And while that message was a really important message, it became confusing. We needed to get back to basics and let the citizens and politicians at the Convention simply meet a number of lesbian and gay couples and hear them talk about their relationships, and that is exactly what we did.

Anthony[2] and Barry, who were fourteen years together at the time, talked about bringing their dog Frodo for walks. Louise and Sive, and their beautiful twin girls, talked about how they first met in their rowing club. Freda talked about humour bringing herself and Deborah together, and Laura speaking of her love of Gillian singing in the shower every morning, starting her day off perfectly and making her smile, made us all smile.

In the three and a half minutes of film we got to know these people and got a great sense of their lives together in the way that only film can do. We saw how they sat together, how they looked at each other, how the two-year-old twins crawled all over their parents in the way that two-year-old children do.

It took only two minutes to set up four couples and give a decent snapshot of their lives. And in the last ninety seconds each had this to say, unrehearsed, from the heart:

'Marriage is important to us because it gives recognition that we're committed to each other and we have a family and we're really serious about our commitment.'

'Marriage is important to us because we want to be equal to everybody else.'

'Our siblings are married, our friends are married, we don't see why we shouldn't have the same rights as they do'.

'I feel excluded here in Ireland and I don't like that. I want to be included. I am legally married in Canada and I want to be legally married here in Ireland. It means the world to me.'

'We're very proud to be Irish, and very proud of our country and we just want our country to accept us for who we are and be treated the same as everybody else.'

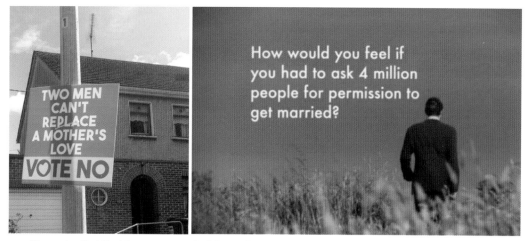

No poster, Dublin, May 2015.   Still frame from *Sinead's Hand*, the Marriage Equality video produced in 2009 by Linda Cullen and COCO TV, which currently has more than 650,000 views on You Tube.

'It's true, it's honest. That's marriage.'

And the very final message read, 'Every love story deserves a happy ending', in the lovely purple ME colour. This little video became an incredibly useful voice along with those other brave and important live voices in the short time allowed for ME and the other equality groups to make their presentation to the Constitutional Convention in 2013. I wasn't at the Convention, there were only a few allowed attend, but it was a great day when the 79 per cent vote calling on government to hold a referendum on marriage equality came in our favour.

Six months prior to the Convention, Feargha and I had become civilly partnered. It was a low-key affair. We decided we needed to solidify our relationship in a legal way for the children. It didn't give me or the children any rights to each other (as their non-biological parent), but it did, from a legal perspective, show intent. And that was important. We lived together, created this family together and wanted legal acknowledgment and recognition of our family. And in the absence of legal recognition for our family, we decided it was wise to have legal recognition of our adult relationship or partnership to at least show our intent about protection of our children. It was a very bitter-sweet day.

Others in this book will give more detail about the various things ME did and how we did it, the 'Out To Your TD' campaign; the Voices of Children conference; the 'Just Love' campaign; and the LGBT parenting conference, just to name a smattering of all the strategies and events that were devised, organised and implemented by the staff, the Board, volunteers, friends and supporters of the ME campaign.

Still frames from two of the series of five *Marriage and Family Matter* videos created by Linda Cullen and COCO TV for the Yes Equality campaign; *(above)* 90-year-old grandmother Madeline Connolly and *(below)* five GAA hurlers speak about why they are voting Yes. May 2015.

There was so much achieved by this small group of dedicated people. Starting with KAL (Katherine and Ann Louise), moving through to the formation of ME and finally galloping to the end with Yes Equality. And in that final year, there were people in every county in Ireland working hard to bring ME over the line. ME, GLEN and the ICCL (Irish Council for Civil Liberties) were all working together, extraordinarily and surprisingly well. It felt like this huge boulder that a small group of us had been pushing up a hill was becoming lighter and lighter and that many of us could step back as others came with new energy, ideas and strength to push it over the edge and see it gathering speed as it rushed to cross the line.

I certainly stood back when Yes Equality took over and became in some ways an interested but passionate supporter, getting involved when asked. Key people in ME worked harder than ever, however, and led the charge with the other groups of fresh and fantastic supporters, activists and volunteers.

My final specific film input was four weeks out from the referendum when Gráinne Healy asked me to come into the Yes Equality office and meet Noel Whelan, along with Moninne Griffith and Andrew Hyland (who had always played key roles in these visual outputs).

At this point in the campaign we were moving just beyond getting lesbian and gay couples to talk about their lives (though that was always and will always be useful), we knew what we were asking for, people now knew what civil marriage was. Research and polls had been done and we knew who we needed to talk to, who we needed to convince, who was sitting on the fence. Crucial groupings of people to whom we wanted to send messages directly. And we knew who we wanted to carry those messages.

So I turned to my workmates again. Anna Nolan (Head of Development in COCO) came to the meeting with me and we undertook to make three videos that would be sent to clubs and groups and would, of course, be spread across social media. The social media machine of Yes Equality was strong, clever and lively.

Happily, lots of people were making various pieces of visual material in support of ME at this stage (2015). Some were scripted productions, like the superb and hilarious online short drama *Armagayddon*, where a gay couple had barricaded themselves in their own house in fear of their very sweet and helpful gay neighbours, following the fictional introduction of gay marriage. Who can forget the 'calling my Nanna' clip on YouTube, a simple single shot of a young gay man, James Mitchell, calling his granny to ask her to vote Yes in the referendum. These were fantastic pieces of material, with brilliant and important messages.

However, there was still the need to directly target the people identified by Yes Equality at this point, immediately before the referendum – the people of Ireland. In these videos, we were looking to straight people in the general population and wanting to stir up the reasons they were voting Yes.

Irish Times front-page photo, 23 May 2015. Linda Cullen and her partner, Feargha Ní Bhroin, at Blackrock polling station with their children, Tess and Rosa.

We filmed mass-going, ninety-year-old Madeline Connolly, mother of fourteen, grandmother of twenty-five children and great-grandmother of four, and she gave her reasons for voting Yes. We filmed her in our back garden (shout out to Joanne McGrath and all the crews) on a beautiful sunny day with the look of hope and light and colour. She was clear about why she was voting Yes. 'God made us all and he made us all equal, everybody should have the opportunity to get married,' she said, gazing into the camera.

We also filmed GAA hurler Conor Cusack and a group of young hurlers on a sunny Sandymount Strand (the GAA wouldn't let us use any of their pitches or grounds for the shoot). These powerful young sportsmen told us their reasons for voting Yes. One of them said, 'As a team we've experienced wins and losses, I've been through a lot with my team, I wouldn't want to feel that my gay team mates couldn't experience the right to marriage that I have.'

And the third video was Paddy and Pat O'Brien who were fifty-five years married and talked about their daughter Joan who'd been with her partner, Olivia, for sixteen years. They spoke beautifully of their own marriage and their children and they really nailed it when Pat said, 'There's nothing to lose by voting Yes, only to gain happiness, for a lot of people.' And Paddy finished off by saying, 'I wouldn't like to deny her that opportunity, if you vote No you're denying her that opportunity. I certainly don't want to do that.'

We ended up making five videos rather than three in the end – we were on a roll and brave families were prepared to become involved. The final two were made with Orla Howard and Gráinne Courtney's wider family, showing the intergenerational diverse nature of modern families in Ireland. We also made a lovely one with Anna Nolan's own family speaking about why they were voting Yes. Beautiful snapshots of these supportive families, who looked just like any family. All these people spoke very personally and spoke directly to many of the people we feared might not vote Yes. Their images appeared in the final campaign Household Leaflet that went into every home in Ireland the week before the vote – they were brave and effective images, of brave and loving families.

All these messages were important, crucial, even, to the success of the campaign. From the notion that we had to ask 'permission' to get married, to seeing real gay couples talk about their everyday lives and express how much marriage meant to them, through to the broader mainstream Irish community voting Yes and saying why, making a clear statement about the Ireland they wanted to live in.

Being a part of the Marriage Equality campaign has been an incredible experience. Sometimes deflating, often humbling but always a great privilege. Our children and their friends talk in a way that we never could. They talk with absolute ease about their family unit, their two mums. And they can do that because their six-year-old counterparts have an understanding that there are lesbian and gay people, and those lesbian and gay people can be parents and get married, just like their own parents.

Dáil visitors to see the safe passage of the Marriage Bill through the Oireachtas, September 2015. *From left:* Moninne Griffith, Seamus Dooley, Andrew Hyland, Katherine Zappone, Ann Louise Gilligan, Brian Sheehan, Alan Hatton, Linda Cullen and Davin Roche.

Brian Sheehan (above) and Kieran Rose

GLEN and the Remarkable Journey to Marriage[1]

The remarkable journey to marriage for same-sex couples has taken many years. Many people and organisations have played significant parts in building towards the extraordinary outcome in the Marriage Equality Referendum, including Marriage Equality (ME) and the Irish Council for Civil Liberties (ICCL), with whom the Gay & Lesbian Equality Network (GLEN) formed Yes Equality to campaign jointly in the referendum. This is the GLEN story about that journey, particularly across the decade from 2005.

The campaign for legal recognition goes back much further, at least to 1990, with the publication of the ICCL report, 'Equality Now for Lesbians and Gay Men'.[2] This recommended gay law reform on the basis of equality, equality legislation and domestic partnership legislation stating that:

> The right to form an intimate association in a domestic partnership is a fundamental issue for lesbians and gay men. Marriage is a legal status which is not open to persons of the same sex … and is an important social status in our society. The commitment implies stability and responsibility. Marriage is also a public statement of family relationships based on love. In our view, the law should formally recognise lesbian or gay domestic partnerships, and give them equal access to the various benefits conferred on married heterosexuals.

The report also went on to deal with issues of child custody and adoption.

The Civil Partnership Bill is signed by Minister for Justice Dermot Ahern,
with Kieran Rose of GLEN, December 2010.

Outside the Oireachtas after the commencement of the Civil Partnership Bill, 2010. *From left:* Brian Kearney Grieve (Atlantic Philanthropies), Chris Robson, Marie Hamilton, Senator Ivana Bacik, Odhran Allen, Kieran Rose, Eoin Collins, Sandra Irwin Gowran, Brian Sheehan, Tiernan Brady and Senator Jerry Buttimer.

Other significant milestones prior to 2005 in which GLEN was involved include the GLEN/LOT (Lesbians Organising Together) seminar on Partnership Laws (2000); Senator David Norris's Civil Partnership Bill (2003–5); Fine Gael Civil Partnership policy (2004); Joint Oireachtas Committee on the Constitution where GLEN's submission recommended civil marriage (2005–6); the Equality Authority supporting access to marriage; and Christopher Robson of GLEN leading the successful campaign to reform capital gains tax so that the surviving partner of a couple was not penalised by onerous taxation, achieved in the 2000 budget of Finance Minister Charlie McCreevy. Christopher was also strongly engaged with the group which formed to support the Zappone/Gilligan case – then known as the KAL Group – and went on to become a Board member of ME.

THE TAOISEACH LAUNCHES GLEN'S STRATEGIC PLAN

In 2005, with significant funding from Atlantic Philanthropies, GLEN was able to develop a very ambitious strategic plan to transform the situation for lesbian, gay and bisexual people in Ireland and to hire highly talented and experienced staff to implement that plan. We invited Taoiseach, Bertie Ahern to launch the plan in April 2006, and there he gave a powerful speech that got widespread publicity, partly because he was the first Taoiseach to speak at an LGBT event. He said: 'Our sexual orientation is not an incidental attribute. It is an essential part of who and what we are. Sexual orientation cannot, and must not, be the basis of a second-class citizenship. Our laws have changed, and will continue to change, to reflect this principle.' This strong commitment to progress, we were later told by officials, was critical in opening the door to legislative and institutional change.

Writing in *The Irish Times* at that time, GLEN Chair Kieran Rose said:

> The key outstanding legal issue for lesbians and gay men is the recognition of our intimate relationships. There is no reason why there should not be an equality of rights and responsibilities for all, in other words civil marriage for same-sex couples ... So in the recognition of gay relationships, our aim should be to become the sixth country in the world after Spain and South Africa to provide for civil marriage for lesbians and gay men.

THE COLLEY GROUP RECOMMENDS CIVIL MARRIAGE

The previous year, in August 2005, Brian Sheehan was Director of the Dublin Lesbian and Gay Film Festival, when the festival controversially invited Michael McDowell, then Minister for Justice, Equality and Law Reform, to open the festival. GLEN publicly supported this decision as an important opportunity for engagement with government. In his speech at the launch, the Minister proposed a very limited form of domestic partnership rights for all mutually dependent couples, including siblings, and said that, in his experience, lesbian and gay people did not want marriage. Following the festival, GLEN sought and was granted a series of meetings with the Minister in September and November 2005. At these, GLEN emphasised that, contrary to the Minister's perception, access to civil marriage was the desired equality option for lesbians, and gay men and suggested the establishment of a group to explore the issue.

In December, Minister McDowell established a Working Group on Domestic Partnership, chaired by former Progressive Democrat TD Anne Colley, to identify the categories of relationships and partnerships outside of marriage to which legal recognition might be accorded. The Minister nominated Eoin Collins, Director of Policy Change in GLEN, to the Working Group which also included senior civil servants and Eilis Barry, legal officer of the Equality Authority.

Protesting against the Civil Partnership Bill outside Dáil Éireann, 30 June 2010.

Preparing together for the Constitutional Convention. *Back from left:* Brian Sheehan and Tiernan Brady (GLEN), Clare O'Connell and Orla Howard (ME), Muriel Walls (GLEN), Dawn Quinn (ME), Stephen O'Hare and Wlater Jayawardene (ICCL). *Front from left:* Conor Pendergrast, Moninne Griffith and Gráinne Healy (ME), March 2013.

Yes Equality Meeting standing up: Cathy Madden, media advisor; Yes Equality Steering Committee members Ailbhe Smyth, Brian Sheehan, Mark Kelly and Kieran Rose, April 2015.

In early 2006, while the group were working, GLEN commissioned Lansdowne Research to do the first opinion poll specifically focused on public attitudes to relationship recognition for same-sex couples. The poll showed significant support for legal recognition, with 84 per cent in favour of relationship recognition for same-sex couples; 51 per cent in favour of civil marriage and a further 33 per cent in favour of civil partnership, but not civil marriage. On a tight nine-month timeframe, the Colley Working Group met twenty times and, after detailed analysis and public consultation, the Minister published the group's report in November 2006. The report noted that the exclusion from marriage had important implications for the status and standing of same-sex couples and 'contributing to a perception that their relationships lacked value and were unequal to others'.

Eoin Collins and others on the Working Group had successfully made the case that their recommendations should go beyond their original remit to consider just domestic partnership and that the relationships between same-sex couples and their children had to be included. This was a crucial turning point on the road to full civil partnership and civil marriage. The Group proposed just two options for same-sex couples: marriage and full civil partnership. Marriage, they said, would 'achieve equality of status with opposite sex couples and such recognition that would underpin a wider equality for lesbian and gay people'.

The Group noted that should marriage be vulnerable to constitutional challenge (the Zappone/Gilligan case was underway), full civil partnership was possible and would at least give equivalent rights and obligations of marriage to same-sex couples, though they noted that civil partnership would not give constitutional protection to same-sex couples and their families. An important aspect of the Group's report was the highlighting of the particular inequalities faced by a growing number of children now being parented by gay couples, particularly women, and a strong recommendation that the possibility of applying for adoption should be open to lesbian and gay couples.

The following month, December 2006, the judgement was handed down in the constitutional case taken by Katherine Zappone and Ann-Louise Gilligan to have their Canadian marriage recognised in Ireland. Unfortunately, the High Court ruled that there was no constitutional right to enter into a same-sex marriage. GLEN described the rejection by the court as a lost opportunity to affirm the status of lesbian and gay people as full and equal citizens under the Constitution.

THE LABOUR PARTY INTRODUCE A CIVIL UNIONS BILL

In a remarkable coincidence, on the same day as the Zappone/Gilligan case was lost in the High Court, the Labour Party launched their Civil Unions Bill for same-sex couples. GLEN strongly welcomed the publication of the bill, which aimed to give same-sex couples the same rights and obligations as married couples. As the GLEN press release noted, it was not marriage and constitutional protection, but it was a very welcome and significant step towards full equality. The Labour Party had accepted legal advice that the introduction of civil marriage would be contrary to the Constitution and would require a referendum. However, civil union was considered by the Labour Party as a constitutionally feasible way of delivering the same legal consequences available from civil marriage to same-sex couples. The Explanatory Memorandum noted that the bill was based on an analysis that accorded with the Colley Working Group.

A few weeks earlier, GLEN had met with Labour Party leaders and urged them to introduce a bill that would provide civil marriage for same-sex couples. Labour Party leaders replied that the legal advice they had received was that marriage would not pass constitutional scrutiny and, therefore, would not make headway in the parliament. (After the High Court decision, it was difficult to disagree with the Labour Party's position.) The Labour Party had sought GLENs support for their Civil Unions proposal and, in an inflection point in our campaign, we accepted that there was near-unanimous legal and other opinion that there was a perceived constitutional barrier to opening out civil marriage to same-sex couples. We also got the sense at the meeting that if we did not support the Civil Unions Bill, it would not be published or progressed.

Noel Whelan during the last weeks of the Yes campaign.

The Yes posters go up, 30 April 2015.

From left: Noel Whelan, Gráinne Healy, Brian Sheehan and Cathy Madden arrive at the RDS count centre, Dublin, 23 May 2015.

The GLEN strategy for civil marriage now shifted to getting full civil partnership enacted as soon as possible and all other legislation such as taxation, immigration and family recognition and protection in place so that civil partners would have all the statutory rights and responsibilities of civil marriage, although not the constitutional status. This strategy was modelled on the second successful divorce referendum where all the necessary legislation for separation was put in place first and then the referendum was about the right to remarry and not 'divorce', as such. The corollary was that when the marriage referendum was held, it would not be about taxation or immigration or parenting, but purely about equality under our Constitution and opening out the constitutional status of marriage to same-sex couples; this is how things turned out in 2015.

In February 2007, the Dáil debate on the Labour Party Bill commenced, with support in principle from all parties. A government wrecking amendment, based on waiting for the Supreme Court appeal in the Zappone/Gilligan case, meant that the bill was defeated, which, as GLEN noted in our press release, was a 'failure of political nerve on the part of the government ... which would cause considerable hardship for many lesbian and gay couples'. However, it should be said that the bill had a powerful impact in pushing the issue up the political agenda, allowing for well-considered Dáil debates that brought greater understanding of the issues and principles involved, and raised the expectations of LGBT people.

DELIVERING CIVIL PARTNERSHIP[3]

Prior to and during the election of 2007, GLEN worked to build support among all parties for equality-based legal recognition of same-sex couples and families, and all political parties included a commitment in their written manifestos to some form of legal recognition. In June, GLEN urged the parties negotiating the new Programme for Government (Fianna Fáil, the Green Party and the Progressive Democrats) to include a commitment 'to implement the recommendations of the Colley Working Group regarding same-sex couples and to introduce legislation at the earliest opportunity'. Following the negotiations, the new government agreed only to go as far as civil partnership. It is the final commitment in the Programme and, problematically, was conditional on waiting for the Supreme Court appeal in the Zappone/Gilligan case.

The Labour Party reintroduced their Civil Unions Bill into the Dáil in October 2007, but the government stuck to the position of waiting for the appeal judgement. Eoin Collins of GLEN met with Brian Lenihan, then Minister for Justice, Equality and Law Reform, and persuaded him to change his mind. This was a huge breakthrough, as the Supreme Court case could have taken years, as it did. Invited to speak at the launch of GLEN's annual report in December 2007, the Minister said that, given the urgency of the issue for lesbians and gay men, it was no longer his policy to await the outcome of the Supreme Court appeal and announced that he would quickly bring forth proposals for civil partnership for same-sex couples. The minister also stated that his advice was that marriage for same-sex couples would require constitutional change, though Kieran Rose pointed out that marriage was the full equality option for which GLEN would continue to strive. In June 2008, the Minister published the 'Heads' of the Civil Partnership Bill, which proposed two key models of recognition: a civil registration scheme for same-sex couples, providing equivalent rights and obligations to married couples, and a redress scheme for cohabitants, opposite sex or same-sex, who do not marry or register their partnerships.

Welcoming the 'Heads', we highlighted, and continued to campaign on, the very critical omission in relation to lesbian and gay families, which was entirely absent. Our campaigning on this issue continued and included roundtables and Dáil presentations with the Children's Rights Alliance (CRA) on the issues arising for the growing number of children being parented by same-sex couples. A backlash by Senator Jim Walsh, and thirty backbenchers within Fianna Fáil, seeking to reverse the government decision to go ahead with a bill was averted when GLEN quickly appeared twice in the one week on *Morning Ireland* and emphasised Fianna Fáil's proud tradition of republican principles, which includes treating everyone equally. Writing in his column in *The Irish Times*, Noel Whelan noted that '[Senator Jim] Walsh and others in the Parliamentary Party who oppose civil partnership for same-sex couples were clearly relying on the traditional strategy of those who oppose reform – delay'. The new Taoiseach, Brian Cowen, defending the bill, told journalists that civil partnership was a commitment in the Programme for Government and noted that 'My predecessor made an important speech in this whole area generally, which I would commend to everybody' (the speech by Taoiseach Bertie Ahern at the launch of GLEN's strategy in 2006).

The new Minister for Justice, Equality and Law Reform, Dermot Ahern, published the Civil Partnership Bill in June 2009. The bill provided comprehensive rights and responsibilities for same-sex couples who registered their civil partnership and the Minister stated that additional bills covering equal treatment for civil partners with the social welfare codes and the taxation systems would also be brought forward. As coalition partners, the Green Party had played a critical role in the delivery of the Civil Partnership Bill, which they described at the launch of the bill in GLEN's offices as an historic reform and a major step towards equality.

Brian Sheehan speaking at the Yes Equality victory party, Ballsbridge Hotel, Dublin, 23 May 2015.

Kieran Rose Sheehan at the press conference following the referendum result on Sunday, 24 May 2015, Radisson Hotel, Dublin.

While the bill offered very significant protections for lesbian and gay couples on a par with those available for married opposite-sex couples, the critical omission in the Heads of Bill was continued in the bill itself, with no provision for children being parented by same-sex couples. While we welcomed the bill as an achievement that would deliver real and immediate change for lesbian and gay couples, we highlighted the lack of recognition of children being parented by same-sex couples and urged the Green Party and the government to address this as the bill progressed through the Oireachtas.

There was a significant public campaign against the bill, including from the Catholic bishops, who restated their opposition to the Civil Partnership Bill as being 'marriage in all but name', and the Primate of All Ireland who warned that a legal challenge would be taken if the bill were enacted. Many of those who campaigned against the bill, including the Iona Institute, asked for extensive exemptions for public officials and religious organisations from the provisions of the bill. Such exemptions would have fatally undermined the spirit of the bill, and were eventually rejected by the Minister and the Oireachtas.

The Civil Partnership Bill and GLEN were also criticised from a different direction on a number of grounds, including on the basis that civil partnership was not marriage and would delay the introduction of marriage. In calculating how to respond to criticisms, GLEN faced some difficult choices. If we stated our strong belief that the legislation was the most effective stepping stone to marriage, we risked fuelling conservative opposition inside and outside of parliament and delay in getting the bill passed. As was noted subsequently, 'our clear understanding is that, had GLEN persisted with its preferred option (i.e. full marriage), civil partnership was at risk of going off the political agenda completely. GLEN understood this risk and made a calculated decision to pursue civil partnership and the legislative protections it brought'.[4]

When the bill was first debated in the Dáil in December 2009, in the midst of the political turmoil of one of the worst recessions ever seen in Ireland, a gallery packed with LGBT people heard very fine contributions by TDs, many stating that civil marriage was the ultimate equality option. That same evening, however, others protested outside the Dáil that the bill would be a barrier to civil marriage. In enacting civil partnership legislation, the government, supported by all parties in the Oireachtas, sought to provide a model of legal recognition as close to marriage as the prevailing understanding of constitutional limits would allow. Speaking in the Dáil, Alan Shatter TD said:

If, instead of using the formula 'civil partnership', the Bill referred to marriage simpliciter, there would have been a serious risk of a constitutional challenge to the legislation and therefore a substantial delay in its enactment. The Minister therefore had no choice other than to use the formula in the legislation. In other words, the relationship is marriage in everything but name.

Finally, in July 2010, the Civil Partnership and Certain Rights and Obligations of Cohabitants Act passed the Dáil with the support of all parties and, shortly afterwards, passed in the Seanad by a vote of forty-eight to four. An amendment drawn up by GLEN's Dr Fergus Ryan, and proposed by Senator Norris and the Labour Party in the Seanad, to expand guardianship of children to include civil partners was defeated, but attracted support from all parties. Later that year the accompanying Social Welfare Act passed, and in early 2011, following a tumultuous general election, the new government passed the Finance Act (No. 3) which provided for equal treatment in taxation matters for civil partners. Crucially, GLEN had been able to make a case to the government that children in a civil partnership should be entitled to the same tax treatment as children in a marriage, which was then included in the Finance Act, and established the principle of equal recognition of children in lesbian and gay families.

Brian Sheehan at the Yes Equality press conference following the referendum result on Sunday, 24 May 2015, Radisson Hotel, Dublin.

Success in retrospect is often seen as inevitable, but it's rarely the case. Speaking in July 2010 at the launch of a report on LGBT community issues as Minister for Community, Equality and Gaeltacht Affairs, Pat Carey said, 'There was never an element of inevitability about the introduction of civil partnerships in this country ... To be honest, when the Bill was introduced last year, many of us thought that it would not get through Dáil Éireann without a vote, and there was a serious danger that it wouldn't get through at all.'

CIVIL PARTNERSHIP AS A CATALYST FOR MARRIAGE

The momentum for further progress continued as a result of civil partnership, not, as some had feared, that marriage would disappear from the political agenda. The first civil partnerships were held in April 2011, to extensive media coverage and widespread public approval. At the end of the first year, nearly 800 couples had entered a civil partnership and an unknown number of couples who had foreign civil partnerships or marriages were automatically able to avail of the rights and entitlements applying to civil partnership in

Ireland. GLEN had engaged extensively in spring 2011 across the general election and the negotiation of a new Programme for Government between Fine Gael and the Labour Party, which included a commitment to a Constitutional Convention, that would explore, among other issues, marriage for same-sex couples.

On the anniversary of the first civil partnership, in April 2012, GLEN stepped up its campaign for civil marriage including stating in an op-ed in the *Irish Times* in April 2012 that 'The right to marry is a basic human right, as set out in the UN Charter of Human Rights and other human rights treaties. In a democratic republic based on equal citizenship, civil marriage should be open to all citizens, including lesbians and gay men.' Political engagement by GLEN and others continued and in 2012 the Fianna Fáil Ard Fheis supported marriage for lesbian and gay couples, joining the Labour Party, Sinn Féin and the Green Party. GLEN supported the establishment of the Fine Gael LGBT group which was launched in April by Jerry Buttimer TD, the group's Chair and the first publicly gay Fine Gael member of the Oireachtas. Subsequently, the Fine Gael Ard Fheis passed a motion to prioritise marriage in the Constitutional Convention.

The public momentum for marriage further increased, spurred by the hundreds of couples across the country who registered their civil partnerships. By June 2013, more than a thousand couples from all counties in Ireland had registered their partnerships and a further 200 couples had already given notice for their civil partnerships. The public enthusiastically welcomed civil partnerships being celebrated throughout the country. As an editorial in the *Longford Leader* stated: 'For many people the term "civil partnership" has become interchangeable with the term marriage. As far as they are concerned they are attending the 'wedding' of their gay or lesbian friends. The reality is that the tide of public opinion had just shifted towards an acceptance of gay marriage.' Breda O'Brien subsequently wrote in *The Irish Times* during the marriage referendum that 'It must be the most successful acculturation in Irish history.' In a heartfelt editorial in *Gay Community News* (*GCN*) in August 2012, editor Brian Finnegan wrote how he was at a civil partnership ceremony and 'suddenly I realised I was at a wedding' and that 'gay and lesbian couples who have civil partnerships are the ones driving the acceptance of marriage equality home'.

GLEN continued to campaign on parenting and children's issues, working with the new Justice Minister, Alan Shatter, building on the commitment in the Programme for Government to reform Family Law. In 2012, the Minister said:

I am acutely aware that we need to reform family law to secure equal citizenship for lesbian and gay parents and the best interests of their children. This reforming focus must also ensure that children in lesbian or gay family units are able to form a legal connection with their non-biological parent and that kindred relationships flow from such legal connection. Reforms are also needed in the areas of guardianship, custody and access, and to ensure maintenance and inheritance rights for the children of civil partners.

The campaign for legal recognition and protection continued with the strong support of the Children's Rights Alliance, LGBT groups and other civil society groups who sought to prioritise children's rights and protections. Minister Shatter published a comprehensive briefing note in November 2013 which fully included lesbian and gay parenting and which was followed by a Heads of Bill in January 2014 that was finally enacted in April 2015.

The Constitutional Convention announced that they would explore the issue of marriage during their April 2013 sitting. There were thousands of submissions from individuals and from civil society groups supporting and opposing marriage. GLEN's submission, 'The Remarkable Journey Towards Equality and Civil Marriage for Lesbian and Gay People in Ireland', called for marriage as the next step in that remarkable journey:

> GLEN, ME and the Irish Council for Civil Liberties joined forces in the presentation of the 'Yes'
> side to the Convention which, after an intensive weekend of debating, voted overwhelmingly
> to propose to the Government that the Constitution be changed to allow same-sex couples
> to marry. In a further remarkable outcome, the Convention voted by a larger majority to
> request the Government to bring forward legislation to recognise and support children
> growing up in lesbian and gay headed families.

'Bráinne': Brian Sheehan and Gráinne Healy as Dublin Pride Grand Marshalls, June 2015.

The three groups subsequently went on to set up the Yes Equality campaign, which was publicly launched in March 2015. Speaking at the Yes Equality launch, Kieran Rose Co-Chair of GLEN said: 'Walking up O'Connell Street this morning past the GPO where the Proclamation of our Democratic Republic was declared in 1916, where equality for all citizens was a central principle, I thought it would be a truly fitting celebration of the ideals of the Proclamation if we voted Yes to opening out civil marriage to all citizens.'

While there were, understandably, a number of disagreements and difficulties along the way, the Yes Equality campaign was soon highly professional and effective with Co-Directors Gráinne Healy and Brian Sheehan; Noel Whelan as the principal strategic advisor; a highly skilled and experienced advisory group; staff from the three organisations; and an extensive team of committed volunteers in HQ and in more than seventy Yes Equality groups all across the country. The campaign generated great enthusiasm, energy and hope from all sectors of society as Dublin City Councillor Críona Ní Dhálaigh wrote:

> It has been the most positive campaign I've ever been involved in. Yes, there were low points and ugly comments, but too few to mention. South West Inner city flat complexes were overwhelmingly voting Yes and looking forward in a lot of cases to voting for the first time. We were in Oliver Bond (a flats complex) on Wednesday night and there was a great atmosphere, all the young kids were looking for Yes badges and residents shouting down 'we are all voting Yes'.

Michael Barron

21

BeLonG To and Marriage Equality

On Saturday, 23 May 2015, the Irish people took a strong and determined stand for social justice, by securing a resounding Yes vote in the Marriage Equality Referendum. That day changed forever what it would mean to grow up Lesbian, Gay, Bisexual and Transgender (LGBT) in Ireland. The Irish people, via the ballot box, gave each and every LGBT child and young person in Ireland — and across the world — a strong and powerful message that they were loved, cared for, and didn't need to change who they were.

Many LGBT community organisations and activists, and many thousands of LGBT people and our allies drove the social change, for forty years or more, which resulted in the referendum victory. The establishment of Marriage Equality (ME) as a focused advocacy organisation in 2008 provided the central locus and drive for what was to become one of Ireland's most successful social change movements. It was also the beginning of a very strong working relationship between the two organisations – BeLonG To and ME. In many ways, there was a meeting of minds between the groups and a shared, positive, generous and open approach to our shared work. David Carroll (former Executive Director) and myself at BeLonG To developed very close links with both Moninne Griffith and Andrew Hyland at ME. We supported each other's campaigns and media work, developed joint funding applications and even submitted a joint complaint to the Press Complaints Commission at one stage! Beyond the mechanics of the work, we were all very personally supportive and encouraging of each other. Moninne and Andrew were particularly influential in BeLonG To's decision to become actively involved in the marriage equality campaign proper.

BeLonG To's journey as the national organisation for LGBT young people, aged between fourteen and twenty-three is the tale of a decade-long battle to deliver youth empowerment in towns and villages the length and breadth of Ireland. A battle that challenged ingrained societal homophobia, and helped set a foundation stone from which to fight for marriage equality.

ESTABLISHMENT OF BELONG TO

At the turn of the millennium, I worked in Dublin as a youth worker for Focus Ireland, the national homelessness charity. During that time, I also became the de facto worker for homeless LGBT young people, mainly because I was the only out gay member of staff. In a short space of time, it became clear that sexuality was a determining factor in the circumstances in which young LGBT homeless people found themselves. With no Irish research in this area of work, I relied on studies from other jurisdictions and my own experience that homophobia was endemic and a clear, contributing factor to these young people finding themselves on the streets.

Unable to keep up with demand, it became glaringly obvious that LGBT young people were being badly let down, as existing organisations were unable to fully support them. Focus Ireland was primarily focused on homelessness, while OutYouth, a voluntary youth group that had been meeting in Dublin under various guises since the 1980s, was not in a position to work with homeless young people.

Together with Fran McVeigh, Billy Rabbitte, Paul Rudden and Denise Croke, we founded BeLonG To, providing dedicated supports, and safe space for LGBT young people to talk about their complex and intersecting circumstances. We were also absolutely determined to throw a light on the lives of the most marginalised LGBT young people in Ireland and to stop future generations from enduring the same unnecessary trauma and hardship. Our vision for BeLonG To was to go beyond the confines of a youth-work setting, taking it into the area of advocacy. To deliver policy change and to activate a network of young people to stand up for their rights, through offering a positive image of LGBT young people, including Trans young people. We wanted to place at the very heart of the organisation, leadership and social change. Our agenda would be set by young people themselves.

Importantly, we wanted an organisation that did not use the age of sexual consent (17) as a lower age limit. In the early 2000s, young people's sexuality and gender identity were taboo issues, and it was widely believed that, even among other youth organisations, one became LGBT in adulthood only. We now know of course that children, on average, realise they are LGBT from twelve years old. Homophobia and transphobia would not be tackled unless we worked with younger age groups.

Within the first year of BeLonG To, two issues were repeatedly voiced by young people as real issues for them – homophobic and transphobic bullying in schools and their impact on the mental health of LGBT young people. The stubborn persistence of these two issues – they remain issues to this day – provided the platform from which LGBT youth activism would ignite.

On 30 March 2003, BeLonG To became Ireland's first State-supported youth service for LGBT young people. A force for good. A force to be reckoned with. And unbeknown to us then, it was also the start of our own journey towards a marriage equality referendum.

Michael Barron and Jaime Nanci as part of the 'We are Family' Marriage Equality Campaign, 2010.

Image of Michael Barron and Jaime Nanci used on the *Irish Times Weekend Magazine* cover, February 2015.

NURTURING LGBT YOUTH ACTIVISM ACROSS IRELAND

In its first year of opening, in 2003, BeLonG To supported fifty-two people. By 2015, the year of the Marriage Equality Referendum, the organisation was helping over 4,000 LGBT young people and their families across Ireland. These very same young people would go on to bravely tell their stories during the referendum campaign to win the hearts and minds of the Irish people.

Within a few years of BeLonG To's establishment, it quickly transpired that we needed to develop support groups across the country. Young people were making weekly trips from as far afield as Donegal and Mayo to visit our Sunday group in Dublin. BeLonG To received funding in 2007 to develop a comprehensive support infrastructure for LGBT young people across Ireland. Fast-forward to 2015, and our support infrastructure had grown to twenty LGBT youth groups, embedding BeLonG To in local communities from Donegal to Wexford. Through our youth work, LGBT young people were meeting up, many for the first time, in almost every county in the country, supporting themselves and their families. And, they were also getting engaged in BeLonG To LGBT awareness campaigns in their schools and local communities.

By the time the referendum was announced, young people had felt supported enough to come out to their local communities for a number of years. Crucially, they had not felt compelled to leave their homes and, in so doing, helped parents, grandparents, sisters, brothers, aunts and uncles across Ireland to see that the LGBT community was their family, too. Their voices crushed old prejudices. These teenagers, who had spent the last decade coming out in their local communities, were now voters, as were their friends and families. Slowly but surely, a shift was taking place across the country: an attitudinal change towards LGBT young people was taking root. A quiet, unassuming revolution of sorts had taken place in the hearts and minds of parents, teachers, families, the media and young people themselves.

STARTING TO GET INVOLVED IN THE MARRIAGE EQUALITY CAMPAIGN

Although marriage equality was not a central focus for BeLonG To at the time, a young man, Aodhan Gregory, and myself spoke at LGBT Noise's March for Marriage in 2008. The following year David Caroll of BeLonG To and his husband, Gary, along with myself and my soon-to-be husband, Jaime, featured in ME's fantastic poster campaign 'We are Family'. We were beginning, gently, to take a position and a role in the campaign, in part due to our strong and trusting relationship with Moninne, Andrew and all at ME.

BeLonG To launches its Yes campaign, O'Connell Street, Dublin, May 2015.

It wasn't always obvious that BeLonG To would publicly campaign on the Marriage Equality Referendum. Internally, the case was being made that marriage equality wasn't a youth issue, and with so much on our plate, we needed to focus our energies elsewhere – such as supports for LGBT refugees, mental health, and bullying in school. However, once the government announced that a referendum would be held, it became apparent that each and every one of the 4,000 LGBT young people attending our twenty-three youth groups had all been affected by the issue. For them, it remained one of the systematic barriers roaring at them that they were second-class citizens. Together, they made a powerful case to us that this was very much a BeLonG To issue. In discussion with the BeLonG To board, we agreed that we would prioritise the campaign, playing our part in the referendum campaign. However, it was imperative that our campaign linked to a wider picture: creating a fairer and more equal Ireland for LGBT young people.

On a deeply personal level – like so many of my BeLonG To colleagues – I wanted to do right by all of our young people. But I also wanted to do right by the many thousands of young people, now adults, who felt they had no choice but to leave Ireland in the past, because of their sexuality or gender identity.

Above: David Carroll introduces a Yes event
for BeLonG To, April 2015.
Left: Moninne Griffith, Michael Barron and
Andrew Hyland, March 2015.

The stakes, we believed, were high. Listening to young people, it was obvious that losing the referendum would reconfirm to them that their all too common experiences of homophobic and transphobic bullying and rejection were acceptable and appropriate in Ireland. In truth, the fear of the damage a No vote would cause to young people became our main motivation. In terms of messaging and winning over supporters, we turned this fear into an opportunity to support LGBT young people, but a very high level of anxiety about the outcome stayed with us until the outcome was clear.

As an organisation, we agreed to use our reserves, in the region of €60,000 from our fundraising, to fund the BeLonG To Yes campaign. On the suggestion of Tanya Ward from the Children's Rights Alliance, we also reached out to Carys Thomas, who had worked on the children's rights referendum a number of years previously. Carys agreed to take a leave of absence from her job in Wales and come to work with us as communications Director. Carys's experience and passion was key to the success of the BeLonG To Yes campaign.

MESSAGING IS EVERYTHING

Immediately, I gathered a number of key individuals to devise our campaign strategy, including David Carroll; Oisin O'Reilly, Office Manager; Anthony Muldoon, the then Political Adviser to Dominic Hannigan TD; and Nikki Gallagher, former Director of Communications for the Office of the Ombudsman for Children.

BeLonG To champion and former Irish president, Mary McAleese, speaking in favour of a Yes vote, 19 May 2015.

Together, with support from the BeLonG To board, it was agreed that the overall focus of the campaign, 'Bring Your Family With You', would focus on young people and their families, complementing the organisation's existing mission, vision and – crucially – expertise. We carved out a role for ourselves that would play to our strengths and support our vision of empowering LGBT young people to embrace their development and growth confidently and to participate as agents of positive social change. Our campaign would focus on the kind of country we wanted this generation and future generations to grow up in. We determined that the success of our campaign would depend on the quality of our messaging.

Focusing on the views of children and young people meant that we were able to contextualise the referendum as a children's rights issue that had the potential to positively impact on the lives of thousands of people. When the No campaign, in their efforts to alarm the population, spoke about the welfare of children in non-traditional families, BeLonG To was able to react swiftly and effectively with a counterargument. Our decision to reframe marriage equality as a children's rights issue of fundamental concern for all Irish families, and indeed citizens, was, I believe, significant in mobilising support. In May, in the final weeks of campaigning, BeLonG To campaigned on three simple messages, appealing to middle Ireland, parents, grandparents and directly to young people:

- This referendum will create a fairer and more equal Ireland for this generation and future generations of young people;
- Fifteen leading children and youth organisations all support a Yes vote, and have formed the #BeLonGToYES coalition;
- 'Bring your family with you to the ballot box, to change forever what it means to grow up LGBT in Ireland'.

VOTER REGISTRATION

Poll after poll identified 18- to 24-year-olds as the strongest supporters of marriage equality, with some age groups in favour as much as 88 per cent. We knew very early on that we needed to harness this support. One obstacle – a significant obstacle – was the fact that this demographic had been the least likely to register to vote, and the least likely to take their precious vote in hand to the polling booth. Consequently, we invested the necessary time, energy and resources motivating young people to register to vote, working in tandem with many other youth and Yes campaigning organisations, including the Union of Students in Ireland, SpunOut.ie, the National Youth Council of Ireland (NYCI), and Yes Equality.

A visible contribution made by BeLonG To was the production of our influential and emotive short film advertisement, *It's in Your Hands*, which focused on youth empowerment. In the weeks preceding the annual deadline for the Electoral Register, the film attracted over 31,000 views. The film opens with the lines 'Are you ready? This chance won't come

From left: Michael Barron, Senator Jillian Van Turnhout and David Carroll, BeLonG To event, 27 April 2015.

Minister for Justice Frances Fitzgerald and Senator David Norris join the Yes Bus canvass, 14 May 2015.

again. You have the power to change our country. It's in your hands.' The intention was to allow young adults, who had never voted before, to feel the power of their position, to feel connected to the referendum, and indeed to feel responsible for its outcome.

Our combined activities in October and November 2014 secured 40,000 new voter registrations, heralded at the time as the largest ever voter registration drive in the history of the State. Significant queues also formed at registration points across the country, in the window of time that the supplementary register was open in 2015, as 66,000 – predominantly young people registered on the supplementary register, and voted Yes in higher numbers than the general population. People of all ages voted Yes to marriage equality but the numbers were particularly high amongst young people. It would also seem that young people, LGBT and not, had not only activated their political selves in great numbers, but played a role in convincing others to turn out and vote Yes.

THE COALITION: #BELONGTOYES

ME and other LGBT groups had taken on the challenge to convince the people of Ireland, many of whom were brought up to believe homosexuality was a sin, that in voting Yes for marriage equality, it would see them on the right side of history.

Early on, we were sure that children's rights issues would be used by the No campaign to oppose marriage equality. Working in the children and youth sector for a good number of years, including as a board member of the Children's Rights Alliance and in BeLonG To, we had developed strong and trustful relationships with other organisations. We were in a strong position to bring together mainstream children and equality organisations.

Above all, people respected this coalition. It introduced children's rights 'brands', which were household names, to the campaign, which I believe made the issue 'safe' and less contentious. I had the opportunity in 2012 to visit the Minnesota marriage equality referendum campaign (which successfully resisted a constitutional ban on marriage for same-sex couples) and had seen how those opposed to marriage equality could try to use children as their central argument. This same argument had been used against BeLonG To for many years and so it was clear to me that we needed the voices and the organisations most associated in people's minds with protecting children to come out and campaign with us. The central involvement of Tanya Ward and the Children's Rights Alliance, Grainia Long and the ISPCC (Irish Society for the Prevention of Cruelty to Children) and Fergus Finlay of Barnardos, really changed the debate and robbed No campaigners of what they believed to be their trump card. Together we were able to confidently say – Yes, this referendum is about children rights, it is about the rights of LGBT children and young people to grow up in a country that values and respects them.

Major youth work organisations had the ability to reach into every corner of urban and rural Ireland. Activating them, as well as other minority rights organisations, including Pavee Point and the Migrant Rights Centre Ireland, would prove crucial to the success of the marriage equality campaign.

It was a long process, but supporting mainstream children's rights voices to come out for LGBT young people was too important an opportunity to miss. We began canvassing these organisations over a year before the vote. Many of these organisations went on their very own journeys, particularly membership organisations that needed to have their internal constitutional discussions. Delicate negotiations ensued, not unreasonably, as we understood that marriage was not an issue they had a position upon, as it was not an obvious children and youth issue.

However, by 30 March 2015, the BeLonG To Yes coalition was formed, the largest ever coalition of children's rights groups in Irish history. A diverse group, it included fifteen children and young people's organisations, including: Foróige, Youth Work Ireland, Migrant Rights Centre Ireland, Headstrong, Yes Equality, Pavee Point, Loving Our Out Kids (LOOK), Start Strong, UNESCO Child and Family Research Centre (NUI Galway), Barnardos, ISPCC, the Children's Rights Alliance, the NYCI, Empowering Young People in Care (EPIC), the Institute for Guidance Counsellors.

Our coalition partners' vast networks, up and down the country, would now allow us to support young people to talk to their parents and grandparents about marriage equality across the whole of Ireland, like Glenmore in Co. Kilkenny, where I grew up. Coalition partners such as Foróige put out material at a local level in the towns and villages where they were based. This mainstream voice signalled to LGBT young people that they were welcome in their communities and in their homes, and provided a positive and hopeful vision for Ireland's future that appealed to voters.

BRING YOUR FAMILY WITH YOU: ONLINE CAMPAIGN

Our campaign was multi-faceted and included a first-time voter registration drive, and volunteer canvassing, with a whole swathe of booklets, posters, badges and T-shirts, adding vibrancy and life to all proceedings. We also increased our online presence. It is widely accepted that the battle for marriage equality was in part won via social media. The BeLonG To Yes coalition campaign engaged online with 4.7 million individuals in total. This was best exemplified by our *Bring Your Family With You* short film, which was viewed more than half a million times. The film, directed by Aoife Kelleher and Hugh Rogers, and starring a host of well-known Irish actors, tells the story of a small village in rural Ireland. In this village, the young people have convinced their parents, aunties and grannies to come with them to the polling station to vote Yes to marriage equality. It was hugely effective in messaging to young people that they had the power to change their communities. It also featured, as a parody, on the John Oliver show on US television!

At the BeLonG To Yes campaign we also made short films explaining how to vote for first-time voters, developed a WhatsApp campaign to remind young adults to vote on 22 May and negotiated the '1 Voted' application on Facebook. In total, the online component of the campaign reached almost five million people.

Mary and Martin McAleese surrounded by members of BeLonG To advocating for a Yes vote, 19 May 2015.

MARY MCALEESE AND THE 'ARCHITECTURE OF HOMOPHOBIA'

Reaching out to undecided voters involved securing the support of some key and trusted allies. Having worked for the past ten years for the rights of LGBT young people, we were in a strong position to support the Yes Equality campaign in this regard. For example, we hosted the Taoiseach (Irish Prime Minister), Enda Kenny, who made his first appearance at an LGBT organisation during the campaign, garnering valuable media coverage. Significantly this intervention from the Taoiseach, at a key moment just a week before the vote, was themed around the importance of a Yes vote for LGBT young people. He met with young people at BeLonG To, who emotionally told him about how difficult it was for them to witness the No side's campaign, and how devastating a No vote would be for them. He comforted a young woman, Ali, an image and a message which was widely reported and an experience which he recalled a number of times in the closing days of the campaign. Again, the BeLonG To Yes message of the referendum being about LGBT young people had really taken hold.

But the standout moment came in the closing days of the referendum campaign, and it was in the form of our long-time ally, former President of Ireland Mary McAleese. While president, she had been highly supportive of our work to highlight suicidality and mental health among LGBT young people, and we knew that she would be a powerful advocate for the referendum campaign. I initially reached out to Dr McAleese in November 2014. On the same day she was asked, she said yes to working with BeLonG To on a Marriage Equality Referendum event. I tic-tac'd with her team and family over the next six months on messaging. Justin McAleese, who himself played a key role in the referendum campaign by leading the huge Dublin Bay South canvassing team, was centrally involved in this work. Maura Grant and Grainne Mooney, who have worked with the McAleeses since their time in the Áras, were also closely involved, and indeed all were a joy to work with. Symbolism and timing was always going to be key. Together we wanted an intervention that emphasised family and children and which reassured religious people that voting Yes was the right thing to do.

Again, she did not let us down, and delivered a stunning address on 19 May explaining why her family would be voting Yes. She spoke about the power of a Yes vote in chipping away at what she described as 'the architecture of homophobia'. The personal aspect of her speech, speaking of her son Justin, who is gay, was widely covered in the media and struck a chord with the public, as did her razor-sharp takedown of anti-marriage equality arguments. In doing so, she reassured Catholics across Ireland that it was okay to 'vote Yes to marriage equality on Friday and go to mass on Sunday'. Her core message, which again was the BeLonG To Yes core message, was that the only children affected by this referendum are the gay children of Ireland.

International image of Yes: Jaime Nanci and Michael Barron's famous celebratory kiss at the RDS count centre, Dublin, 23 May 2015.

LEGACY

It is still tough growing up LGBT in Ireland. Youth workers have seen a tenfold increase in the number of first-time service users, owing to negative and disturbing comments heard during the marriage equality debate, coming from the No camp. Coupled with the fact that 50 per cent of LGBT young people still consider suicide owing to stigma and homophobic and transphobic bullying, and that one in five LGBT pupils avoid school, we are far from where we need to be. We have huge work to do to end discrimination in our school system, to bring gender recognition to Trans children and to support the most marginalised in our community – including LGBT refugees.

However, in tapping into the quiet revolution that is underway in our towns and villages, often driven by LGBT young people, the Marriage Equality Referendum showcased the best of who we are. Much analysis has yet to be done and it will take time and perspective to do this. I really hope that in years to come we will be able to look back on this time and say with some confidence that the possibilities opened up by the Yes vote have helped further equality in other aspects of our society.

Laura Harmon

22

Working Together
The Student Movement
and Marriage Equality

'Civil partnership is yet another way of saying that gay people can be treated unequally and legitimately discriminated against,' boomed the voice of then Marriage Equality (ME) Board member and LGBT Noise organiser, Anna MacCarthy. I remember vividly the March for Marriage on 22 August 2010, standing with fellow students from University College Cork near the Department of Justice and listening to what was one of the most powerful and memorable speeches during the campaign for marriage equality. 'We will not be settling for second class citizenship,' she said.

And settle we did not. The campaign for marriage equality in Ireland was one that spanned decades and was achieved through the collaborative efforts of many civil society organisations working together. The Union of Students in Ireland (USI) campaigned closely with many organisations, including ME, to ensure the passage of the referendum. ME played a critical role in ensuring the passage of the referendum and, as part of its campaign efforts, provided the much-needed legal and researched arguments as to why civil marriage equality matters, and why civil partnership was not enough. We cannot underestimate the importance of the fact that we had ME – a single-issue organisation working solely to campaign for marriage equality in Ireland, much in the same way that it was vital that we had Transgender Equality Network Ireland (TENI) campaigning predominantly on Trans rights, which ultimately brought about the Gender Recognition Act 2015.

From left: Moninne Griffith, accepting a big cheque from Café, Choral Confusion and Gloria, with Olivia McEvoy, Laura Harmon and Pauline Tracey, June, 2012.

Jason Aughney *(left)*, president of IT Blanchardstown students' union, and James Duffy, president of the National College of Ireland's students' union, give Laura Harmon *(centre)* a little lift on International Happiness Day, 20 March 2015.

The passing of the Civil Partnership Bill in 2010 was welcomed by many as a stepping stone to full marriage equality, but it was stated clearly at the time by the then Minister for Justice, Dermot Ahern, that 'this is not a stepping stone to marriage'. The years 2010 and 2011 were a critical time in the campaign because there was a danger that people might become complacent after the commencement of the Civil Partnership Act, a worry that the public would equate civil partnerships to civil marriage itself, to full equality and the campaign for marriage equality could stagnate.

It was important to recognise the progress associated with the Civil Partnership Act but also to insist that we needed to go much further. In the run-up to the 2011 general election, it was vital to lobby political parties and raise awareness of the differences between civil partnership and access to civil marriage. These issues included financial and immigration issues, and the legal relationship between parents and children and the family home, but it was also critical to highlight that language mattered. Even if civil partnerships had all the rights of civil marriages, calling something by another name was creating a separate and two-tiered system, because the term 'marriage' is the highest status conferred on loving, committed relationships in Ireland. One of the most problematic aspects of the Civil Partnership Act was its complete omission of children and how it ignored the existence of families headed by LGBT parents. ME consistently highlighted these issues to great effect through lobbying, the media and through publications and research, and helped to equip other organisations with the appropriate language and the facts.

ME's 2011 'Missing Pieces' report and campaign, in particular, is one which I associate as having a massive impact and playing a very important role in educating people on why anything short of access to civil marriage was not true equality. For pro-marriage equality spokespersons in other organisations and for the student movement, the 'Missing Pieces'[1] report was a very useful handbook as were the 2010 'Voices of Children'[2] report and the 2013 'LGBT Parents in Ireland'[3] report.

As a student in University College Cork, I considered ME as an important go-to organisation when it came to arming myself with facts about the campaign and about the legal arguments. At that time, Moninne Griffith (Director of ME) was in regular contact with LGBT societies and students' unions on college campuses, and ME delivered many workshops as well as providing vital information and materials to students. I remember our UCC LGBT Society using the 'Out To Your TD' packs and distributing the 'Just Love' badges on campus. The USI and ME always had a strong communication channel over the years and this continued when I worked as USI Equality and Citizenship Officer from 2012 to 2014 and as USI president from 2014 to 2015. ME and USI were close friends and allies and it was a pleasure working together. We shared information and best practice and worked together in partnership on many occasions.

The USI was no stranger to campaigning for LGBT equality and had highlighted the need for LGBT rights as far back as the 1970s. Eamon Gilmore (later Labour Party leader and Tánaiste in government), during his tenure as USI president, had called for marriage equality in 1977. The USI was also active in the lead-up to decriminalisation of homosexual acts in 1993. It was a privilege to be able to work for students and on USI's marriage equality campaign in the three years before the referendum. My colleagues and I were deeply conscious and proud of the work that had been done by student leaders in the past and we knew we had a responsibility to ensure that the student movement did everything in our power to play our part in the referendum campaign.

Over the years, students' unions passed motions on their campuses to support a Yes vote and this ensured that when it came to 2015, the entire student movement was united for the cause. USI had been running Pink Training for over twenty years – the largest student Lesbian, Gay, Bisexual, Transgender and Queer training event in Europe. Hundreds of students gather every year to learn about LGBTQ rights and to build networks. This event was pivotal in mobilising students and over the years, the staff of ME was always integral to the event – delivering workshops and providing materials to the delegates. In turn, students and LGBT societies regularly fundraised for ME on their campuses and volunteered for the organisation.

Laura Harmon takes some questions at the 'I'm Voting Yes. Ask Me Why' launch at the National Library, Dublin, 9 April 2015.

Laura Harmon enjoys a cup of tea with journalist Charlie Bird to promote 'I'm Voting Yes. Ask Me Why'.

The telling of stories was a very effective aspect of the campaign and something that ME always led with, providing case studies and media spokespersons to convey the arguments in real-life terms and bring the human aspect to the debate. In 2013, USI made a submission to the Constitutional Convention. Students told their stories in our submission about why marriage mattered to them and about why civil marriage equality was a student issue. Mental health was a big issue for young LGBT people and students, and we knew that passing the referendum would send out a very positive and validating message to young LGBT people who were struggling with their sexuality and were being oppressed as a result. Again, USI worked closely with ME in relation to the Constitutional Convention itself and in relation to the sharing of information. It was an amazing feeling to be at the Constitutional Convention in April 2013 when its members voted overwhelmingly (79 per cent in favour) that government, in holding a referendum on the issue, would support the extension of marriage rights under the Irish Constitution to all couples regardless of gender. This was another milestone on the way to a referendum.

The same year, USI unanimously passed its 'Towards Marriage Equality 2015' strategy document at our annual Congress. Voter registration, training and canvassing were all identified as some of the core areas where students could make a real impact on the campaign.

Big Love: Volunteers gather to attempt a world-record-sized heart at Smithfield, Dublin, 25 April 2015.

In 2014/2015, student leaders directly registered 27,663 students to vote and handed out tens of thousands of forms. It was recognised by many as one of the most effective voter registration campaigns that had ever been seen in Ireland. Queues and queues of students lined up to register to vote. Student leaders and LGBT societies worked tirelessly to register as many new voters as possible and many college campuses were successful in lobbying to get exam dates moved so that students could travel home to vote.

In January 2015, USI launched the student 'Make Grá The Law' campaign, the title of which was the brainchild of Síona Cahill, the then Welfare and Equality Officer in Maynooth Students' Union. We launched our voteforlove.ie website also. Moninne Griffith and Gráinne Healy (Chairwoman of ME and then Co-Director of Yes Equality) attended our launch in Wood Quay that day, as well as representatives from BeLonG To, politicians and other organisations. We were overwhelmed with the enthusiasm that the student body had for the cause and marriage equality was the student movement's priority campaign for 2015.

Alongside Yes Equality, USI also ran a successful media campaign targeting traditional media and college media and also targeting the Irish language media via our Irish language officer, Feidhlim Seoighe. Throughout the campaign, USI frequently met with Yes Equality and we attended the weekly Yes Equality meetings at their HQ offices, to share information with other organisations on how the campaign was progressing. Moninne Griffith and Andrew Hyland (Co-Directors of ME) shared a great relationship with USI and we worked closely together during the campaign. USI also worked closely with Michael Barron and David Carroll in BeLonG To, in relation to mobilising young people.

One of my most memorable events from the campaign was the Big Love event the Union of Students in Ireland ran in Smithfield to create the biggest human love heart on 23 April 2015. Despite the lashing rain in an otherwise sunny month, over 500 people turned up to show they supported a Yes vote. Among the speakers was Gráinne Healy of Yes Equality. The aerial photograph of our heart made the papers and was a welcome positive lift in a campaign that was often stressful for members of the LGBT community who had to listen day in, day out, to our rights being debated in the national media.

The momentum was building fast in the final weeks. Yes Equality joined USI and SIPTU when we unveiled our giant Students for Marriage Equality 'Yes' banner on Dublin's Liberty Hall in early May and the launch was attended by representatives from Yes Equality. Students were canvassing with their local Yes Equality groups in their communities and talking to their peers and to their families. The USI Equality and Citizenship Officer, Annie Hoey, spearheaded USI's campaign and worked tirelessly to mobilise students across the country. She organised USI's flagship Pink Training event in Cork in November 2014. The weekend conference focused heavily on training students in campaigning for a Yes vote and it was attended by a record number of students. In the months leading up to the vote, she travelled across the country conducting training events for students on messaging and canvassing. Annie also came up with the idea of 'voter motor', a campaign that was launched by USI in the final week of the campaign, to encourage people to give their fellow citizens a lift to the polling stations, if they were in a position to do so.

All of us could rest easy that we had done everything in our power to get the vote out and to promote a Yes vote, but the air was thick and heavy on 22 May. There was a tension in the atmosphere. There was so much at stake. I think we all went to bed that night knowing that the impending result would change our lives forever and, as we tossed and turned, we hoped that tomorrow, Ireland would become a better place.

The sun was warm on our faces as thousands of us, rainbow-coloured and elated, rippled in to the grounds of Dublin Castle and gathered on the streets of Ireland to hear the final results coming through. I remember the feeling of pure joy and acceptance, like no other feeling I had ever felt in my life before. It was clear from the outset that we had won when the first of the ballot boxes were opened in count centres across the country. I watched eagerly that morning to see the results of my home constituency of Cork North West coming through, where I had voted Yes with all of my family the day before in the primary school in which I spent my childhood.

Big Love: The USI's 'Make Grá the Law' attempt at the world's biggest human heart, Smithfield, Dublin, 25 April 2015.

I remember the trepidation and the excitement, as we watched the votes being counted. We held our breath and hoped desperately that with every box that was opened we would find the keys to a brighter future. The Irish people had spoken and love had won out handsomely in the end. Couples kissed, friends embraced, glitter was thrown, cameras flashed, tears of happiness were shed and we all breathed a collective sigh of relief. It was a proud day to be Irish and to be a member of the LGBT community. For the first time in our lives, we were equal; we were family.

'Achieving marriage equality won't create a perfect society, there will still be homophobia, transphobia, bullying and homophobic attacks.' Anna MacCarthy was right when she said this in her 2010 speech, but equal access to marriage was one of the most important steps along the way to full equality and acceptance of our LGBT citizens in Ireland. We have a long way to go yet to ensure equality for all in our LGBT community but the future is looking very bright.

Thalia Zepatos

Hands Across the Water
Freedom to Marry and Marriage Equality

PARALLEL MOVEMENT

Freedom to Marry, a US-based organisation founded in 2003, has served for years as an informal clearing house of information and strategies to marriage movements worldwide. Evan Wolfson, our inspiring founder and president, had been in contact with Marriage Equality (ME) Ireland since its inception in 2008, exchanging information and ideas via email and by phone. Soon after the state of Massachusetts secured its victory as the first US state to win marriage, Marc Solomon (of Mass Equality and later Freedom to Marry) came to Ireland and helped shape a strategy which focused on ensuring that every Irish TD and Senator would receive visits from marriage supporters in their constituency or office.

In late 2010, Evan travelled to Ireland to meet with marriage equality advocates and lawyers, sharing his perspective on how the soon-to-be-enacted civil partnership law could serve as a springboard to winning full marriage equality in Ireland. Soon after his return from Ireland, Evan asked me to begin sharing research and messaging resources with Moninne Griffith, Director of ME.

As the Director of Research and Messaging for Freedom to Marry, I had two primary roles in the American movement to win marriage for same-sex couples. By 2010, our movement had lost thirty-one statewide votes on marriage, and we all knew that we needed to fundamentally shift the conversation we were having with voters. I hired a research team, organised a collaborative research consortium with colleagues, and together we 'cracked the code' on why we were not connecting better with voters in the US. Our movement had been talking primarily about 'rights and benefits' of marriage, which resonated with our supporters, who were the very people being denied those rights and benefits. But the average American had a different concept of marriage, it seemed.

Our research found that most Americans defined marriage in terms of 'love and commitment' and that the legal rights of marriage were subsidiary to those ideals. In fact, by emphasising legal rights, we realised we may have been making the case for domestic or civil partnership, and not strongly making the case for marriage. Over time, we had inadvertently created the impression that same-gender couples wanted to marry for different reasons than straight couples did. By changing our messaging, we could win over new supporters and start driving our polling numbers up nationwide, which was a crucial part of our national strategy.

A second key role for me was to help in winning legal marriage, state by state. Our national strategy also called for building momentum through a steady stream of state victories, in preparation for the day when we would make our case at the Supreme Court in order to secure a nationwide decision. Every year we would study the map and evaluate the political dynamics of each state, then choose several states where we would push to win marriage. We had achieved victory in some states through court cases, and others by passing bills through state legislatures. Yet our opponents taunted us with the idea that we had never yet won a statewide vote of the people to legalise marriage for gay and lesbian couples.

When I came to Freedom to Marry, I was a veteran of many statewide referenda campaigns – fighting to maintain legal abortion in US states, and to defend the lesbian, gay, bisexual and transgender community from attacks in my home state of Oregon, and beyond. Another important focus for my work was to help turn around our long string of losses in high-profile campaigns like California's Prop 8 (a 2008 ballot proposition that stated that 'only marriage between a man and woman is valid in California'). We had to show that we could win the popular vote in one or more statewide referenda on marriage.

In 2010 and 2011, I focused on developing a public education campaign called 'Why Marriage Matters', which began telling the stories of same-sex couples who wanted to marry for reasons similar to other couples. Quietly, we were also working on ways to respond to and undermine fear-based attacks from the opposition. In high-profile campaigns like Prop 8 in California, we had seen how fear-based messaging from opponents could upset and alienate supporters who had been leaning toward voting for our side. Attack ads that focused on threats to children were particularly effective. It was common for our opposition to create ads stating that legalising marriage for gay people would mean that children would be taught about homosexuality at a young age, or to claim that children who were raised by a same-sex couple would somehow be irreparably harmed. We conducted research that helped us understand some of the underlying concerns, so that we could respond more effectively to those attacks.

By 2012, Freedom to Marry had four states preparing to go to the ballot on marriage equality issues to vote on marriage – Maine, Maryland, Minnesota and Washington. Many states were employing the 'Why Marriage Matters' messages in public education efforts, and we had evidence that it was working. We provided each of the referenda campaigns with all of our research, and pre-tested strategies on how to push back on opposition charges that marriage for same-sex couples would be harmful to children. In November 2012, we won a clean sweep in all four states, which helped boost momentum for marriage in the US.

In 2013, the US Supreme Court invalidated a key component of the Defense of Marriage Act (DOMA) which had been in place since 1996. The Defense of Marriage Act barred the federal government from recognising same-sex marriages, which were legal in some US states, and numerous federal protections of marriage were withheld from legally married couples. Edie Windsor, whose wife Thea Spyer had died, sued the government after being forced to pay excessive taxes when she inherited Thea's estate. Victory in the Windsor decision in 2013, unleashed a series of pro-marriage decisions in lower courts, which would put us on the fast track to return to the Supreme Court only two years later.

During this period, the fight for marriage equality in Ireland was also rapidly heating up. We had cheered from afar as our colleagues from ME joined the Gay & Lesbian Equality Network (GLEN) and the Irish Council for Civil Liberties (ICCL) to win support at the April 2013 Constitutional Convention to place a referendum on marriage for same-sex couples before the voters of Ireland. Momentum was building quickly in Ireland, just as it was in the US. In 2014, both countries were heading into the final crucial stages of our national efforts.

HANDS ACROSS THE WATER

My email discussions and Facetime conversations with Moninne were becoming more frequent. Dublin was eight hours later than the time at my home office in Portland, Oregon, so I would often talk with Moninne late in the evening when she had returned home after another busy day as Co-Director of ME. As our list of topics grew, I suggested that it might be time for me to come to Dublin and meet with Moninne and her colleagues in the wider campaign for a few days.

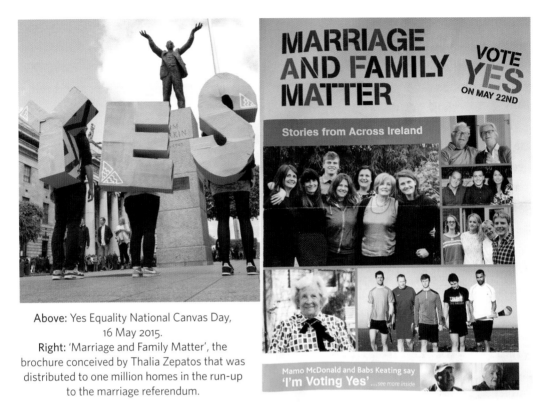

Above: Yes Equality National Canvas Day, 16 May 2015.
Right: 'Marriage and Family Matter', the brochure conceived by Thalia Zepatos that was distributed to one million homes in the run-up to the marriage referendum.

I travelled to Dublin in September 2014, along with my friend and colleague Aisling Coghlan. Aisling was Irish by birth, and was a stalwart ally of the LGBT community in Oregon. She had managed the statewide campaign to defeat a 'one-man, one-woman' marriage amendment in Oregon in 2004, and had been strategising ever since on how to win marriage for same-sex couples in our state. I knew she could help bridge the differences between campaigning in the US and Ireland, and together we spent several days in meetings set up by ME Co-Directors Andrew Hyland and Moninne Griffith.

What struck me initially as we talked with our Irish colleagues were the stark differences in the legal rules around campaigning. In Ireland, paid political ads on broadcast television were not allowed, while we relied on that type of advertising heavily in our US-based campaigns. We rarely engaged in head-to-head debates with our opponents on radio and television in the US, since we felt those provided opportunities for our opponents to spread attacks and misinformation. In Ireland, we were told, scores of broadcast and radio debates would be a central part of the referendum campaign.

As we talked about the building blocks of successful campaigns, I was relieved to hear that there were many parallels, as well. Grassroots conversations – what we had come to describe as 'long-form' conversations – had been the backbone of our success at the ballot in 2012 in the US. When we found voters willing to engage with us, our volunteers were instructed to answer their questions and talk with them at length. It was wonderful to learn that door-to-door canvassing was a strong component of the Irish political tradition, with many political party regulars willing and able to knock on doors.

In America, our movement was surging because of the support of young people, and one of the most exciting meetings during our time in Dublin that September was a joint meeting with BeLonG To and the Union of Students of Ireland, to discuss voter registration as a key strategy to engage Irish students and young people in the marriage movement.

One evening at dinner with Gráinne Healy, Chairwoman of ME, we discussed the likelihood that opponents would continue to raise fears about the referendum's impacts on children, as they had during the Constitutional Convention. In the United States, we had learned that telling voters our personal stories and speaking to them about core values was our most effective means of responding to fear-based attacks. And while I could share the values that resonated with American voters, we all agreed that it would be crucial to identify and speak to deeply held Irish values during the upcoming campaign. This would be important work for Irish-based research firms on behalf of the campaign.

In the months after that September 2014 trip to Dublin, Freedom to Marry maintained contact as the coalition between ME, GLEN and ICCL continued to prepare for their joint referendum campaign. As the lists of questions and discussion topics grew, Freedom to Marry invited the Irish coalition groups to send a team of representatives to our New York office for information sharing and discussion.

In mid-January 2015, Moninne Griffith and Andrew Hyland, Co-Directors of ME; Tiernan Brady, the Policy Director of GLEN; and Karen Ciesleski of ICCL, flew to New York for three days of intense meetings at Freedom to Marry headquarters. Holly Pruett of Freedom to Marry organised and facilitated the sessions as we worked through an agenda that allowed our Irish colleagues to meet face to face with our President, Evan Wolfson, our Campaign Director, Marc Solomon and experts from our national team. Andrew and Moninne brought copies of a comprehensive campaign plan, which they had drafted – the Roadmap to Marriage Equality.

In three short days, we Americans attempted to convey to our Irish visitors all we had learned as we won marriage in state after state across the US. Richard Carlbom discussed his experience in building a massive movement-based campaign to win Minnesota (a state slightly larger than Ireland); our Communications Director, Kevin Nix, reviewed strategies for engaging the media; Michael Crawford and the online team discussed digital organising and Field Director extraordinaire Amy Mello detailed canvassing strategies and the logistics of voter engagement on a massive scale. We brainstormed ideas for grassroots fundraising in Ireland, as the culture around donating money to campaigns seemed significantly different from what we were accustomed to in the US. Between the meetings, we shared meals and told war stories from previous campaigns. Some things are universal, after all.

TRAVELLING TO CAMPAIGN HEADQUARTERS

Social media made it easy for me to follow developments from day to day. I became alarmed after Andrew sent me the link to an early debate on *Claire Byrne Live*, and then relieved after watching video footage of Gráinne Healy at the Yes Equality Campaign launch, declaring that Yes Equality was the family values campaign. It was no surprise when I opened the link to the opposition's campaign website – their committee was called Mothers and Fathers Matter – that message was directly taken from our opposition's playbook in the United States.

Spring 2015 was heating up as a busy time for our efforts in the US, as well. After years of working in parallel, it seemed that our two national movements would now be moving towards conclusion within a month of each other. By that time, we had won marriage in thirty-seven of the fifty American states and public support was polling at almost 60 per cent. Mary Bonauto, a brilliant movement legal strategist, would go before the Supreme Court to argue on behalf of Jim Obergefell (and fourteen same-sex couples) that marriage was a fundamental right guaranteed by the Federal Constitution. Oral arguments on the case were scheduled for the Supreme Court on 28 April, with a decision expected in late June. The Irish government scheduled the marriage referendum for 22 May, at the mid-point between those two events.

Not only would a win on the Yes Equality campaign be a tremendous victory for Ireland, it could send a powerful signal to observers in the US at a very crucial time.

I talked with Evan, and while we had a tremendous amount of work leading up to the Supreme Court, we agreed that I should spend a week working alongside our colleagues in Ireland. They had sent me the address of the campaign office on Clarendon Street, and I booked a flight and a hotel room nearby. I was determined to try and be of assistance and not create extra work for them by showing up at a very busy time. I found my way to the campaign office about six weeks before the election, rang the buzzer and came upstairs. The giant room was easy to recognise as a campaign office – dozens of people clustered around tables, clicking away at laptops or walking the halls while talking rapidly on the phone. I recognised the faces of colleagues I had met and worked with in Dublin and New York, now surrounded by many others who had taken on supportive roles as the campaign expanded.

Thalia Zepatos with Noel Whelan *(left)* and Paula Fagan *(foreground)* at Yes Equality HQ, 9 April 2015.

Brian and Gráinne, now Co-Directors of Yes Equality, welcomed me warmly, and introduced me to Noel Whelan, an experienced political party operative who was now advising the campaign. They briefed me on their opening campaign message, 'I'm Voting Yes. Ask Me Why.' I thought the approach was terrific, because it set a very positive tone and invited the kind of back-and-forth conversation that would provide the opening for LGBT people and straight allies to invite others to join in support. Noel suggested I talk individually with staff, then pitch in and work for a couple of days, after which they offered to sit down and hear my thoughts about how the campaign was progressing.

One staffer pointed me to an open spot at a table and pushed a rolling chair in my direction. I introduced myself around the table, shook hands, plugged in my laptop, and got to work. My first conversation was with Andrew, who was serving as Director of Communications of the now formally titled Yes Equality campaign. Andrew was now leading a much larger communications team, aided by other professionals who had taken leave from their jobs and were volunteering full-time. He clicked open a couple of videos that were making the rounds, of young people calling their grannies and asking them to vote Yes. Despite the lack of paid ads on television, I could see how videos shared online would be the key to storytelling for the campaign.

Andrew and the Communications team had begun collecting press coverage of the Yes and No campaigns to send out via a daily email, and I tossed out a concept I had seen used in US campaigns – lead off each email with a 'message of the day' to focus campaign staff, partners and key volunteers on the single most important proactive message or point of rebuttal each day of the campaign. 'Love it! We'll do it!' Andrew said, as he turned back to his work.

There are never enough hours in a campaign day, and I didn't want to randomly engage staff in conversation that might take them away from important deadlines. I relied instead on Bráinne (as co-Directors Brian and Gráinne were now called) to point me towards people they thought I should be working with.

'Thalia, can you chat with Denise Charlton about fundraising ideas? She's working with Karen on that ...'

'Can you tell Orla Howard what you had been saying about signature ads in local newspapers?'

Yes, of course.

'Here's Seamus Dooley, he's working on the Messaging Bible, take a look.' After I'd read his draft materials and shared some thoughts, Seamus (General Secretary of National Union of Journalists, on leave to be part of the campaign) brought me to a meeting which he had scheduled to discuss possible responses to the opposition's already relentless messaging that 'children need a mother and a father'. Campaign spokespeople and academic experts crowded around the table and, as they offered ideas about how to respond, I found that I had strong opinions about what they were saying but being so new to the Irish context, I really questioned whether I should weigh in with these Irish experts. After listening carefully to the discussion for a while, I offered what I had learned from years of paid research and voter engagement in the US: when voters are overtaken by fear-based arguments, we can't calm their fears or change their minds by presenting facts or statistics to undermine the opposition case. We must move to a discussion of higher values, in a non-confrontational way, to help voters resolve their concerns.

For two days, I sat in on meetings, grabbed a quick meal when invited, and made notes about how the campaign was doing. As I walked up and down Grafton Street, someone invariably noticed my Yes Equality badge and asked where they could get one. More often than not, I took the button from my lapel and handed it to them after a brief chat about the importance of helping the campaign. Gráinne took me along one evening to a campaign debate in Dublin City University, which provided a chance for me to see the opposition (as well as our spokespeople) in action. On another evening, she brought me along to a campaign organising event in Ratoath, Co. Meath.

Dublin GAA star Rory O'Carroll (*left*) and Anna Nolan launch 'Marriage and Families Matter', 7 May 2015.

The next morning, as I came into the office, I saw Noel. He suggested that I join him, Brian and Gráinne for lunch. 'Let's have a meal and talk about how the campaign is going.' Shortly afterwards, I took out a pad of paper and drew a line up the middle. I made a list on the left side of all the things that I thought were progressing well in the campaign. On the right, I listed ideas for things to add or change. I thought carefully about that second list, because I felt I needed to prioritise the strategies that were most crucial to victory. I crossed off several items that didn't make the grade.

Four of us went across the street for lunch, catching up on campaign news and developments. About the time we had almost finished eating, Noel turned to me and asked me to share my thoughts about the campaign. I started out by listing the many things I thought the campaign was doing well. There was a clear plan laying out priorities for the team, with direct lines of communication and clarity about assignments. While there was a general hubbub in the crowded campaign office, there was not any confusion. Decisions were being made quickly and conveyed clearly. This was especially important, and a great relief, since the campaign had adopted a Co-Director structure, which could have led to extra time making decisions or resolving issues. By then, Brian and Gráinne were already operating like clockwork, and things were moving swiftly along.

The research and messaging work had gone well. The team had identified Irish values, such as inclusion, fairness and equality that would be pre-eminent during the campaign. While in the US we had defined marriage as 'love and commitment' in the Irish context, it was a 'foundation of society', which had unique constitutional protection. They had created a campaign message that was uniquely Irish, based on principles that I believed to be very sound.

I went on to say that message discipline seemed to be strong, with the daily briefing book and messaging bible, and impressive senior level staff in place to handle key aspects of the campaign. As I looked back at my list of 'what's going well', Noel held up his hand and thanked me for the positive feedback.

'Let's move on,' he said, 'Tell us what we're not doing right ...'

I took a deep breath. While I had gotten to know Gráinne and Brian a bit more over time, I really did not know Noel well. Although he had invited my feedback, how would he take to an American flying into Dublin and offering potential criticism of an Irish campaign?

I started by talking about the mindset of the conflicted voter, as we had come to understand them in the US. They may know someone who is gay or lesbian, and want to be fair to that person, yet they may have some unconscious fears or misperceptions about who gay people are, and why they want to get married. They might want to show they were tolerant of gay people by voting Yes, but they were very vulnerable to attacks from the opposition, which wanted to make the campaign all about how children would somehow be negatively affected. Voters could easily be diverted from Yes to a No vote. The campaign's job was to keep them with us, throughout several challenges already in play.

First of all, the campaign had to develop a stronger approach to an easy 'out' that we also encountered frequently in US campaigns: if same-sex couples wanted legal protections, didn't Ireland already have civil partnerships in place? Shouldn't more time be allowed to see how they worked, or to fix any problems associated with civil partnership? The leadership team had already been thinking about that. Civil partnership had been a signal achievement for GLEN. While no one intended to criticise civil partnership, it would be important to clarify the difference between it and marriage. The campaign needed to sharpen that difference and be clearer about it.

Beyond that, I raised a deeper concern. While I thought the canvassers would be prepared to have very positive conversations with voters at their doorsteps, I was concerned that most voters would be likely to see multiple televised debates, and the tone of the debates kept nagging at me. I acknowledged that we did not use debates as a key persuasion strategy in the US, but also conveyed my concern that the style of the debates would ultimately work against us.

The debates I had seen on video and in person had an aggressive tone, with both sides putting their champion debaters forward to try and score points against their opponents, however they could. To be consistent with the storytelling and values approach of the campaign, I made the case that the Yes presenters had to speak less directly against opponents on the stage, and instead aim their comments at the voters at home or in the audience. Irish voters who did not know gay people well might not react positively to a gay debater with an aggressive tone, even if that presenter was only matching the tone of the person representing the No side. The Yes campaign representatives would be watched and judged especially carefully. If they acted derisively towards opposition sentiments, some of which undecided voters might share, then they might alienate the very voters we were trying to persuade. I suggested that it would help to have less polished or experienced debaters, even adult children raised by same-sex couples, using debate time to tell their personal stories and move away from focusing on facts. This would be a useful way to undercut arguments against us, and reinforce the positive and welcoming tone adopted by the rest of the campaign.

Given the back and forth nature of the attacks, I also pitched my most important new idea: the Yes campaign should develop and deliver to every household in Ireland a single piece of campaign literature that would sum up the stories of our key messengers, as well as respond clearly to the key arguments of the opposition. In order to create and deliver this campaign newsletter to every home in Ireland, Brian said, the likely cost would be up to €100,000 or more. The campaign simply could not afford it.

I made the case that the campaign would have to find the money to do it. We needed to put material summarising our case on the kitchen table of every household in Ireland, for voters to read before they went to the polls. It would be the Yes campaign's closing argument, and given the difficulty of controlling the debates, it seemed crucially important to find the money to produce it.

Noel, who had been quiet as I suggested changes to the campaign, turned to Brian and Gráinne and said, 'She knows what she's talking about. We should do these things.' I felt a great relief that Noel, an expert in Irish campaigns, was open to my ideas. We went back to the office and started working to put these plans in motion.

FINDING MONEY AND MESSENGERS

Days flew by quickly. I had a memorable afternoon with Gráinne, Brian and Noel, sharing what we had learned at Freedom to Marry about effective messengers for marriage. We discussed the power of 'journey stories', i.e. finding people who had once been against the idea of marriage for same-sex couples to publicly explain why they had changed their minds. Those messengers could model for others that it was indeed possible, in fact a good thing, to assess your position in light of your personal values, and make a change. We also identified a growing list of what we came to term our 'unlikely messengers'. Those were people who most voters would not expect to be on our side of the vote. These messengers were a crucial component of our ongoing efforts to break down assumptions about LGBT people, and who would be supportive. These were messages which we had shared already with Andrew and Moninne, reinforcing them now with the Yes Equality leaders seemed important.

I opened my laptop to share some examples with Bráinne and Noel. We had made some ads we thought of as 'bands of brothers', groups of straight men who were strong and masculine, and willing to voice their support of a gay colleague. In the US, groups of military veterans or firefighters told their stories very effectively. Who would be best to do that in Ireland? 'Gaelic footballers and hurling stars,' Gráinne said.

I felt that we could respond to the idea that 'children need a mother and father' by showing multi-generational families, where it was clear that children raised by a lesbian couple would still have male role models available, in the form of uncles and granddads. So we brainstormed a list of families in which a picture would be worth a thousand words of debate. It was crucial, we had learned in the US, not to show same-sex couples in isolation from family, friends or co-workers. These are not couples that have been rejected by their communities, but part of extended families and broader communities, just like the average voter. Plans to make video and still images in this manner were quickly made.[1]

We went on to talk about other messengers who would be important; elderly people who attended Mass regularly, as well as other people of faith; parents who accepted their gay children; adult children who had been raised by gay men or a lesbian couple, and turned out just fine. These would be the stories that the campaign would feature in videos, and also in the newsletter that would go to every home in Ireland.

I had one idea for raising money for the newsletter, although I doubted it would pay for the entire cost. Since I'd arrived in Dublin I had been asked over and over again on the street for Yes or Tá campaign badges. The campaign was giving them away by the thousands, and yet people everywhere seemed desperate to get their hands on one. 'Why not start selling the badges?' I asked. 'It's something our campaigns have done in the US with wonderful success. Perhaps you could ask some friendly bookshops to sell Yes materials near the cash register and hand the money over to the campaign.' I suggested taking over an empty table in the lobby of the campaign headquarter in Clarendon Street and turning it into a campaign sales shop. They went one better than this and opened a pop up shop in nearby St Stephen's Green Shopping Centre where hundreds of thousands of badges and campaign materials were bought by campaign supporters contributing much needed funds to the campaign.

The week went by quickly. I was honoured to be invited to address the organisers of the regional canvass teams that convened on a Saturday in Dublin, and to speak to coalition members one evening at the campaign office. I travelled to Galway for a wonderful campaign fundraiser, and then it was time to go home.

WATCHING AND HOPING

Once I returned home, I followed developments on social media and tried not to pepper the Yes campaign's leaders with too many emails. I was thrilled by reports about the campaign's pop-up shop in the St Stephen's Green Centre. I loved the picture on social media of the 500,000th badge being given out on Grafton Street by Bráinne. I avidly followed the progress of Moninne, who had spent years helping to organise and inspire local activists nationwide and was now leading a bus tour across Ireland to energise the final stages of the campaign and demonstrate the high level of support outside of Dublin.

From left: Senator David Norris, Evan Wolfson (Freedom to Marry US), Thalila Zepatos and her husband Mike Barela at the Road to Equality Summer School, Dublin, July 2016.

I continued to assist from afar and, of course, answered requests for help quickly. Brian emailed multiple drafts of the campaign newsletter, which he and Gráinne were working on. It was warm and engaging, informative and inviting – exactly the tone we needed. We discussed a few final wording changes before it went to print. Gráinne sent images of a new set of campaign posters that featured portraits of Irish people who said, 'I am your daughter/sister/brother/co-worker, and you can let me marry, too.' The campaign was personalising its message to the very end. These posters would be held up on the key bridges across Dublin on the eve of polling day to encourage drivers to vote Yes.

I sent one final email to Bráinne and Noel, encouraging them to calm the discourse during the crucial final days of the campaign, and to set a tone that would ensure that voters would feel comfortable aligning with the Yes campaign. I wished them well and regretted that I could not be back in Ireland for referendum day.

Instead, on polling day in Ireland I joined millions of people across the world, tearing up frequently as I followed the news from my home office in Portland. Andrew sent links to stories detailing the thousands of Irish people flooding home to Ireland in time to vote, joining thousands of students who had registered and voted for the first time, alongside thousands of parents and grandparents, who were part of the 1.2 million good people of Ireland who generously voted Yes for fairness, love, inclusion and equality. The campaign had created and empowered a social movement, which sent a message around the world on the day of the count on 23 May 2015. It was a uniquely Irish campaign, based on Irish values. Yes Equality had taken the best of what we had to offer, and all of us at Freedom to Marry were happy to have helped in whatever ways we were able.

I felt sure that the Justices of the US Supreme Court were watching, too, as they finalised their written opinion that would legalise marriage in all of the United States, just thirty-four days later. In Ireland and in the United States, we had made history in 2015.

Notes

CHAPTER 1

1 This article is based on our oral presentation to 'Summer School 2016: The Road to Marriage Equality' led by Denise Charlton and Gráinne Healy. See also our memoirs, *Our Lives Out Loud: In Pursuit of Justice and Equality* (Dublin: O'Brien Press, 2008).

2 BeLonG To is the national organisation for LGBT young people, aged 14–23.

3 Miriam O'Callaghan is a well-known Irish broadcaster who hosts political and entertainment programmes on RTÉ, the national radio and television station.

4 This is the constituency in which the authors live and in which Katherine subsequently ran in and won a seat in the Dáil in 2016 to become a member of the Dáil and a TD.

CHAPTER 2

1 Gráinne Healy is a co-founder and Chairwoman of Marriage Equality, the organisation which formed in 2008 to seek civil marriage rights for same-sex couples in Ireland. She completed a PhD on same-sex relationship recognition and its meaning at DCU in 2015 – this chapter is a version of a paper she gave in 2014 which she developed as part of her studies and it provides the reader with some insights into the socio-political changes that took place in the decades leading up to the achievement of Marriage Equality and the context within which the Marriage Equality campaign began its advocacy journey a decade before the hundred days of the Yes Equality campaign in 2015.

2 Some ninety-one same-sex marriages were recorded in Ireland from November–December 2015 (CSO, April 2016).

3 The National Women's Council of Ireland (NWCI) cites childcare as a major obstacle to women's equality in their 2016–20 strategic plan 'Driving Women's Equality'. It remains to be seen if the recent introduction of statutory parental leave from September 2016, on the same basis as maternity leave payments, but for two weeks only, a small but welcome development, affects childcare problems in any significant way.

4 Similarly, in the 2015 marriage referendum, 1.2 million people voted Yes to marriage equality contrary to the Catholic Church's stated opposition – this maturity of Catholic opinion is a phenomenon worth further study.

5 The significance of the Fr Brendan Smyth affair was that it led to the fall of the Albert Reynolds-led Fianna Fáil/Progressive Democrats government later that year when it emerged that the State had been involved in the protection of this serial child abuser.

6 David Norris took a case against the Irish State to recognise his right to privacy at the European Court of Human Rights in 1988. He won and this case subsequently led to the transposition of the judgement and the decriminalisation of homosexuality in Ireland in 1993.

7 GLEN (Gay and Lesbian Equality Network) was founded in 1988 and is committed to securing legislative change and bringing about equality for the lesbian, gay and bisexual population in Ireland (www. glen.ie).

8 Marriage Equality was founded to support the KAL case (Katherine Zappone and Ann Louise Gilligan's case for recognition of their Canadian marriage). Marriage Equality advocates for access to civil marriage for same-sex couples in Ireland (www.marriageequality.ie).

9 NLGF (National Lesbian and Gay Federation), founded in 1979, seeks to work towards elimination of discrimination against lesbian, gay, bisexual and transgendered people in Ireland (www.nxf.ie).

10 LGBT Noise was founded in 2007 and works for civil marriage, parenting and reproductive rights and gender recognition and religious ethos removal from Irish law.

REFERENCES

Advisory Committee on Equality for Lesbians, Gays and Bisexuals, *Implementing Equality for Lesbians, Gays and Bisexuals* (Dublin: Equality Authority, 2002).

All Party Oireachtas Committee on the Constitution, *The Tenth Progress Report: The Family* (Dublin: Government of Ireland, 2006).

BBC News Documentary, *Suing the Pope* (BBC, 2002).

BBC Panorama Documentary, *Sex Crimes and the Vatican* (BBC, 2006).

Bourdieu, P., *Distinction: A Social Critique of the Judgement of Taste* (London: Routledge, 1984).

Brady, C., 'RTÉ history of television screened out bigger picture', *Irish Times*, 27 July, 2012.

Breen, R.; Hannan D.F.; Roffman, D.B. and Whelan, C. (eds), *Understanding Contemporary Ireland* (Dublin: Gill and Macmillan, 1990).

Canavan, J., 'Family and Family Change in Ireland: An Overview', *Journal of Family Issues,* 33, 1 (2012), pp. 10–28.

Central Statistics Office, *This is Ireland: Highlights from Census 2011 Part 1* (Dublin: Government of Ireland, 2012).

Cloyne Report, *Cloyne Report by the Commission of Investigation into Catholic Diocese of Cloyne* (Dublin: Government of Ireland, 2010).

Colley, A., *Options Paper presented by the Working Group on Domestic Partnership to the Minister for Justice, Equality and Law Reform* (Dublin: Government of Ireland, 2006).

Connolly, L. and O'Toole, T., *Documenting Irish Feminisms: The Second Wave* (Dublin: The Woodfield Press, 2005).

Cosgrove, A. (ed.), *Marriage in Ireland* (Ireland: College Press, 1985).

Dillon, M., *Catholic Identity: Balancing Reason, Faith, and Power* (Cambridge: Cambridge University Press, 1999).

Duffy, M., *Voices from the Hinterland: Lesbian Women's Experiences of Irish Health Care* (Germany: Lambert Academic Publishing, 2011).

Fagan, P., *Missing Pieces: A comparison of the rights and responsibilities gained from civil partnership compared to the rights and responsibilities gained through civil marriage in Ireland* (Dublin: Marriage Equality, 2011).

Ferns Report, *The Ferns Report Presented by the Ferns Inquiry to the Minister for Health and Children* (Dublin: Government Publications, 2005).

Ferriter, D., *Occasions of Sin: Sex and Society in Modern Ireland* (London: Profile Books, 2009).

Fine-Davis, M., *Attitudes to Family Formation in Ireland: Findings from a Nationwide Study* (Dublin: Family Support Agency, 2011).

Foucault, M., *The History of Sexuality: Volume 1: An Introduction translated by R. Hurley* (London: Allen Lane, 1978).

— *The History of Sexuality Vol. 3 The Care of the Self translated by R. Hurley* (New York: Random House, 1986).

Gilligan, A. and Zappone, K., *Our Lives Out Loud: In Pursuit of Justice & Equality* (Dublin: O'Brien Press, 2008).

GLEN, *Statement of Strategy 2008–2010* (Dublin: Dept of Community, Rural and Gaeltacht Affairs & GLEN, 2007).

— 'Civil Partnerships in Ireland: Figures from April 2011 to 30th June 2013': http://www.glen.ie/attachments/Civil_Partnership_Statistics_to_June_2014.pdf (accessed 14 March 2017).

— *Civil Partnerships in Ireland: Figures from April 2011 to 30th June 2013* [Online]. Available from: www.glen.ie/attachments/Civil_Partnerships_Statistics_To_June_2013.PDF [Accessed 22 July 2013].

Hannan, D. and Katsiaouni, L., *Traditional Families?: From Culturally Prescribed to Negotiated Roles in Farm Families* (Dublin: ESRI, 1977).

Healy, G.; Sheehan, B. and Whelan, N., *Ireland Says Yes: The Inside Story of How the Vote for Marriage Equality Was Won* (Kildare: Merrion Press, 2016).

Hug, C., *The Politics of Sexual Morality in Ireland* (New York: Palgrave Macmillan Press, 1999).

Inglis, T., 'Foucault, Bourdieu and the Field of Irish Sexuality', *Irish Journal of Sociology,* 7, (1997), pp. 5–28.

— *Lessons in Irish Sexuality* (Dublin: UCD Press, 1998).

— 'Religion, identity, state and society' *in* J. Cleary and C. Connolly (eds) *Cambridge Companion to Modern Irish Culture* (Cambridge: Cambridge University Press, 2005).

Kennedy, F., *Cottage to Crèche: Family Change in Ireland* (Dublin: IPA, 2001).

Kilfeather, S., 'Irish Feminism' *in* J. Cleary and C. Connolly (eds) *Cambridge Companion to Modern Irish Culture* (Cambridge: Cambridge University Press, 2005).

Law Reform Commission, *Law Reform Commission Report 2004.* 26. Law Reform Commission, 2004.

Law Reform Commission, *Law Reform Commission Report 2006.* 28. Law Reform Commission, 2006.

Layte, R.; McGee, H.; Quail, H.; Rundle, K.; Cousins, G.; Donnelly, C.; Mulcahy, F. and Conroy, R. (eds), *The Irish study of sexual health and relationships Summary Report* (Dublin: Crisis Pregnancy Agency and Department of Health and Children, 2006).

Lunn, P.; Fahey, T. and Hannan, C., *Family Figures: Family Dynamics and Family Types Ireland, 1986-2006* (Dublin: ESRI, 2009).

McGarry, P., 'Survey finds Ireland second only to Vietnam in loss of religious sentiment' *Irish Times,* 8 August, 2012.

Marriage Equality, *Outline of research on same-sex parenting and the outcomes for their children* (Dublin: Marriage Equality, 2012).

Murphy Report, Report of the Commission of Investigation into Catholic Archdioceses of Dublin, Minister for Justice and Equality (Dublin: Government of Ireland, 2009).

Navarro, Z., 'In Search of Cultural Interpretation of Power', *IDS Bulletin,* 37, 6, (2006), pp. 11–22.

Nic Ghiolla Phádraig, M., 'The Power of the Catholic Church in the Republic of Ireland' in P. Clancy, S. Drudy, K. Lynch and L. O'Dowd (eds) *Irish Society: Sociological Perspectives* (Dublin: IPA, 1995).

Norman, J.; Galvin, M. and McNamara, G., *Straight Talk: Researching Gay and Lesbian Issues in the School Curriculum* (DCU: Centre for Educational Evaluation, 2006).

O'Gorman, C., *Sex Crimes of the Vatican: Suing the Pope*, BBC documentary (broadcast 2002 & 2006).

Pillinger, J. and Fagan, P., *LGBT Parents in Ireland Report from a study into the experiences of Lesbian, Gay, Bisexual and Transgender People in Ireland who are parents or who are planning parenthood* (Dublin: LGBT Diversity, 2013).

Raftery, M., *Suffer the Little Children: The Inside Story of Ireland's Industrial Schools* (Bloomsbury USA Academic Press, 2002).

— *Do They Think We're Eejits?* (Dublin: New Island Books, 2013).

— and O'Sullivan, E., *Suffer the Little Children* (Dublin: New Island Books, 1999).

Rose, K., *Diverse Communities: The Evolution of Lesbian and Gay Politics in Ireland* (Cork: Cork University Press, 1994).

RTÉ *Prime Time* Documentary, '*Cardinal Secrets*' (RTÉ, 2002).

Ryan Report, *Report of the Commission to Inquire into Child Abuse Office of the Minister for Children and Youth Affairs, Department of Health and Children* (Dublin: Government Publications, 2009).

Ryan, F., *Civil Partnership: An Overview* (Dublin: GLEN, 2010).

Ryan, P., *Asking Angela McNamara: An Intimate History of Irish Lives* (Kildare: Irish Academic Press, 2012).

Smyth, A., 'States of Change: Reflections on Ireland in Several Uncertain Parts', *Feminist Review*, Vol. 50, No. 1 (1995), p. 24.

Williams, J.; Greene, S.; McNally, S.; Murray, A. and Quill, M., *Growing Up in Ireland: The Infants and their Families,* Offices of Minister for Children and Youth Affairs (Dublin: Stationery Office, 2010).

CHAPTER 3

1 Home of Zappone and Gilligan.
2 http://www.gao.gov/new.items/d04353r.pdf.
3 http://www.marriagequality.ie/download/pdf/missing_pieces.pdf.
4 One Family works to provide high-quality, much-needed services to the many different one-parent families in Ireland and the professionals working with them.
5 Women's Aid is a voluntary organisation working with women and children who are suffering physical, mental or emotional and/or sexual abuse and works to end domestic violence.
6 Barnardos is an independent children's charity working in Ireland.
7 LGBT Diversity was an LGBT initiative supported by The Atlantic Philanthropies seeking to build an effective infrastructure for LGBT groups in Ireland, including commissioning research on LGBT life.
8 Children's Rights Alliance (CRA) works to change the lives of children by ensuring their rights are protected and respected.
9 Equality for All Families (2006) ICCL, Dublin.

10 Irish Council for Civil Liberties.

11 The Iona Institute promotes the place of marriage and religion in society.

12 This refers to a comment made by a Fianna Fáil TD, Martin Mansergh, during early Dáil debates on the issue.

13 A short video made for the Convention audience by COCO Television.

14 Kathleen Hunt was HQ office administrator for Yes Equality and played a hugely significant role in ensuring that campaign logistics of all sorts were overseen and leaflets, posters and campaign materials were delivered effectively.

15 Former Minister for Justice who oversaw the decriminalisation of homosexuality when in government in 1993 and is now EU Commissioner for Research, Innovation and Science.

CHAPTER 4

1 *Irish Independent* columnist and Director of the Iona Institute.

2 AOH is an Irish Catholic organisation established in 1836 and now has its largest membership in the US where it was founded, in New York.

CHAPTER 5

1 Freedman, L., *Strategy: A History*, Oxford University Press, 2015, ix. http://www.justice.ie/en/JELR/OptionsPaper.pdf/Files/OptionsPaper.pdf, 7.20.

2 'It's No Joke: Civil Marriage Rights for Lesbians and Gay Men in Ireland', Marriage Equality, 2009. http://www.justice.ie/en/JELR/Pages/PR15000009.

CHAPTER 7

1 *Katherine Zappone and Ann Louise Gilligan v The Revenue Commissioners*, Ireland and The Attorney General (2008) 2 IR 417.

2 The 34th Amendment of the Constitution (Marriage Equality Act) 2015 and Marriage Act 2015.

3 The Children and Family Relationships Act 2015.

4 The Gender Recognition Act 2015.

5 The Equality (Miscellaneous Provisions) Act 2015, s. 11; this section amends the Employment Equality Act 1998, s. 37.

6 *Zappone and Gilligan v The Revenue Commissioners*, Ireland and The Attorney General (2008) 2 IR 417 (the KAL case).

7 Two of the reforms which stand out from this period are the Employment Equality Act 1998 and Equal Status Act 2000 which prohibited discrimination on grounds of sexual orientation in employment and vocational training and in the provision of goods and services respectively. Furthermore, Ireland has been credited with drafting the final text of Article 19 TFEU (ex Article 13 TEC). This Article in the Treaty on the Functioning of the European Union was inserted during the negotiation of the Treaty of Amsterdam (See Mos (2014), p. 643). This Article established for the first time in an EU Treaty a competence to address discrimination on various grounds, including sexual orientation, in the European Union. This provision allowed for the enactment of the Framework Directive, which now prohibits

discrimination on a variety of grounds including sexual orientation in employment and vocational training in all twenty-eight EU Member States.

8 Civil Partnership and Certain Rights and Obligations of Cohabitants Act 2010.

9 *Ryan v Attorney General* (1965) IR 294 (HC) 313 (Kenny, J.) mentioned the right to marry as an example of a personal right inherent in Article 40.3; *McGee v Attorney General* (1974) IR 284 (SC) 301 (FitzGerald, C.J.); In a dissenting judgement, the Chief Justice observed that the right to marry was protected by Article 40.3 of the Constitution and had been recognised in 'most, if not all, civilised countries for many centuries'. See further, G. Hogan and G. Whyte, *J.M. Kelly: The Irish Constitution* (Dublin: Butterworths, 2003), at 7.6.12.

10 Art 40.1.

11 *Foy v An tArd Chláraitheoir* (Unreported, High Court, McKechnie, J., 9 July, 2002). In a case concerning gender recognition, Justice Kechnie observed that 'Marriage as understood by the Constitution, by statute and by case law refers to the union of a biological man with a biological woman.' However, it has since become clear from *Goodwin v United Kingdom* [2002] 35 E.H.R.R. 447 that transsexual people have a right to marry in accordance with their gender identity, under the European Convention on Human Rights.

12 *Zappone and Gilligan v The Revenue Commissioners* (2008) 2 IR 417 at 505 (the KAL case).

13 Ibid., at 504.

14 *Hyde and Hyde v Woodmansee* [1866] LR 1 P&D 130 (Lord Penzance) 133, 'marriage, as understood in Christendom may ... be defined as the voluntary union for life of one man and one woman, to the exclusion of all others'.

15 For example, pursuant to the Fifteenth Amendment of the Constitution Act, 1995 which inserted Article 41.3.2 thereby making provision for divorce, marriage is no longer for life.

16 The KAL case (n 10) at 513.

17 Ibid., at 506–7.

18 A classic example for this issue area is provided by the Judgment of the Court of Justice of the European Union in Case C-249/96 *Lisa Jacqueline Grant v South-West Trains Ltd.* (1998) ECR I-621 at para 8. The case concerned the refusal by an employer, South-West Trains, to grant a travel concession to the same-sex cohabiting partner of one of its employees in circumstances where the pass would have been granted to the couple had Grant's cohabiting partner been male. Rather than drawing this comparison the Court of Justice instead concluded that a man with a same-sex partner would similarly have been refused the travel pass. In effect, the Court compared the treatment of a lesbian to a hypothetical gay man and then concluded that there had been no discrimination.

19 The KAL case (n 10) at 499, 'It is worth noting having said that, however, that none of the studies carried out to date have demonstrated any adverse impact on children involved in the particular studies.'

20 In *Murray v Ireland* (1985) IR 532 (SC) the fact that the couple in question could neither consummate the marriage nor have children was not referred to in the judgment as a barrier to marriage.

21 *Murray v Ireland* (1985) IR 532.

22 *United States, Petitioner v Edith Schlain Windsor, in Her Capacity as Executor of the Estate of Thea Clara Spyer, et al.* 133 S. Ct. 2675 (2013) at 22–23 per Justice Kennedy, 'By creating two contradictory marriage regimes within the same State ... [the Defense of Marriage Act] undermines both the public and private significance of State-sanctioned same-sex marriages; for it tells those couples, and all the world, that

their otherwise valid marriages are unworthy of federal recognition. This places same-sex couples in an unstable position of being in a second-tier marriage. The differentiation demeans the couple … [a]nd it humiliates tens of thousands of children now being raised by same-sex couples.'

23 See for example, Amicus Brief of American Psychological Association et al, in *Dennis Hollingsworth v Kristen M. Perry et al.*, 133 S. Ct. 2675 (2013). http://www.apa.org/about/offices/ogc/ amicus/hollingsworth-perry.pdf, accessed 20 February 2016.

24 Seanad Debate, 16 February 2005, vol. 179, col. 675. Senator David Norris sought to introduce a civil partnership bill into the Seanad in 2004.

25 Report of the United States General Accounting Office, GAO/OGC-97-16, Defense of Marriage Act Update to Prior Report (Jan 23, 2004). http://www.gao.gov/new.items/d04353r.pdf, accessed 3 March 2016.

26 This argument, grounded in feminist critiques of opposite-sex marriage as a profoundly unequal institution for women and children, has undoubted historical pedigree and in many parts of the world still holds true today. The same can be said of the argument that privileging marriage over other family forms can of itself produce unequal outcomes. In so far as scholars have critiqued marriage, their arguments are often compelling but, in my view, do not provide a justification for the exclusion of couples in same-sex relationship from marriage, an outcome that does nothing to advance equality for anyone else but instead carries legal, social and economic consequences for an already disfavoured minority (See, for example, Polikoff, 2005, Franke, 2006).

27 Seanad Debates, 7 July 2010, vol. 204, col. 255.

28 'Ahern Welcomes Coming Into Law of Civil Partnership and Certain Rights and Obligations of Cohabitants Act 2010' Press Release, 19 July 2010. http://www.justice.ie/en/JELR/Pages/Press-releases?OpenDocument&start=41&year=2010, accessed 19 February 2016.

29 Ibid.

30 The Missing Pieces Report, *A Comparison of the Rights and Responsibilities Gained from Civil Partnership Compared to the Rights and Responsibilities Gained Through Civil Marriage in Ireland* (Dublin: Marriage Equality, 2011).

31 LGBT poster reads: 'Half measures? Dorothy ordered a gin and tonic at the bar, but the bartender only gave her the tonic. Civil Partnership is not equality, don't settle for half measures. On 22 August 2010 March for Equal Rights, March for Civil Marriage'. http://goo.gl/QN34tX, accessed 24 February 2016.

32 These comments were made by Justice Ruth Bader Ginsburg in the United States, *Petitioner v Edith Schlain Windsor, in Her Capacity as Executor of the Estate of Thea Clara Spyer, et al.* 133 S. Ct. 2657. For a more detailed account of this case and of the comments made by Justice Bader Ginsburg, see Kaplan, 2015, p. 261.

33 A sign held up at the 2011 March for Marriage. https://goo.gl/pmi6Mn accessed 24 February 2016.

34 LGBT Noise is an independent non-party political group founded in November 2007, which campaigned for access to civil marriage irrespective of sexual orientation or gender identity.

35 See for example, the LGBT Noise Poster for the March for Marriage, 18 August 2013 (https://goo.gl/uoZecd, accessed 24 February 2016) and 'LGBT Noise 4th Annual March for Marriage 12 August 2012 3pm City Hall be There! Get Equal', *GCN,* Issue 271 (Dublin, July 2012) at 9.

36 This poster was displayed on behalf of Marriage Equality on an admobile throughout Dublin in 2011. https://goo.gl/ryX85V, accessed 24 February 2016.

37 Art 41 provides: 1° The State recognises the Family as the natural primary and fundamental unit group of Society, and as a moral institution possessing inalienable and imprescriptible rights, antecedent and superior to all positive law. 2° The State, therefore, guarantees to protect the Family in its constitution and authority, as the necessary basis of social order and as indispensable to the welfare of the Nation and the State.

38 A number of cases have been brought before the European Court of Human Rights, concerning Ireland's treatment of families other than those based on marriage. See *Johnson and others v Ireland* App no 9697/82 (ECHR, 18 December 1986) (an illegitimate child) *Keegan v Ireland* App no 16969/90 (ECHR, 26 May 1994) (an unmarried father).

39 *McD. v P.L. and B.M.* {2010} 2 IR 199 at 270 and 274.

40 Civil Registration Act 2004, s. 2(2)(e).

41 Civil Partnership and Certain Rights and Obligations of Cohabitants Act 2010, s. 97. Children are, however, mentioned in the legislation with reference to conflicts of interest and ethics in public office legislation.

42 Pursuant to the Guardianship of Infants Act 1964, s. 7, the surviving partner could be appointed testamentary guardian upon the death of their life partner if provision was made for this in the deceased's will. However, in the event that there was a surviving parent who objected to the appointment, s. 7(5) provided that the court could 'refuse to make an order (in which case the surviving parent shall remain the sole guardian)'.

43 Adoption Act 2010, s. 20(1) and 33(1).

44 An earlier Law Reform Commission Consultation Paper had made no mention of children parented by couples in same-sex relationships.

45 Law Reform Commission, *Report on the Legal Aspects of Family Relationships* (LRC 1-2010), 41 (italics in original).

46 Department of Justice and Equality, 'General Scheme of a Children and Family Relationships Bill' (2014) (General Scheme of a Children and Family Relationships Bill).

47 General Scheme of a Children and Family Relationships Bill, Head 10(5) provided as follows: '(5) This Head applies in relation to a child born through assisted human reproduction using eggs, sperm or an in vitro embryo provided by a donor whether before or after the commencement of this Part.'

48 This aspect is now addressed in the Children and Family Relationships Act, s. 20(1)(b) which addresses children who were 'born as a result of a DAHR procedure that was performed before the date on which this section comes into operation'. This section retains the original intent of the General Scheme in that it provides for the recognition of the family relationships of children born prior to the commencement of the legislation. These changes were introduced to address issues arising regarding the rights of known donors. This section allows for an application to be made to the District Court for a declaration as to the parentage of the child.

REFERENCES

Article 19 TFEU (ex Article 13 TEC).

Boele-Woelki, K., 'Legal Recognition of Same-Sex Relationships Within the European Union', *Tulane Law Review*, 82 (2008), pp. 1949–81.

Council Directive 2000/78/EC of 27 November 2000 establishing a general framework for equal treatment in employment and occupation, OJ L 303 (Framework Employment Directive).

Della Porta, D. and Diani, M., *Social Movements: An Introduction* (Blackwell Publishing, 2009).

Epp, C.R., *The Rights Revolution: Lawyers, Activists, and Supreme Courts in Comparative Perspective* (Cambridge University Press, 1998).

Franke, K.M. 'The Politics of Same-Sex Marriage Politics', *Columbia Journal of Gender & Law*, 15 (2006), p. 236.

Kaplan, R.A. and Dicky, Lisa, *Then Comes Marriage: Windsor v United States and the Defeat of DOMA* (WW Norton & Company, 2015).

McCann, M.W., *Rights at Work: Pay Equity Reform and the Politics of Legal Mobilization* (*University of Chicago Press*, 1994).

Mos, M., 'Of Gay Rights and Christmas Ornaments: The Political History of Sexual Orientation Non-discrimination in the Treaty of Amsterdam', *JCMS: Journal of Common Market Studies*, 52, 3 (2014), pp. 632–49.

Paris, M., *Framing Equal Opportunity: Law and the Politics of School Finance Reform* (Stanford University Press, 2010).

Polikoff, N.D., 'For the Sake of All Children: Opponents and Supporters of Same-Sex Marriage Both Miss the Mark', *New York City Law Review*, 8 (2005), p. 573.

Scheingold, S.A., *The Politics of Rights: Lawyers, Public Policy, and Political Change* (University of Michigan Press, 2010).

— and Sarat, A., *Something to Believe In: Politics, Professionalism and Cause Lawyering* (Stanford University Press, 2004).

Vanhala, L., *Making Rights a Reality?: Disability Rights Activists and Legal Mobilization* (Cambridge University Press, 2010).

— 'Legal Opportunity Structures and the Paradox of Legal Mobilization by the Environmental Movement in the UK', *Law & Society Review*, 46, 3 (2012), pp. 523–6.

CHAPTER 8

1 The KAL case (the Katherine Zappone and Ann Louise Gilligan case taken to have their Canadian marriage recognised in Ireland) being one of the main exceptions to this.

2 In particular, designer Peter Clifford created a wonderful series of pop art posters to promote the March for Marriage.

3 The most successful of these videos, *Armagayddon*, went viral with over 450,000 hits on YouTube. Written by Tara Flynn and Kevin McGahern and produced by Like Minded Productions, 2014.

4 Una Mullally, *In the Name of Love* (The History Press, 2014), p. 155.

5 Even after the referendum in 2015, the Dublin Pride Board, despite asking me to write an article for their Pride Guide about the Noise campaign, refused to publish any such details for fear of publicly offending GLEN according to Pride Chairperson Jason Flynn.

6 Panti, speaking as Rory O'Neill on a late-night chat show, was threatened with a defamation suit, which resulted in RTÉ paying out large sums of money to high-profile individuals he alleged were homophobic.

CHAPTER 9

REFERENCES

Burning Issues: Listening to the Voices of the LGBT Community in Ireland, National Lesbian and Gay Federation, 2009c.

Full & Equal Rights – Lesbian & Gay Marriage & Partnership Rights in Ireland: Symposium Press Release, National Lesbian and Gay Federation, 2007a.

Full & Equal Rights – Lesbian & Gay Marriage & Partnership Rights in Ireland: Symposium Opening Speech, National Lesbian and Gay Federation, 2007b.

Marriage Matters for Lesbian and Gay People in Ireland: Diary Notice, National Lesbian and Gay Federation, 2009b.

Marriage Matters for Lesbian and Gay People in Ireland: Symposium Proceedings, National Lesbian and Gay Federation, 2009a.

(Revised) Policy Position Paper on Marriage Equality, National Lesbian and Gay Federation, 2010.

CHAPTER 12

1 O'Connell, A., (2006) Submission on Domestic Partnerships on behalf of LINC (Lesbians in Cork) to the Working Group on Domestic Partnership, Dept JELR. Working Paper.

CHAPTER 15

1 Fire is a well-known Dublin restaurant in Dawson Street.

CHAPTER 16

1 Ombudsman for Children (July 2010) Advice of the Ombudsman for Children on the Civil Partnership Bill. http://www.oco.ie/publications/advice-togovernment.html.
2 http://www.marriagequality.ie/justlove/.
3 http://www.marriagequality.ie/download/pdf/missing_pieces.pdf.
4 http://www.marriagequality.ie/news/2011/10/06/marriage-equalitys-october-advocates-of-the-month/.
5 http://www.failsafefilms.ie/project/marriage-equality/.
6 https://www.youtube.com/watch?v=BZU-HQ_c8bg.

CHAPTER 17

1 Bus Éireann is the national bus company supplying bus services outside Dublin to all regions of Ireland.
2 Father Ted's house was used in the comedy series *Father Ted*, set in a fictional Craggy Island, featuring the antics of three priests and their housekeeper Mrs Doyle.

CHAPTER 18

1 The Constitutional Convention consisted of sixty-six people taken from the electoral register randomly and thirty-three elected representatives from the Dáil and Seanad and the remaining place was held by the Chairman Tom Arnold.

CHAPTER 19

1 Feargha Ní Bhroin has been part of the ME Board and wrote a very significant paper that was published early on in ME's lifetime 'Feminism and the Same-Sex Marriage Debate' (2009, Marriage Equality, Dublin).
2 See Anthony Kinahan's piece elsewhere in Chapter 13.

CHAPTER 20

1 The Gay & Lesbian Equality Network's submission to the Constitutional Convention on Marriage was titled 'The Remarkable Journey towards Equality and Civil Marriage for Lesbian and Gay People in Ireland'. http://www.glen.ie/attachments/GLEN_Submission_to_the_Constitutional_Convention.PDF.
2 The report was the work of the ICCL Working Party on Lesbian and Gay Rights. The Working Party which completed this report included: Ursula Barry, Tom Cooney (Chair), Éadaoin Ní Chléirigh, Christopher Robson and Kieran Rose. Tom later was advisor to Minister Alan Shatter in a key period when the Children and Family Relationships Bill was being drafted and other foundations were being laid for the referendum.
3 A case study of the civil partnership campaign is available in 'Civil Partnership and Ireland: How a Minority Achieved a Minority': http://www.glen.ie/attachments/GLEN_and_Civil_Partnership_Case_Study.PDF.
4 GLEN Evaluation, 2010: http://www.atlanticphilanthropies.org/research-reports/report-evaluation-building-sustainable-change-programme.

CHAPTER 22

1 Paula Fagan, 'Missing Pieces: A comparison of the rights and responsibilities gained from civil partnership compared to the rights and responsibilities gained through civil marriage in Ireland' (Dublin: Marriage Equality, 2011).
2 Iris Elliott, 'Voices of Children Report' (Dublin: Marriage Equality, 2010).
3 Jane Pillinger and Paula Fagan, 'LGBT Parents in Ireland: Report from a Study into the Experiences of Lesbian, Gay, Bisexual and Transgendered People in Ireland Who are Parents or are Planning Parenthood', (Dublin: LGBT Diversity, 2013).

CHAPTER 23

1 See details of the making of these videos in Linda Cullen's chapter.

Contributors

CAROL ARMSTRONG works within the School of Physics & Clinical & Optometric Sciences, DIT, and has volunteered with various LGBT groups for many years. Carol was involved in Marriage Equality's successful 'Out To Your TD' campaign from its inception and also worked on training and organising the Marriage Equality volunteers to keep the campaign moving forward, ultimately becoming a member of the Marriage Equality Board.

MICHAEL BARRON is the Executive Director of EQUATE: Equality in Education, and was Founding Director of BeLonG To – Ireland's national LGBT youth organisation (2003–15). During his time at BeLonG To, he directed the development of a national network of LGBT supports and successfully advocated for significant policy and legislative change in the areas of children and young people, education, bullying, mental health, drug use and equality. He directed the BeLonG To Yes campaign – a national coalition of children and youth rights organisations which played a significant role in the campaign for a Yes vote in Ireland's referendum on marriage equality in May 2015.

DARINA BRENNAN opened and established the very successful Fire Restaurant and venue at the Mansion House, Dublin. She is currently the Executive Head Chef for the Clayton Hotel Group. Over the years, she has cooked for many celebrities including, Rhianna, John Hurt, Ralph Fiennes, Kevin Spacey, Sean Penn, Danny DeVito, U2 and the Irish rugby, soccer and Olympic teams, to name a few. Darina did stints on Ireland AM, City channel and featured on the Rachael Ray European show. Her recipes have been featured in major Irish publications. She has a number of awards including being shortlisted for Best Event Caterer 2015 (Event Industry Awards), shortlisted for Best Chef, Best Restaurant 2013 Fire Restaurant (RAI Awards), and Business Person of the Year 2010 (GALAS).

DENISE CHARLTON has twenty-five years' experience in the field of equality, human rights and anti-discrimination and integration issues, at a senior management level. Former Director of Women's Aid and CEO of Immigrant Council of Ireland, she has been involved in several European Commission projects, specifically in the area of integration, immigration and human trafficking. At EU level, her roles have included country co ordinator for E NOTES, an EU observatory on human trafficking, exploitation and slavery. Currently, she is the Irish Expert nominated to the European Commission Expert Group on

Trafficking in Human Beings. Denise was a co-founder of Marriage Equality and a Co-Chair for many years. She has worked with different anti-discrimination bodies and has worked on various governmental and NGO committees and commissions.

NIALL CROWLEY was chief executive officer of the Equality Authority from its establishment in June 1999 until January 2009. He currently works as an independent equality and diversity expert. He is author of *An Ambition for Equality*, published by Irish Academic Press in 2006 and *Empty Promises: Bringing the Equality Authority to Heel*, published by A&A Farmar in 2010.

LINDA CULLEN is an enduring and committed programme maker. She is Head of Television and co-owner of COCO Television. She has been directing, writing, producing and executive producing TV programmes since 1985. She collected two IFTA's (Irish Film and Television Awards) for COCO's work in 2016. Since becoming a partner in COCO Television in 1997, Linda has been responsible for executive producing, originating, and steering the success of numerous popular household TV brands. Some of her recent and current credits include *Room to Improve* (RTÉ), *CrimeCall* (RTÉ), *First Dates* (RTÉ), *Norah's Traveller Academy* (BAI), *Northern Ireland's Greatest Haunts* (BBCNI), *Pat Kenny In the Round* (UTV Ireland), *Mahagonny* (SKY Arts) and *1916* (documentary series BBC, RTÉ, PBS and various worldwide channels). Linda has served on the boards of Marriage Equality, Women's Aid and Screen Producers Ireland. She is author of the lesbian novel *First Kiss* (published by Attic Press in 1990) and has been a lesbian activist from then until now.

PAULA FAGAN currently works as national coordinator with the LGBT Helpline, where her responsibilities include expansion of the Helpline's support services, and working in partnership with a wide range of LGBT organisations and groups across the country. Paula has been an activist on LGBT issues for many years: she was a founding Board member of Marriage Equality and has authored a number of seminal research reports in the area of LGBT rights, including the 'Missing Pieces Report' (2011) and 'The LGBT Parenthood Study' (2013). Paula has extensive experience in volunteer management and led the volunteer engagement team for the National Yes Equality campaign in 2015. She is a graduate of University College Dublin, with an MA in Women, Gender & Society Studies, and is a Fellow of the Association of Certified Chartered Accountants. Paula lives in Dublin with her partner Denise and their two children.

RONAN FARREN was a campaign communications consultant and then a Board member of Marriage Equality. He currently works in Public Policy for Coca Cola.

ANN LOUISE GILLIGAN is a philosopher and former senior lecturer in St Patrick's College, Dublin City University. She established and directed the Education Disadvantage Centre at St Patrick's College, and established and chaired the National Education Welfare Board. Along with Katherine Zappone, she established The Shanty/An Cosán. Together, as litigants, they challenged the failure of the Irish State to provide for marriage equality in *Zappone and Gilligan v Revenue Commissioners [2008]* 2 IR 417. She co-authored her memoirs with Katherine, *Our Lives Out Loud: In Pursuit of Justice and Equality* (Dublin: 2008, the O'Brien Press.) She is currently a member of the Quality and Qualifications Ireland Board, and is writing a book on neuroscience and brain recovery through personal narrative.

ROSS GOLDEN-BANNON was educated in Britain and France, and is a graduate in politics, economics and French. He worked in the House of Commons in the UK before returning to Dublin in 2000, where he pursued a successful career in the food sector while maintaining his commitment to social justice issues. His voluntary involvement includes the Dublin Rape Crisis Centre; One Family; The Irish Food Writers' Guild; and the Board of NCAD. He is a long-time Board member of Marriage Equality Ireland. He believes he has probably gained far more than he has given.

MONINNE GRIFFITH is Executive Director of BeLonG To Youth Services, the national organisation for Lesbian, Gay, Bisexual and Transgendered (LGBT) young people, aged between 14 and 23. Before joining BeLonG To Moninne worked as Director of Marriage Equality since its launch in February 2008. During the marriage equality referendum campaign Moninne devised the 'Roadmap to Victory' and was Director of mobilisation for the Yes Equality campaign. As well as developing the mobilisation strategy for Yes Equality she led the work engaging with a broad base of partner organisations and allies across Ireland and running the hugely successful and wonderfully colourful Yes Bus that travelled 11,000 km to 80 locations across 26 counties in 29 days. Before Marriage Equality, Moninne worked as a solicitor in general practice for almost ten years and volunteered with FLAC (the Free Legal Advice Centres), and Women's Aid. She has an MA in Women's Studies from UCD and is a former Chairperson of the National Women's Council of Ireland. She lives in Dublin with her partner, Clodagh, and their daughter, Edie.

LAURA HARMON was president of the Union of Students in Ireland (USI), 2014/15, during the Marriage Equality campaign. The USI mobilised and registered tens of thousands of new voters ahead of the referendum with their 'Make Grá The Law' campaign. She served for two years as USI Vice-President for Equality and Citizenship, 2012–14. A graduate of University College Cork, Laura has been an LGBT activist since her student days when she was LGBT Rights Officer in UCC Students' Union. In the run-up to the 2016 general election, she worked as Women's and Equality Officer with the Labour Party. In 2016, Laura contested the Seanad Éireann elections on the NUI panel. She was unsuccessful in winning a seat but came fifth out of thirty candidates. Laura now works as a PR Account Manager.

GRÁINNE HEALY is Chairwoman and co-founder of Marriage Equality. A former Chairwoman of National Women's Council of Ireland and Vice President of European Women's Lobby, she is also co-author of *Ireland Says Yes* (Merrion Press, 2016) and completed her Phd at DCU in 2015. See www.grainnehealy.ie.

ORLA HOWARD is a Board member and Deputy Chair of Marriage Equality. She has been involved in LGBT activism for many years and, along with her long-suffering family, has been to the fore of the campaign for equal marriage.

ANDREW HYLAND was a communications consultant to Marriage Equality in the early years and later returned as Co-Director with Moninne Griffith to see the campaign across the line in the referendum. He was also Director of Communications for the Yes Equality campaign. He currently works for Google.

ANTHONY KINAHAN is an actor/teacher from Louth. He is happily married to Barry Gardiner (36), a Special Needs Assistant, also from Louth. Anthony and Barry live with their foster child and their dog Frodo.

ANNA MACCARTHY is an activist and lawyer who works in the IT sector. Anna has a wide range of experience of LGBTQI rights campaigning, from grass roots level activism and student politics, to working in the Oireachtas for a number of years on social justice issues. Anna was an organiser with LGBT Noise from 2008 to 2014; a Board Member of Marriage Equality from 2010 to 2013, and a board member of Transgender Equality Network Ireland (TENI) from 2011 to 2014.

OLIVIA McEVOY, Chairwoman, National LGBT Federation (NFX). The NXF is an Irish community organisation striving to advance equality and end the discrimination of LGBT people in Ireland and internationally. The NXF aims to achieve this social change through advocacy, publications, such as *Gay Community News*, digital platforms, symposia and events that celebrate our vibrant and diverse community including, the GALAS. Olivia McEvoy was the elected voluntary Chair of the National LGBT Federation, 2013–16 and has been a member of that Board since 2008. She is also a Board member of Marriage Equality.

KATE MOYNIHAN, a Kerry native, is the co-ordinator of LINC (Lesbians in Cork). With a long-held interest in community work and social justice, Kate enrolled in University College Cork as a mature student in her mid-forties, graduating with a degree in social work. She joined the steering group of LINC in 2005 and, following work with other marginalised groups, took up her present position in 2013. Kate was one of the founding members and Directors of Yes Equality Cork.

ÍDE B. O'CARROLL, PhD, is an Irish-born social researcher and writer who lives in Amherst, Massachusetts (USA), and summers in Lismore, Co. Waterford. In 2014, she retired her consultancy business in order to concentrate on writing (see www.ocainternational.com). She is the author of *Models for Movers: Irish Women's Emigration to America* (Cork University Press, 2015) and *Irish Transatlantics* (forthcoming, 2017). She is currently a Visiting Scholar at Ireland House, New York University.

RICHARD O'LEARY grew up in Cork and is an author and performer. He was a university lecturer in sociology at Queen's University Belfast until 2010 when he became a full-time carer for his late partner, the Reverend Mervyn Kingston. In 2006, as a same-sex couple, they took a successful landmark equality case, supported by the Equality Authority, against the Department of Social and Family Affairs. In 2007 they co-founded the pro-LGBT faith group, Changing Attitudes Ireland. Richard has written an autobiographical one man show called *There's a Bishop in my bedroom*, which he will be performing in 2017.

KIERAN ROSE is Co-Chair of the Gay and Lesbian Equality Network (GLEN) since its foundation and a long-time LGBT rights campaigner. He works for Dublin City Council in the Planning Department.

JUSTINE SCHÖNFELD-QUINN practised as a barrister in Ireland for six years and lectured in law. She holds a Bachelor of Law from Trinity College Dublin and a Master of Law from the London School of Economics and Political Science. In addition, Justine has been called to the bar of New York. During her time in practice as a lawyer in Ireland, she worked as a researcher on the European Commission-funded Equal Jus Project based at the University of Udine in Italy, co-financed by the European Commission Programme 'Fundamental Rights and Citizenship 2007–2013', supported by partners in Italy, France, Poland and Lithuania. She first volunteered to work for Marriage Equality in 2009 and worked on the 'Missing Pieces' project, before joining the Board of Marriage Equality the following year. She now lives in Berlin and is writing her thesis on legal mobilisation and institutional overlap in regime complexes as a PhD candidate at the Faculty of Social and Behavioural Sciences at Leiden University.

BRIAN SHEEHAN was Executive Director of the Gay & Lesbian Equality Network (GLEN) until November 2016 when he took up the post of General Secretary of the Social Democratic Party; he was also, with Gráinne Healy, Co-Director of the Yes Equality campaign, which successfully led to the introduction of marriage equality for same-sex couples in Ireland in 2015.

AILBHE SMYTH has been active in feminist, LGBT and radical politics for many years. The former head of Women's Studies at UCD, she has published widely on feminism, politics and culture. A founding member of Marriage Equality, she was centrally involved in the 'Yes Equality' campaign. Ailbhe has been campaigning for women's right to choose for over thirty years, and is Convenor of the Coalition to Repeal the Eighth Amendment.

DR KATHERINE ZAPPONE is an America-born feminist theologian and independent politician. She is currently Ireland's Minister for Children and Youth Affairs. She and her wife, Dr Ann Louise Gilligan, founded An Cosán, which supports individuals and communities to actively engage in the process of social change through transformative education. Zappone was a member of the Irish Human Rights Commission, Chief Executive of the National Women's Council of Ireland, and a lecturer in the fields of ethics, theology and education at Trinity College, Dublin. With her Seanad nomination in 2011, Zappone became the first openly lesbian member of the Oireachtas and the first member in a recognised same-sex relationship. In February 2016, she also became the first openly lesbian Teachta Dála (TD) (member of parliament) and, by her own reckoning, the world's 32nd lesbian to be elected to parliament. In May 2016, after a delay in government formation due to prolonged talks in which she played her part, Zappone became Ireland's first openly lesbian government minister and the first minister to have been openly gay at the time of first appointment to cabinet, when Enda Kenny appointed her as the Minister for Children and Youth Affairs.

THALIA ZEPATOS was Freedom to Marry's Director of Research and Messaging. She is widely recognised as the 'message guru' who led the marriage movement's messaging shift, resulting in exponential growth in support for gay marriage in the US that paved the way for a Supreme Court victory. Zepatos has a long track record in fighting anti-gay and anti-choice ballot measures and played a key role in devising tactics for the crucial 2012 ballot victories on gay marriage in November 2012 – the first-ever victories at the ballot. She was an advisor to the YES Equality national referendum campaign in Ireland, and has been consulting internationally with other campaigns and social movements. Zepatos is the co-author of *Women for a Change: A Grassroots Guide to Activism and Politics* (1995) and is the author of two travel books for women. She lives in Portland, Oregon with her husband, Mike.

Index

abortion 32, 36, 37, 38

Adams Auctioneers 222

adoption 70, 72, 73, 116, 127, 149, 182; Colley Group and 282; UK and 200–1

Adoption Authority of Ireland 204

Ahern, Bertie 159, 279, 285

Ahern, Dermot 122, 123, **278**, 285, 309

Alder, Alejandro 145

Amendment of the Constitution (Marriage Equality) Bill (2015) 98

Amnesty International **26**, 55, 56, 64

Ancient Order of Hibernians 80, 194

Anglican Christians 57

ARC International 144

Armagayddon (video) 273

Armstrong, Carol **210**, 211–17; Dublin Pride and 211; fundraising 215; Marches for Marriage and 214; ME and 211–12, 215–17; 'Out to Your TD' and 211–12; referendum result 217; Yes Equality and 215–16

Arnold, Tom 175

'Art for Marriage Equality' **220**, 221–2, **223**; works donated by artists 221–2

Atlantic Philanthropies 109, **278**; GLEN and 108, **278**, 279; KAL case and 159, 253; ME and 98, 107, 143, 225

Bacik, Ivana 151, **170**, **278**

Badgett, M.V. Lee 62, 104, 111

Barnardos 51, 182, 301, 302

Barrington, Brian 46

Barron, Michael 95, **292**, **295**, **300**, **305**; BeLonG To and 293–305; USI and 313; *see also* BeLonG To; BeLong To Yes; Twitter, #BeLonGToYes

Barry, Eilis 69, 80, 280

Barry, Evan 49, 125, 234, 235

BBC 129, **262**

'Believe in Equality' 50

BeLonG To 14, 61, 88, 293–305; establishment of 294–5; funding 296; homophobia and 294, 295; ME and 293–4, 296–8; transphobia and 295; USI and 313, 321; Yes campaign launch **297**; Yes Equality and 304; young LGBT people and 294–5; youth activism 296

BeLonG To Yes 298–303; Bring Your Family With You 299, 302–3; *Bring Your Family With You* film 303; children's rights and 299; *It's in Your Hands* film 300–1; voter registration and 300–1; *see also* Twitter, #BeLonGToYes

Ben & Jerry's **54**, 65

Benedict XVI, Pope 83

Benson, Sarah 55

Bent, Emily 49, 95

Big Love **312**, 313, **314**

Bird, Charlie **311**

Blackwell, Noeline 46

Boele-Woelki, K. 117

Boland, Eavan 103

Bonauto, Mary 18, 322

Bourdieu, Pierre 35

Brady, Conor 30, 32

Brady, Tiernan **27**, **149**, **278**, **281**, 321

Bráinne **39**, 261, **290**, 324, 328, 329, 330

Breen, Richard, et al. 22, 28

Brennan, Darina **121**, **218**, 219–27; 'Art for Marriage Equality' **220**, 221–2, **223**; civil partnership and 219–20; employment 225; marriage equality and 219–20; ME and 219, 220, 221–4, 226–7; *Sinead's Hand* video and 220

Brennan, Seamus 77

Bring Your Family With You (film) 303

Broadcasting Authority of Ireland 227

Broderick, Karl **224**, 227

Browne, Vincent 262

Bruton, Richard 253–4, 261

Buckley, John, Bishop of Cork and Ross 248

Burke, Micheál 180

Burrows, Michael, Bishop of Cashel, Ferns and Ossory 242

Burton, Joan **13**, **165**, 167, 168, 169

Butler, Brendan 241, **242**

Buttimer, Jerry 63, **85**, **109**, **145**, 151,

278; Fine Gael LGBT Group and 289; Yes Bus and **159**

Byrne, Claire 261, 322

Byrne, Gay 179

Cahill, Síona 312

'Call Your Granny' 112, 273

Canada 10, 41, 117, 221

Canavan, John 22, 24, 27, 34

Carey, Pat 288

Carroll, David 96, **171**, 293, 296, **298**; BeLonG To Yes and 298, **300**; USI and 313

Case Against 8, The (film) 58

Casey, Eamonn, Bishop of Galway 37–8

Casey, Gerard 79

Catholic Church: changes in Irish society and 25; clerical sexual abuse 22, 36, 37, 112; Constitution and 22; education and 35; homosexuality and 37, 83; influence of 6, 22, 35; Irish identity and 34; laity and 36; Marriage Equality Referendum and 112, 183; priesthood, homosexuals and 78; secularism and 35; sexual discourse and 35; sexual morality and 28, 32, 34; State and 35; women, role of 30

Catholic *habitus* 35–6, 38

censorship board 35

Census (2011) 26, 36

Central Statistics Office (CSO) 24, 26, 29, 36

Changing Attitudes Ireland 57, 241

Charlton, Denise 13, **19**, 49, 90, **228**, 229–39; children, LGBT families and 230, 232–4; father's last vote 237, 266; KAL case and 231; letter to *Irish Times* 229; Marriage Equality Referendum and 237–8,

239; ME and 107, 160; No campaign, views on 237

child abuse 22, 36, 37, 38, 112

children: #BeLonGToYES coalition and 301–2; BeLonG To Yes campaign and 299; Civil Partnership Act and 309; civil partnership and 41, 123, 126–7, 189, 233, 287; Civil Partnership Bill and 286; illegitimacy and 193; legislation and 126–7; lesbian parents and 192–3, 195, 230; LGBT families and 59, 231, 232–6; LGBT parents and 88, 91, 95, 197, 231, 232–4, 235; marriage equality debate and 145; Marriage Equality Referendum and 197, 235; multi-generational families and 328–9; No campaign and 299, 301, 327; non-biological 41, 125; non-recognition of family relationships and 128–9; rights of 192, 195, 234, 236, 290, 299; same-sex parents and 118–19, 126, 127–8, 163–4, 193

Children and Family Relationships Act (2015) 49, 115–16, 129, 195

Children and Family Relationships Bill 52–3, 128–9, 204, 236, 237

Children's Rights Alliance 52, 53, 285, 290, 298, 301, 302

Choral Confusion **308**

Ciesleski, Karen 321

civil marriage 133–4; benefits 120; GLEN and 279, 284, 289; NXF and 146; perception of 267, 269; rights and 88; same-sex couples and 28, 40, 41, 56, 72, 118, 121; statutory differences, civil partnership and 120, 124, **174**; versus civil

partnership 133–4, 309, 327; Working Group on Domestic Partnerships and 80–1; *see also* Marriage Bill

civil partnership 14, 21, 26, 27, 40, 219; catalyst for marriage 288–91; children and 41, 123, 126–7, 233, 287, 289; Dáil debates on legislation 123, 164; equality and 124, 135–6, 281–2, 307; Fianna Fáil and 285; GLEN and 122, 163, 174, 175, 257, 267–8, 284–8, 327; Ireland and 111, 145; legislation, absence of family and 195; legislation, introduction of 145; ME and 93, 108; number registered 42; opposition to **158**; perception of 124; political parties and 164; rights and 48, 87, 88, 120, 135–6, 233; statutory differences, civil marriage and 120, 124, **174**; UK and 200; versus civil marriage 133–4, 309, 327; versus marriage equality 175; Working Group on Domestic Partnerships and 80–1

Civil Partnership Act (2010) 195, 309

Civil Partnership Act (NI 2004) 77

Civil Partnership Bill 93, 108, 120, 123, 233, 284–8; children and 286; criticism of 287; GLEN and 136, **278**; heads of 285, 286; LGBT Noise and 135–6; Norris and 279; opposition to 286; passing of 309; publication of 285; signing of **278**

Civil Partnership and Certain Rights and Obligations of Cohabitants Act (2010) 40, 41, 48, 108, 117, 121, 123–4, 126–7; GLEN and 287; NXF's view on 141; passing of 287

Civil Partnership Scheme 88

Civil Registration Act (2004), Section 2(2)(e) 126

Civil Unions Bill (2007) 40, 132, 158, 282, 284

Clifford, Kieran 56

Cloyne Report (2011) 38

COCO Television **78**, 96, 126, 267, 270–5

Coghlan, Aisling 320

Colley, Anne 192, 280

Colley Group *see* Working Group on Domestic Partnership

Colley Report 40, 281

Collins, Eoin 80, 105, 108, 144, **278**, 284; Working Group and 280, 281

Colton, Paul, Bishop of Cork 242

Combat Poverty 105

Community Foundation Ireland, The 95

Connell, Desmond, Archbishop of Dublin 37

Connolly, Linda 30

Connolly, Madeline **272**, 274

Connor, Stephen **94**

Constitution of Ireland (1937) 117, 118; Article 41, families and 118, 126; Catholic Church and 22, 34; Eight amendment 14; marriage and 118, 126; women and 29

Constitutional Convention **27**, 95, 175, 177, **213**, **254**; establishment of 14, 42; film, same-sex couples and 270–1; Fine Gael/Labour coalition and 59, 289; GLEN/ME/ICCL and 59, 290; GLEN's submission to 290; LINC and 195; marriage equality and 42, 212, 257–8, 290; ME and 215; participants 42, 270, **281**; referendum and 166, 167, 195, 196, 234; USI submission 311; *Yes to Love* video 96, 204

contraception 25, 32, 36

Conway, KerryAnn (Conway Communications) 64

Cooney, Anne 185

Cork, LINC and 191–7

Cosán, An, Jobstown 7–8

Courtney, Daire **78**, 96, **252**, 253–4, 261

Courtney, Gráinne 90, **179**, 251, 252–3; video and 275; 'We Are Family' 95–6; Wedding in New York (2013) **156**, 258

Cowen, Brian 285

Criminal Law (Sexual Offences) Bill (1993) 38–9

Crowley, Niall **68**, 69–81, **77**, **78**, 146

Cullen Byrne, Tess and Rosa **267**, 275

Cullen, Linda 90, **264**, 265–75; civil partnership and 271; COCO Television and 96, 126, 267, 270–5; daughters 269, 275; family **274**; *Irish Times* photo and 266; marriage, viewson 265; ME and 266–7, 269–70, 273, 275; referendum and 266; *Sinead's Hand* and 268–9, **271**

Cusack, Conor 274

Dáil Éireann **216**; Civil Partnership Bill **280**, 288; debates 122, 164; Marriage Bill **37**, **97**, **259**

Daly, Paul 58, 159–60

D'Arcy, Ray 203

Della Porta, D. and Diani, M. 116

Denard, Hugh 241, **242**

Denham, Susan 126

Department of Enterprise, Trade and Employment 70

Department of Environment and Local Government 70

Department of Finance 70

Department of Health 70

Department of Justice, Equality and Law Reform 70, 128

Department of Social, Community and Family Affairs 70, 75, 77

Devlin, Patricia 204, 241, **242**

Diamond, Donogh 54

digital media 96, 134, 321

Digital Revolutionaries 55

Dillon, Michele 25

discrimination: indirect 5; legislation and 39, 69; LGBT people and 90, 131, 305; national study and 105; same-sex couples and 235; sexual orientation and 75, 76

diversity 29, 38, 51, 72, 150, 238; legal reform and 71; recognition of diverse identities 73–4

divorce 25, 36; 'gay' divorce 62; referendum 284

Doctors for Yes **256**

Domestic Partnership *see* Working Group on Domestic Partnership

Donoghue, Emma 106

Dooley, Seamus **92**, **275**, 324

Doris, Des 226

Dublin Bus, posters and 95, 96, 98

Dublin City University (DCU) 62, 111, 324

Dublin Lesbian and Gay Film Festival 279

Duffy, Marcella 28

Duke, Tom 55

Dundalk Outcomers 199–200, 203, 205

Dunne, Elizabeth 117–18, 231

Dwyer, Lisa-Anne 186

education: Catholic Church and 35; early childhood 7; second-chance 7; second-level, access to 32

Egan, Ailbhe 195
Electric Picnic (2014) 204, **225**
Elliott, Iris 49–50, 59, 95, 204
employment: legislation and 31; marriage bar and 30; married women and 31; sexual orientation and 39; women and 29, 30
Employment Equality Acts 69, 70, 76; (1977) 31; (1998) 39, 106, 116; (2004) 106
Empowering Young People in Care (EPIC) 302
Epp, Charles R. 116
Equal Pay Act (1974) 31
Equal Status Acts 39, 69, 75, 76, 77, 106
equality: civil partnership and 124, 135–6; concept of 73; Irish people and 86; legislation and 173–4; lesbians and 39; LGBT community and 315; same-sex relationships and 124; substantive 73
Equality Authority 40, 69–81, 196; advisory committee 70, 72; budget cuts and 81; case work 74–7; concepts and 73–4; diverse identities and 73–4; housing 70; institutional change and 79; leave entitlements 70; legal reform 71; marriage and 279; national debate and 78–9; National Economic and Social Forum and 74; NXF and 144; parenting/fostering/adoption rights 70; partnership rights 70, 72, 79; Strategic Plan (2006–8) 73; tax reform 70; Vatican Directive (2005) and 78–9; welfare benefits 70
Equality Rights Alliance 55
EQUALS 137
EROSS Centre 111

European Convention of Human Rights 76
European Economic Community (EEC) 30–1
European Union (EU) 106; legislation, same-sex couples and 144; marriage equality and 162

Facebook 96, 181, 188, 189, 248, 303
Fagan, Gary 96, 296
Fagan, Paula 41, 48, 50, 51, 90, **228**, 229–39; children, LGBT families and 230, 232–4; equality 41, 42; 'Just Love' launch **25**; KAL case and 231; letter to *Irish Times* 229; Marriage Equality Referendum and 237–8; 'Missing Pieces Report' 48, **52**, 123–4, 125, 128, 235; No campaign, views on 237; referendum result and 239
Fail Safe Films 96, 125, 235
Faith in Marriage Equality 57, 62, 241–3, 248, 249
'Faith for Yes' 242, 243, 244, 246, 249
families: Article 41 and 118, 126; changes in 24, 29, 38; cohabiting male/female couples and 29; lesbian parents and 195; one-parent 29, 56
family law 115–16; guardianship and 290; reform 289–90
Family Resource Forum 55
Farrell, Eamonn **89**, 90
Farrell, Michael 46
Farrelly, Dave 179–80
Farren, Ronan 55, 58, **154**, 155–71; family background 155–6; KAL case and 159–160, 162–3; Labour Party and 157, 158, 166, 167–9; ME and 160–6, 170–1; MEPs and 162; 'Out to Your TD' and 161; politics and 155–6;

Yes Equality celebrations 170
Farren, Sean 155–6
Feeney, Chuck 107; *see also* Atlantic Philanthropies
feminism 30; marriage, perception of 146, 192
Ferns Report (2005) 38
Ferriter, Diarmaid 21–2, 30, 35, 36
Fianna Fáil 132, 285, 289
Fianna Fáil/Green Party 164, 285
Finance Act (No.3) (2011) 287
Fine Gael 40, 164, 167, 279, 289
Fine Gael/Labour coalition 59, 165, 166, 175, 289; Constitutional Convention and 289; Marriage Equality Referendum and 167, 169
Fine-Davis, Margret 27
Finlay, Fergus **166**, 301
Finnegan, Brian **142**, 289
Fire Restaurant 220, 221, 222, **225**
Fisher, John 144
Fitzgerald, Frances 14, **17**, 52, **97**, 98, 151; draft legislation and 128; Yes Bus **63**, **300**
Fjoser, Kirsten 84
Flanagan, Ross 64, **125**
Fledglings Early Childhood Centres 7–8
Focus Ireland 294
Foróige 302
foster carers 203
Foucault, Michel 22, 35
Fr Ted's House 248
free travel passes 75
Freedman, Lawrence 84
Freedom to Marry 18, 111, 214, 231, 238, 317, 331; ME/GLEN/ICCL and 321–2; messengers for marriage and 328; national strategy 318, 319; Roadmap to Marriage Equality 321; strategies 321–2, 328
Furey, Finbar 224

Gaffney, Maureen 70, 74, **166**
GALAS **23**, **127**, 150–1, 153
Gardiner, Barry 90, 199–200, **213**; adoption issue and 200–1; canvassing and 206; civil partnership and 199, 200; Dublin Pride **201**; fostering and 203; homophobia and 207–8; marriage to Anthony 209; ME and 201–2; ME Louth and 203, 205; media and 203, 204, 209; 'Out to Your TD' and 201, 203; referendum result 208; #VoteWithUs videos 208; Yes Equality Louth **204**, 206, 208; *Yes to Love* video and 203–4, **209**
Garrett, Mark 165, 166–7
Gaughan, Martin 270
Gay Catholic Voice Ireland 241
Gay Community News (*GCN*) 147–8, 150–1, 153, 251, 289
Gay and Lesbian Awards (GALAS) **23**, **127**, 150–1
gender recognition 138, 305
Gender Recognition Act (2015) 116, 307
General Election (2011) 59
Genockey, Darragh 17
Germany 129
Gilligan, Ann Louise **2**, 3–12, 18, 214, **275**; Boston College and 4–5; An Cosán, Jobstown 7–8; European Parliament visit 162; GALA award 151; High Court case 40, 81; illness 266; indirect discrimination and 7; life in Ireland 6–8; life-partnership vows 5; marriage equality and 9–10, 41; marriage to Katherine 10–11, 16, 41, 83, 106; *Our Lives Out Loud* **8**, **77**; Revenue Commissioners and 9, 11, 83; Road to Equality Summer School **19**; St Patrick's College

6, 7; The Shanty 7, 45, 231, *see also* KAL/KAL Advocacy Initiative; KAL case
Gilmore, Eamon 146, **156**, **162**, 257, 310; marriage equality and 165, 166–7, 169–70
Ginsburg, Ruth Bader 124
GLAD (Gay and Lesbian Advocates and Defenders) 18
GLEN (Gay and Lesbian Equality Network) 27, 41, 59, 106, 132, 277–91; children, civil partnership and 285, 287, 289; civil marriage and 279, 284, 285, 289, 290; civil partnership and 122, 163, 174, 175, 255, 257, 267–8, 284–8, 327; civil partnerships registered 42; Civil Unions Bill and 282; Colley Working Group and 279–82; Freedom to Marry and 321–2; funding 279; GLEN/LOT seminar (2000) 279; KAL case and 284; Labour Party and 282; LGBT Noise and 136; ME and 255, 258, 259, 260–1; national study 105; strategic plan 279; Working Group on Domestic Partnerships and 80–1, 194; Yes Equality and 83, 175, 215–16, 277
Glennon, Brian 204, 241, **242**
Gloria Choir **145**, 223, **308**
Golden-Bannon, Ross **52**, **172**, 173–89; canvassers' experiences 185–7, 189; canvassing and 178–80; civil partnership versus marriage equality 175; Constitutional Convention and **27**, 175, 177; Facebook update and 188; Faith in Marriage Equality **243**; Howth-Sutton-Baldoyle group 178–84, 188; ME Board and 173, 177; messaging and briefing,

Yes Equality and 181–4; 'Out to Your TD' and **176**; RDS count centre and 188–9; 'So long, and thanks for all the Noes' 188; Yes Bus and 177; Yes Equality and 177–84, **215**
Golombok, Susan 192
Green Party 40, 284, 285, 286, 289
Greene, Sheila 145
Greenham Common Air Force Base 16
Grieve, Brian Kearney **278**
Griffith, Moninne **15**, **37**, **44**, 45–67, **145**, 241; BeLonG To and 293, 294; Constitutional Convention and **27**, 59, **281**; 'Just Love' launch **25**; March for Marriage **121**; 'Marriage Audit' 48; ME and 45–67, 84, 160–1; Roadmap to Victory **66**, students' unions and 309; USI and 313; Yes Bus and **60**, **63**, 67, **159**, 177; Yes Equality and 45, 56, 59, 60–7, **125**; Zepatos, Thalia and 319–20

habitus, Catholic 35–6, 38
Hackett, Edel 160, 162
Hannan, D. and Katsiaouni, L. 29
Hannigan, Lisa 269
Harmon, Laura **306**, 307–15; 'I'm Voting Yes. Ask Me Why' **310**, **311**; UCC LGBT Society and 309; USI and 307, 309–14
Harvard Family Research Project 109
Hayden, Karl 50, **205**, **226**, **259**
Hayes, Joanne 37
Hayes, Kate 70
Healy, Gráinne 13, **20**, 21–43, **37**, **40**; Catholic *habitus* 35–6; Constitutional Convention campaign **27**, **281**; EEC, Ireland and 30–1; families, changing 24–5; GALA award

(2015) **23**, 151; GLEN, ICCL and 255; Ireland, changes in 34–5; *Ireland Says Yes* 108; legislative progress, gay and lesbian 38–42; March for Marriage **28**; ME and 107, 112, 146, 160, 164; media, change and 32, 34; men, changing roles of 29; National Women's Council and 106; NXF symposium and 144; polling day (2015) **34**; same-sex headed households 26–7; Sheehan, Brian and 260–1; social changes in Ireland 28; socio-sexual issues 36–8; 'We are Family' **24**, 95; women, changing roles of 29; women's movement 30; Yes Equality **31**, **125**, 323, 325; *see also* Bráinne

Healy, Ronan 95, **121**
Heffernan, Tony 155, 158
Hibernian Consulting 98
Higgins, Michael D. 16, **142**
Higgins, Sabina 16, **142**
Hogan, Linda 242, 243
homelessness, LGBT community and 294
homophobia 185, 186, 207–8, 234, 305; BeLonG To and 294, 295, 298; schools and 75, 83
homosexuality: Catholic Church and 37, 83; decriminalisation of 36, 37, 38–9, 83, 105; legislation and 36, 37, 38; Vatican and 78
Howard, Amy **260**
Howard, Orla **37**, 90, **142**, **179**, **250**, 251–63; Constitutional Convention and **27**, **254**, **281**; GLEN/civil partnership and 255, 257; 'Just Love' launch **25**; ME and 253–4, 257; NLGF and 251, 253, 254, 257; NXF and 143; parenting and 252–3; politicians and 253–4; strategy versus the

objective 255; video and 275; 'We Are Family' 95–6; Wedding in New York (2013) **256**, 258; Yes Equality **125**, 179, 258–63
Hudson, Chris, Rev. 144
Hug, Chrystel 30, 31, 36, 37
Hughes, Alan **224**, 227
Hunt, Kathleen 64, **125**, 263
Hyland, Andrew 51, **82**, 83–101; BeLonG To and 293, 294; civil partnership and 93; digital media 96; Freedom to Marry and 321; Marriage Bill and **37**, **275**; ME, communications and 48, 83–101, 219; media handbook 93–4; media training and 89; posters and 95–6; USI and 313; Yes Equality **89**, **90**, 178, 273, 323–4; Zepatos, Thalia and 320
Hyland, Eithna and Andy **31**
Hyland, Lisa **125**, 263

ICCL (Irish Council for Civil Liberties) 52, 59, 83, 108, 112, 175; 'Equality Now for Lesbians and Gay Men' report 277; Freedom to Marry and 321–2; ME and 255; Yes Equality and 83, 175, 215–16
'I'm Voting Yes. Ask Me Why' **15**, **64**, 206, **310**, **311**
immigration rights 14, 41, 108, 112–13, 284, 309
'Implementing Equality for Lesbians, Gays and Bisexuals' (2002) 70, 74
Incitement to Hatred Act (1989) 36
Independent 188
Inglis, Tom 22, 30, 34, 35, 36
Institute of Guidance Counsellors 302
International Happiness Day **308**
International Lesbian and Gay Association (ILGA) 145

Iona Institute 53, 286
Iredale, Breda 178, 180, 189
Ireland: modernisation and 25; sexuality and 21–2; social changes in 28; socio-political changes in 21
Ireland Says Yes: The Inside Story of How the Vote for Marriage Equality Was Won (Healy *et al.*) 43, 108, **113**
Irish Congress of Trade Unions 55, 79, 249
Irish Examiner 248
Irish Human Rights and Equality Commission 81
Irish Independent 79, 90, 203, 222
Irish Lesbian and Gay Organisation (ILGO) 106
Irish Queer Archive 251
Irish Times 251; 'Art for Marriage Equality' 222; article by Olivia McEvoy 152; Charlton, Denise and Fagan, Paula 229; 'Families come out for Gay Marriage' 253; GLEN 279, 289; KAL case 4, 5, 11–12; Kevin Myers 73; LGBT family photo 266; marriage equality 203, 289; RTÉ history of television 30, 32; Vatican Directive 78
Irwin, Conor **24**
Irwin-Gowran, Sandra **125**, 263, **278**
Irwin-Murphy, Christine 50
ISPCC (Irish Society for the Prevention of Cruelty to Children) 301, 302
IT Blanchardstown Students' Union **308**
'It's No Joke: Civil Marriage Rights for Lesbians and Gay Men in Ireland' 94–5
It's in Your Hands (video) 300–1

Jayawardene, Walter **27**, **89**, **281**

Joint Oireachtas Commission on the Constitution 279
Jones, Stella, Rev. 241, **242**
'Just Love': Gig for Marriage Equality 223–4; headpiece 222; launch of **25**, 235; poster campaign **49**, 96, 125, **161**; UCC LGBT Society and 309

KAL/ KAL Advocacy Initiative 13, 45, 106, 144,159–60, 253, 273, 279
KAL case 4, 5, 11–12, 13, 43, 106–7, 115; GLEN and 284; High Court judgement 117–18, 126, 158, 231, 282; influence of 119, 120, 253; NGLF and 253; NXF and 143; Supreme Court appeal 126, **179**, 284, 285
Keenaghan, Celia 49, 95
Kelleher, Aoife 303
Kelly, Mark **27**, **33**, 144, **281**
Kelly, Ruth Esther 48, 120
Kennedy, Brian **52**, 223, 224, **224**, **225**, 227
Kennedy, Finola 24, 29, 30, 36, 38
Kenny, Enda 14, 42, 52, **159**, **205**, 259, 304
Kenny, Mary 79
Kerwick, Lavinia 37
Kilfeather, Siobhan 35, 37, 38
Kinahan, Anthony 90, **198**, 199–209, **213**; adoption issue and 200–1; canvassing and 206; civil partnership and 199, 200; Dublin Pride **201**; family support and 200, 208; fostering and 203; homophobia and 207–8; marriage to Barry 209; ME and 201–2; ME Louth and 203, 205; media and 203, 204, 209; No campaign and 205–6; 'Out to Your TD' and 201, 203; referendum result 208; #VoteWithUs videos 208; Yes Equality Louth **204**,

206, 208; *Yes to Love* video and 203–4, **209**
Kingston, Mervyn, Rev. 69, 77, 248
Knock 246–7

Labour Party 14, 58, 59; Civil Unions Bill (2007) 40, 132, 158, 164, 282, 284; GLEN and 282, 284; LGBT group 157; Marriage Equality Referendum and 165, 166, 167–9; Press Office 157; referendum strategy 167–9
Lansdowne Market Research 85, 87, 94
law reform 71, 115–16
Law Reform Commission 13, 128
Layte, Richard, et al. 34, 38
Leeson Street says Yes **235**
legal mobilisation, marriage and 116–17
'Legal Status of Co-habitants and Same-Sex Couples' (2006) 80, 194
Lenihan, Brian 284–5
Lesbian and Gay Visions of Ireland: Towards the Twenty-First Century (1995) 105–6, **107**
lesbians: acknowledgement of 105; equality and 39; visibility and 232
Lesbians in Cork (LINC) 106, 191–7; Constitutional Convention and 195; domestic partnerships and 192–3; feminism and 192; 'Marriage and Lesbian and Gay Families' conference 194–5; objectives 191–2; parenting group 192
Lesbians Organising Together (LOT) 106, 279
Lewis, Maeve 112
LGBT community: 'Burning Issues' survey 149–50; canvassing and 185; coalition

of organisations 146, **149**; equality and 315; freedom 14; *GCN* and 147–8; homelessness and 294; invisibility and 99; isolation and 173; marriage equality and 16, 315; perception of 46; political tensions 163; referendum result and 315; rights and 123, 138, 139, 144–5; unequal treatment of 124; visibility and 150–1, 153, 195, 265; *see also* young LGBT people
LGBT Diversity 51
LGBT Film Festival 58
LGBT Noise 41, 58, 88, 89, 93, 121, 132–9; equal rights and 133–4, 257; founded (2007) 132; funding and 134; GLEN's criticism of 136; Marches for Marriage 124–5, 137–8, **213**, 214, 296, 307; ME and 135, **216**; poster campaign 124; protests and 136, 139; social media and 134; USI and 135; Yes Equality and 139
LGBT parenting study *see* 'Voices of Children'
'LGBT Parents in Ireland' 51
LGBT Platform 61, **149**, 258–9; *see also* Platform for Equality
LGBT-parented families 24, 41, 49–51, 204, 232–6; rights and 231, 235, 236; visibility and 231, 232, 233, 238
LGBTI families 232–4
Logan, Emily 233
Logan, Johnny **168**
Longford Leader 289
Lough Derg 245–6
Lovett, Ann 37
Loving Our Out Kids (LOOK) 302
Lynch, Patrick 143, 253
Lyons, John **32**, 63, **109**, 212, **215**

McAleese, Justin 3–4, 237

McAleese, Mary 151, 237, 251, **299**, **303**, 304

McCamley, Christopher 79

McCann, Des 225, 227

McCann, Michael W. 116

McCarron, Mark 90, 146

MacCarthy, Anna **130**, 131–9, 315; civil partnership, rights and 135–6; Dublin Pride and 135–6; LGBT Noise and 132–9, 307; ME and 131, 135; 'Out to Your TD' and 131

McCarthy, Joan 105

McClenaghan, Brendí 105

McCreevy, Charlie 279

McDaniel-Miccio, Kris 243

McDermott, Mary **60**, 64, **149**, **247**

McDonagh, Jeanne 53, **215**

McDowell, Brian 167

McDowell, Michael 80, 192, 194, 279–80

McEvoy, Olivia **27**, **140**, 141–53, **308**; GALAS 150–1; *GCN*, marriage equality and 147–8; *Irish Times* article 152; NXF and 141–53; Yes X 10 campaign 152–3

McGarry, Patsy 38

McGrath, Finian 253, 254

McGurk, Myra 69, 76–7

McKenna, Mary 226

McNamara, Helen 183–4

McQuaid, John Charles, Archbishop of Dublin 35

Maguire, Anne 106

Mahony, Geraldine 183

Malone, Michelle 212, **213**

Mannion Farrell, Steven 90, 221

Marches for Marriage **28**, 58, **119**, **121**, 124–5, **132**; BeLonG To and 296; first March (2009) 137–8; LGBT Noise and 124–5, 137–8, **213**, 214, 306

'Mario and the singing waiters' 227

Markey, James 178

marriage: American concept of 318; change in attitudes towards 29; civil partnership as catalyst 288–91; Constitution of Ireland and 118; definition 118; exclusion from 86, 88, 270, 281; feminist critique of 146, 192; Ireland and 35, 86; legal mobilisation and 116–17; patriarchal nature of 72, 192, 265; perception of 72, 121, 265; rights and 270, 289; sustaining momentum for 123–5; traditional interpretation of 159

Marriage Bill **97**, **100**, 112, **179**, 209, **259**, **275**; USA and 214

marriage equality 9–14, 21, 146; Canada and 10, 41; Constitutional Convention and 42, 212, 257–8; European campaigners 162; *GCN* and 147–8; significance of 14, 16; Spain and 145, 194; support for 62; versus civil partnership 175

Marriage Equality Louth 203, 205

Marriage Equality (ME) 17–18, 41, 45–6, **52**, 83–101; advocacy evaluation (2009–10) 98, 109–13; American influences 106–8; BeLonG To and 293, 294, 296–8; board of 16; civil partnership 93, 108; communications and 48, 53–4, 83–101, **161**; Constitutional Convention and 215; digital media 96; establishment 12, 13, 107; evaluation 98, 103–13; foundations: strategy and research 84–8; Freedom to Marry and 321–2; funding/fundraising **51**, 107, 110, 143, **145**, **308**; fundraising 219, 220, 221–4, 226–7; GALA awards **127**, 151; GLEN and 255, 258, 259, 260–1; importance of ME 307; launch of **23**, **47**, 163, 164, 253; leadership 16; legacy 99, 101; legal strategies 46, 48, 50–3, 116–17; LGBT Noise and 135, **216**; litigation strategy 117–19; media and 53, 97–8; media handbook 93–4; media training 89; message development 88; mobilisation and political strategy 54–8; NXF and 141, 143–6, 152–3; opinion poll 232–3; political strategy 55–6; political work 58–9; politicians and 99; posters 95–6, 125; reports 94–5; research 85–8; staff (2008) 84; stories, sharing and 90–1, 311; strategies 46; tactics 91; TV and radio debates 53; videos 96, 125, 126; volunteers 212, **213**

Marriage Equality Media Handbook 93–4

Marriage Equality Referendum 14, 16, 42, 52, 53; BeLonG To and 297; campaign 17–18, 129, 139, **147**, 152–3, 237–8; Catholic Church and 112, 183; children and 197, 235, 293; Constitutional Convention and 166, 167, 195, 196, 234; Dundalk Count Centre 208; *GCN* and 148; Labour Party and 165, 167–9; media coverage, balance and 53; No campaign and 148, 237; RDS count centre **92**, **122**, 129, 188–9, **283**, **305**; research and 87–8; result 67, 72, **85**, **92**, 98, 101, 208, 217, 249, 262, **263**, 293; Service of Thanksgiving 249; success of 116, 189, 239, 331; support for 226; voting date 167, 177

Marriage and Family Matter 96, **147**, **272**, **320**, **325**
'Marriage and Lesbian and Gay Families' conference 194–5
'Marriage Matters' (NXF 2009) 142, 144–6, 257
MassEquality 161, 317
Matthews-McKay, Rachel 203, 222
ME *see* Marriage Equality (ME)
media: catalyst for change 32, 34; Equality Authority report and 78–9; LGBT community and 90–1, 203, 204; LGBT issues and 93–4, 204; posters 95–6; social change and 32, 34, 35–6; women's movement and 30; *see also* digital media; social media
Mee, John 72
Meldon-Hugh, Ann 221–2
men: changing roles of 21, 29; male breadwinner model 31
Migrant Rights Centre Ireland 302
'Missing Pieces' 56, 120–2, 123; Report (Fagan) 48, **52**, 123–4, 125, 128, 235, 309
Moynihan, Kate **190**, 191–7; Cork Pride **194**; LINC and 191–7; marriage equality and 196–7
Mullally, Una 266
Murphy Report (2009) 38
Myers, Kevin 73, 79

Nanci, Jaime 95, **295**, **305**
National Economic and Social Forum (NESF) 70, 74
National Lesbian and Gay Federation (NLGF) (now NXF) 88, **142**, 251, 254, 257
National LGBT Federation (NXF) 106, 141; 'Burning Issues' survey 149–50; Equality Authority and 144; first symposium (2007) 143–4; 'Full and Equal Rights' symposium (2007) 143–4; GALAS 150–1;

GCN, marriage equality and 147–8; 'Marriage Matters' (2009) 142, 144–6; ME and 141, 143–6, 152–3; Platform for Equality and 144, 146, 257; policy position 141–2; thirty-fifth birthday (2014) **148**; Yes X 10 campaign 152–3
National Volunteer Day 61
National Women's Council 55, 64, 106
National Youth Council of Ireland (NYCI) 300, 302
Ní Bhroin, Feargha 89, 90, 266, 269; civil partnership and 271; daughters **267**, 275; family **274**
Ní Dhálaigh, Críona 291
Nic Ghiolla Phádraig, M. 34, 35
NLGF *see* National Lesbian and Gay Federation (NLGF)
No campaign 205–6, 208, 322; children and 181–2, 299, 301, 327; effects on LGBT community 305; 'Faith for No' 242, 246; *GCN* and 148; Novena for a No vote 246, 249; posters **182**, **271**; press coverage 324; surrogacy and 181–2, 237
Nolan, Anna 273, 275, **325**
non-discrimination legislation 117
Noon, Claire 221
Norman, J. et al. 38
Norris, David 38, 40, 151, 249, 287, **330**; Yes Bus and **165**, **182**, **300**
NXF *see* National LGBT Federation (NXF)

Obama, Barack 18, 211, 215
O'Brien, Breda 289
O'Brien, Joan **147**, 274
O'Brien, Kieran 49
O'Brien, Paddy and Pat **147**, 274
O'Callaghan, Miriam 16
O'Carroll, Íde B. 98, **102**, 103–13;

'Marriage Equality: A Case Study' 103, 108, 111, **113**; ME advocacy evaluation (2009–10) 109–13; ME, American influences and 106–8
O'Carroll, Rory **325**
O'Connell, Angela 192
O'Connell, Clare **78**, 96, **252**, 253–4; Constitutional Convention and 95, 234, **254**, 258, **281**; *Late Late Show* panel 261; 'Voices of Children' and 59
O'Connor, Eamon 222, 226
O'Connor, Hugh 96, 269
O'Connor, Patricia (Trisha) **24**, **34**, 95, **127**
O'Gorman, Colm 22, **31**
O'Hare, Stephen **27**, 64, **281**
Ó hÉigeartaigh, Seán 74
Oireachtas Commission on the Constitution (2006) 13
Oireachtas Joint Committee on Justice, Defence and Equality 128
O'Kane, Padraic 222
O'Leary, Richard 57–8, **240**, 241–9; civil partnership and 77; Faith in Marriage Equality 241–3; 'Faith for Yes' 242, 243, 244; letter to the *Irish Examiner* 248; Pilgrimage for Yes 244–9
Ó Mathúna, Ciarán 241, **242**
One Family 51, 56
One in Four 112
one-parent families 29, 56
O'Neill, Rory (aka Panti Bliss) 135, **137**, 139
O'Reilly, Oisín **149**, 298
Ó Riordáin, Aodhán 63, 151, **170**, **171**, **256**
O'Toole, Mary 53
'Out To Your TD' 55, 56, 99, 111, 123, 161; effects of campaign 165; 'Families come out for Gay

Marriage' 253; launch of **81**, **176**; Louth and 201; ME and 107, **109**, 135, 161; ME seminar (2012) 203; role of volunteers 55, 211–12; UCC LGBT Society and 309
Outhouse 106, **149**, 212, 221
OutYouth 294

Panti Bliss 135, **137**, 139
Paris, Michael 116
Partnership Laws (GLEN/LOT 2000) 279
partnership rights 70, 72, 79; disadvantages 72; Equality Authority and 70, 72, 79; NESF report and 74
Pavee Point 302
Pendergrast, Conor 27, 50, 59, 95, **234**, **254**, **281**
Pilgrimage for Yes 244–9
Pillinger, Jane 24, 27, 28, 41, 51, **230**
Platform for Equality 144, 146, 257
'Pledge to Vote' 204
'Poverty: Lesbians & Gay Men, The Economic and Social Effects of Discrimination' (1993) 105, **107**
Power, Averil 63, 151, 177–8, 179, 180, 206
Power, Sean 144
Prendiville, Patricia 145
Pride marches 56, **104**, 209; Dublin Pride **47**, 124, 135–6, 157, 158, **176**, **201**, 211, **290**; Dublin Pride Marshalls (2015) **33**, **290**
Pringle, Thomas 63

Quinn, David 53, 54, 72–3, 79
Quinn, Dawn 27, 50, 55, 84, **202**, 211, **281**
Quinn-Patton, Michael 109

Rabbitte, Pat 157, 158
Raftery, Mary 22, 37

Raidió Teilifís Éireann (RTÉ) 30; see also RTÉ
rape 37
Ratzinger, Joseph, Cardinal 83
referendum see Marriage Equality Referendum
religion: decline in 38; religious identity and 34; see also Catholic Church
Residential Tenancies Act (2004) 76
Revenue Commissioners 9, 11–12, 83; see also tax system
rights: children and 192, 195, 234, 236, 290, 299; civil partnership and 48, 87, 88, 120, 135–6, 233; homosexuals and 36; LGBT community and 123, 138, 139, 144–5, 230; LGBT-parented families 231, 235, 236
Road to Equality Summer School **19**, **238**, **330**
'Roadmap to Victory' 60, 61, **66**
Robinson, Clodagh 50, 53, **66**
Robinson, Mary 38, 251
Robson, Christopher **278**, 279
Rogers, Annie G. 103, 112–13
Rogers, Hugh 303
Rogers, John 53
Ronayne, Kaye 72
Rory's Story (video) 96, 125, 235
Rose, Kieran 30, 39, **276**, 277–91; civil marriage and 285, 291; GLEN and 277–91; *Irish Times* article 279; Yes Equality **281**, 291
Royseven 223, 224
RTÉ 11, 169, 204, 209; *Claire Byrne Live* 322; *Irish Times* article 30, 32; *Late Late Show* (RTÉ) 17, 30, 261; *Morning Ireland* (RTÉ) 11, **32**, 285; *Prime Time* (RTÉ) 53, 167, 169
Ryan, Fergus 41, 195, 287
Ryan, Karl 65
Ryan, Paul 29, 30, 31, 32, 35, 36

Ryan Report (2009) 38

St Audeon's Church 249
St Patrick's College, Drumcondra 6, 7, 9
same-sex couples: children and 118–19, 126, 127–8, 163–4, 193; EU legislation and 144; families and 24, 27, 115–16; housing, local authority and 70; multi-generational families and 328–9
same-sex marriage: Colley Report and 281; jurisdictions recognising 117; public attitudes towards 87, 163; support for 268
same-sex parenting, perception of 233
same-sex relationships 24, 27, 116; equality and 124; legislation and 119; parenting and 118; social changes and 28, 29; unequal status and 124
same-sex-headed households 26–7, 125, 177
Schönfeld-Quinn, Justine 53, **114**, 115–29; Children and Family Relationships legislation 126–9; 'Just Love' launch **25**; KAL case appeal 126; March for Marriage (2014) **121**; marriage 129; Marriage Equality Referendum and 129; ME board and 116, 120; 'Missing Pieces' research 120–2, 123; 'Out to Your TD' and 123
Schönfeld-Quinn, Sabrina **122**
schools, homophobic bullying and 75, 83
Seanad Éireann 40, 93, 209, 287
secularism 35, 36
Seoighe, Feidhlim 313
sexual abuse, clerical 22, 36, 37, 112
sexual morality: Catholic